D0667190

I was thrilled to be asked to lend my voice to the ZOE W8 Loss Program. One of the biggest health problems we face in Texas, and the nation, is the epidemic of childhood obesity and diabetes. Ed and Elisa McClure have put forth real, long-term solutions to this truly serious health crisis. Every parent should read this book!

—SUSAN HOWARD, EMMY-NOMINATED ACTRESS
GOVERNOR'S ADVISORY COUNCIL ON PHYSICAL FITNESS,
STATE OF TEXAS

As a busy family physician who advocates good nutrition, quality supplements, and behavioral changes for optimal health, I am pleased to recommend the ZOE W8 Loss Program. It is very gratifying to see that true food experts have made available to everyone this potentially life-changing information through a thoroughly researched book.

—VICTOR VELA, MD
BOARD-CERTIFIED IN FAMILY MEDICINE

I met Ed McClure after he had lost 100 pounds, and I was his physical therapist and trainer while he lost the next 100 pounds. I've seen many people get results with the ZOE W8 Loss Program. The nutritional instruction offered goes hand in hand with anyone starting a weight-training program or improving their quality of life through increased activity. Ed is truly inspirational, and I recommend this program—give it a try!

—HAROLD PHIFER, RMT, PTA, RT, CPT

Believe me, this book contains no "fluff." It is jam-packed with information on physical, emotional, mental, and spiritual health. I'm excited to be a part of the ZOE 8 team and to recommend this life-changing program, which teaches people how to successfully change negative behaviors into positive ones. If you follow the principles spelled out in these pages, you can't stop the results!

—MARK JONES, DMIN, LMFT

You owe it to yourself—and your Creator—to learn the principles found in the ZOE W8 Loss Program. As a young man with a busy schedule, I often robbed myself of living to my maximum potential because of health issues related to excessive weight. Having been introduced to this wonderful way of life, I have enjoyed life more abundantly. If *how* is your question, ZOE 8 is your answer.

—MATTHEW HAGEE, ASSOCIATE PASTOR
CORNERSTONE CHURCH, SAN ANTONIO, TX

Not only did the ZOE 8 program produce immediate results for me (both in my losing a few extra pounds and getting rid of severe heartburn), it also literally saved the life of my sister-in-law. This book is about far more than weight loss; it's about improving health and discovering a quality of life that is unsurpassed—and that's a benefit every reader can experience.

—JIMMY SEWELL, PASTOR
NEW HOPE FELLOWSHIP, BOERNE, TX

I have been through the program myself and refer patients who need to lose weight or improve health conditions. I highly recommend *Eat Your Way to a Healthy Life*—your search for an effective weight-loss and health-management plan is over.

—MICHAEL S. BOSS, DC

When I saw Ed McClure lose what appeared to be half his body weight—without looking like someone who has lost enough weight to be ready for the grave—I asked him what he did. Ed and his wife, Elisa, freely shared with us how we could conquer our weight problem once and for all. We put the information to work, and over the next year I lost more than 100 pounds and my wife lost more than 70. We've kept the weight off, even while serving on the mission field, and our health is great. We are allergy-free and enjoy eating foods that taste great and help maintain our weight loss.

—REV. NEIL AND MARLENE CASSATA
MISSIONARIES TO AUSTRALIA

I have known Ed McClure since 1994, when on a Sunday morning Christ spiritually reclaimed him and placed him on the road to full recovery. Ed's sincerity, humility, and willingness to trust and receive correction have allowed God to accomplish the miraculous! His character has been shaped on the anvil of challenging trials and difficulties, and I believe God has a tempered instrument in Ed to bring deliverance to thousands of lives.

—DUB JONES, PASTOR
BOERNE ASSEMBLY OF GOD

Eat Your Way TO A Healthy Life

ED & ELISA McCLURE

SILOAM
A STRANG COMPANY

Most Strang Communications/Charisma House/Siloam/Realms products are available at special quantity discounts for bulk purchase for sales promotions, premiums, fund-raising, and educational needs. For details, write Strang Communications/Charisma House/Siloam/Realms, 600 Rinehart Road, Lake Mary, Florida 32746, or telephone (407) 333-0600.

Eat Your Way to a Healthy Life by Ed and Elisa McClure
Published by Siloam
A Strang Company
600 Rinehart Road
Lake Mary, Florida 32746
www.siloam.com

This book or parts thereof may not be reproduced in any form, stored in a retrieval system, or transmitted in any form by any means—electronic, mechanical, photocopy, recording, or otherwise—without prior written permission of the publisher, except as provided by United States of America copyright law.

Unless otherwise noted, all Scripture quotations are from the Holy Bible, New International Version. Copyright © 1973, 1978, 1984, International Bible Society. Used by permission.

Scripture quotations marked KJV are from the King James Version of the Bible.

Scripture quotations marked NKJV are from the New King James Version of the Bible. Copyright © 1979, 1980, 1982 by Thomas Nelson, Inc., publishers. Used by permission.

Cover design by Bill Johnson
interior design by Terry Clifton
Author photo©MarksMoore.com

Neither the publisher nor the author is engaged in rendering professional advice or services to the individual reader. The ideas, procedures, and suggestions in this book are not intended as a substitute for consulting with your physician. All matters regarding your health require medical supervision. Neither the author nor the publisher shall be liable or responsible for any loss or damage allegedly arising from any information or suggestion in this book. We highly recommend that you enlist a qualified medical practitioner as a partner in a weight-loss and health-management program. Neither the publisher nor the author makes any guarantee. Individual results may vary depending on commitment and other factors.

The recipes in this book are to be followed exactly as written. The publisher is not responsible for your specific health or allergy needs that may require medical supervision. The publisher is not responsible for any adverse reactions to the recipes contained in this book.

While the author has made every effort to provide accurate telephone numbers and Internet addresses at the time of publication, neither the publisher nor the author assumes any responsibility for errors or for changes that occur after publication.

Copyright © 2006 by ZOE 8
All rights reserved

Library of Congress Cataloging-in-Publication Data:
An application to register this book for cataloging has been submitted to the Library of Congress.
International Standard Book Number: 1-59185-919-0
First Edition
06 07 08 09 10 — 987654321
Printed in the United States of America

Dedication

Ed **I** would like to dedicate this book to my heavenly Father, God. To me, he is love; he is all knowledge, all wisdom, and all might. This book isn't for him; it *is* his and for all his children of every faith, every race, every health condition, every day, and everywhere.

I also dedicate this book to the five people God has personally chosen to share my life in him:

My wife, Elisa. No matter all the specifics of our past or our future, I thank God and you for each day since I met you and every day to come. I love you. No man could ask for more than you.

My daughter and son, Taylor and Ian. May you find in your futures the love and joy you've brought and bring to my life.

My mother, Delyte, so aptly named, who first introduced me to my heavenly Father and who loves me still.

My pastor, Dub Jones, who personally reintroduced me to my heavenly Father twelve years ago. He has taught and loved me well and pastors me still.

Thank you all.

☙

Elisa **FIRST,** I dedicate this book to my family, Ed, Taylor, and Ian, who always display and live the true meaning of unconditional family love.

My mom and dad, brothers Peter, Steven, and John, and sister Jeanne for the foundation of family, love, and fun, and for a culture of hospitality and great family food passed down from the long line of Italian ancestors before us!

Yvonne, my true friend, who encourages me to do what I think I can't.

Then to all of you who read this book, employ the principles, eat healthy whole foods, and embrace the abundant life God has for you in spirit, mind, and body.

Acknowledgments

FIRST, we wish to acknowledge our children, Taylor and Ian, who lived it—and thankfully live it—with us daily.

A work of this magnitude requires the concerted effort of an entire team, and we have been abundantly blessed in that respect. We would like to thank Pastor John Hagee, his wife and partner, Diana Hagee, and Terry Thompson of John Hagee Ministries for referring and encouraging us to share our project with Strang Communications. We thank Stephen Strang, Bert Ghezzi, and Barbara Dycus of Strang Communications for their willingness to take on this project and their shepherding of the finished product. Debbie Marrie not only lent her skills as an editor, but she also took time to travel to Texas for a ZOE 8 seminar and became an enthusiastic supporter not just of this book but of the entire ZOE 8 Weight Management Program.

We also thank Connie Reece, our writer, who throughout the process applied ZOE 8 to her life and became a valuable contributing member not just to the book but also of the ZOE family.

Special thanks are due to Charles Stallcup and Yvonne Olvey, who added additional projects to an already heavy workload in order to facilitate the writing of this book, and to Jason and Leslie Coleman who worked with us in the beginning for many hours organizing our thoughts and documenting them to create our first seminar. Elisa's mom, Diana Travisono, and her sister, Jeanne Travisono—both professionals in the publishing field—volunteered many hours to read the manuscript and offer suggestions, as did our friend Kimberly Smith.

My associate Chris Hagee, along with Pastor John and Diana Hagee, made the initial contact with Mary Colbert on our behalf, and we will forever be in their debt for the introduction and Mary's efforts. The Hagees have taken a personal interest not only in us but also in our endeavors, and we value our association with their family and ministry.

Words are completely inadequate to properly thank Dr. Don Colbert and Dr. Mark Jones, whose words of wisdom and compassionate guidance are reflected throughout these pages. Without these two godly men in our lives, we would not be where we are today.

Finally, we are grateful for those who contributed their personal stories for this book—Gil, Judy, Rusty, Margie, Linda, Oliver, and the Sutton family—and all those who have sought help for health or weight problems through ZOE 8. Sharing our experiences and knowledge with others has become the high calling of God on our lives, and it is a privilege to now bring this information to a larger audience.

Thank you all.

—Ed and Elisa

Contents

Table of Charts

Foreword

ED McClure has been a patient of mine for several years. When I initially saw Ed, he was suffering from morbid obesity, hypertension, reflux esophagitis, sleep apnea, psoriasis, glucose intolerance (prediabetes), asthma, fatigue, osteoarthritis of his knees, allergic rhinitis, and depression. Ed was also taking eight different medicines. I have watched him lose almost 200 pounds and overcome all the health problems that have plagued him for many years; he has also been able to come off all his medication. I have been delighted to see him answer his unique calling to help others lose weight and achieve vibrant health.

The ZOE 8 dietary program addresses many of the components of why people overeat. It takes a whole-person, lifestyle approach to nutrition and weight loss. Especially important is Ed's treatment of the emotional and spiritual elements of overeating. I recommend the ZOE 8 program to all my patients who are overweight. I have seen many individuals reach a healthy body weight and maintain it by following these teachings. Most of them were also able to overcome many of the diseases associated with obesity.

Ed and Elisa make a wonderful team. They are extremely creative when it comes to making new recipes—recipes that are not only healthy but also very tasty. Many obese individuals get tired of eating the same boring recipes. Ed and Elisa have developed some delicious, healthy recipes that make this program exciting and easy to follow. I have found that if patients enjoy their food, they are much more likely to stick to the program. This also fulfills Ecclesiastes 9:7, which says, "Go, eat your food with gladness, and drink your wine with a joyful heart, for it is now that God favors what you do."

Obesity is the root cause of so many diseases—hypertension, sleep apnea, type 2 diabetes, GE reflux, high cholesterol, heart disease, and even cancer, just to name a few—so there has never been a time when *Eat Your Way to a Healthy Life* has been more urgently needed.

—Don Colbert, MD
Lake Mary, Florida

Introduction

PSSST! This book is for you...yes, you!

You see, this is not just a weight-loss book. Oh, the principles inside will melt away the pounds, if that is what you are after. I lost 200 pounds in twelve months and have kept it off for three years now. But the very same principles will just as surely put pounds on you, if that is what you need. And, remarkably, you will automatically promote regulation of your blood pressure, lower your cholesterol, normalize your blood sugar, and clear up many skin disorders. Emotional issues can become a part of your past, and you can enjoy a deeper, more rewarding—and fun—life. That is why the book is called *Eat Your Way to a Healthy Life*, and the "secrets" are all inside.

This book will also benefit people with no health issues at all, particularly children and young adults. Why? They have the most to lose—or gain, if you will—by making sure they never experience any of the serious health problems I once endured.

And if you are a "supertanker," my affectionate term for individuals, like me, who somehow find themselves dangerously overweight—well, you are about to get some remarkable answers to questions that have no doubt haunted you for some time.

Bottom line: the following pages present solutions and prevention strategies to help you reach your individual weight and health goals. As you read, it will help you to know that my wife, Elisa, and I have each written sections of the book from our own perspectives. When the perspective changes from mine to hers, and vice versa, you will be signaled by one of our names at the beginning of the paragraph. Before you start, you need to know three things:

1. The ZOE 8 program addresses the whole you. Let me explain it this way. My name is Ed, I live in a body, I definitely have a mind and emotions, and I am positive there is more to me than you can see: my spirit. I achieved amazing improvements in my physical health by addressing the whole me—body, mind, and spirit. And you can achieve the results you need as well.

2. This is not a diet or a quick fix. The ZOE 8 program is unique because it is a sustainable approach to curing, or preventing, what ails you. Why do diets fail? Because they are not sustainable. Diets are something you start

and stop. But ZOE 8 is different. It is all about balance. Balanced nutrition. Body, mind, and spirit balance.

ZOE 8 is also all about you—not me, and not the latest fad or theory. ZOE 8 is built on solid science—facts that will ring true as you read. Further, ZOE 8 will not try to change who you are. Your ethnicity, your culture, and your food likes and dislikes are essential to a balanced, sustainable lifestyle. This takes a little time, but you—and your loved ones—are worth it.

3. God is a part of our lives. Whoa, don't quit on me now! Please, just for a moment, regardless of your background or spiritual life (if any), hear me out. People of many different faiths and many with no faith or spiritual beliefs at all have benefited from our program. I have already said I am not out to change who you are; I just want you to know where I'm coming from and how I achieved my health objectives.

Many years ago Elisa and I made a personal choice to believe in a God who is almighty, our Creator. We also personally believe that the Bible, the top-selling book for a century or two, is the irrefutable, unalterable, precise Word of God. After all, if you believe in an omnipotent God, it is not much of a leap to believe he can get his message and words right.

Nowhere in this book do we ask you to believe what we believe; we are simply sharing my story and what we have learned about weight loss, balanced nutrition, and an abundantly healthy lifestyle. Neither do we ask you to believe the biblical quotes we have used in the same way we believe them. All Elisa and I ask is that you consider the merit of what is said as you would when reading any book.

We have two children: a daughter, Taylor, and a son, Ian. We know just how much we love them and all the wonderful things we desire for them. Our concept of God is that he loves each of us—you, me, all of us—in a way that transcends our love for our own children.

SO WHO IS THIS ZOE CHARACTER?

Zoe is not a who; it is a what. It is an eight-step program for weight loss and health management—a total health program, we sometimes call it—and here is how the name came about.

In January 2004 a valued and valuable friend, Diana Hagee, listened to a presentation of our program and suggested that Elisa and I pray for a descriptive name. She indicated that she and her husband, John Hagee, who pastors Cornerstone Church in San Antonio, often did this when they were creating or launching "new" visions. "There is a name and a number that is right for your program," she said succinctly. Eight months later, after a number of brainstorming sessions, and after much prayer, the name ZOE and the number eight came to be.

Zoe is the Greek word for life, specifically life as the gift of God. The apostle John, friend and disciple of Jesus, recorded these words that his master spoke: "I have come that they may have life [*zoe*], and that they may have it more abundantly" (John 10:10, NKJV). Jesus was referring to the fullness of life that God intended for his creation—you and me. And it is a life beyond anything we can comprehend.

The number eight signifies a new beginning, regeneration, or resurrection. The ancient Hebrews put a great emphasis on numbers, which are often used in a descriptive way in the Bible. That is why male children were circumcised on the eighth day, for example, signifying the entrance into a covenant with God. That is also why the eighth day, the day following the end of a seven-day feast, signaled the beginning of a new cycle of growth.

So the name ZOE 8 reflects the idea that it is possible for you to have a new beginning for a well-balanced, healthy lifestyle. My new beginning was absolutely necessary, or I would be pushing up daisies now instead of giving a message of hope, peace, joy, and health.

What is an "abundant" life? Like the ZOE 8 program itself, that is an individual issue. But I can tell you what an abundant life is not: I have lived that. It was being so heavy I could barely walk, suffering from high blood pressure, heart arrhythmia, bleeding psoriasis, and all sorts of chronic health conditions. I can also tell what abundant life is for me now. It is having no health issues that steal my money, no limitations on my ability to participate in activities with my family, and no impediments that keep me from enjoying all aspects of my life. I am happy and at peace with myself. It was a long and winding road to get here, and my hope is that reading about my experiences will shorten your route to the abundant life you deserve and desire.

What about weight? It seems that everybody is concerned with their weight. Our recommendation is that you find your ZOE W8 (weight) as part of your zoe life. What is that? It is pretty simple, actually. It is the weight at which you achieve the life I have just described—not some "ideal" weight determined by a chart or a study or the latest diet plan or Madison Avenue or Hollywood; those change all the time.

Frankly, this concept made our publisher a little nervous. It goes against the grain and seems to contradict established medical standards. My first concern is pleasing God, then my family and myself—not pleasing the medical establishment. My desire for writing this book is to help you. But although our food plan may not fully comply with the medical establishment by pinpointing some arbitrary number as an ideal weight, it does embrace and utilize the latest medical and nutritional research. After all, you can't be at your ZOE W8 and enjoy a zoe life if you have high blood pressure, high cholesterol, out-of-control blood sugar, or chronic pain. Let's recognize that people come in all sizes and body types. It is not the outward appearance that counts. It is the inward health—physical, mental, and spiritual. A person can exemplify some standard of ideal weight and still be unhealthy. That is "not zoe."

I am at a ZOE W8 for me. Yet it's possible some people may look at me and say, "But you are still too big." Well, let me put it to you the way I put it to our publisher when we were deciding to do this book together. I have regular checkups, and every single measurement of my blood chemistry is in the normal range. I lift weights—over 20,000 pounds in one training session—and I can do sixty minutes of intense aerobic exercise with great cardiopulmonary function. I feel great, and I have tons of energy.

Consider this. Three years ago I could not obtain adequate life insurance because of my health. I had the highest possible rating; any higher and I would have been uninsurable. Now insurance executives are not doctors, but they are pretty good at what they do, and they employ a lot of doctors and individuals called actuaries, who make a living determining how long someone is going to live. This year I secured almost six million dollars in life insurance coverage, my insurability is guaranteed to age seventy-two, and I will only pay a portion of my past premiums.

That is "pretty zoe," I would say. Oh yes, did I mention I am having fun, I love life, and I am at peace? Well, here's to the same for you—now and in the future.

Take your time reading and examining what is inside. I believe you will find that you truly can *Eat Your Way to a Healthy Life.*

Chapter One

"Ed, You Are Going to Melt"

ON a bleak Tuesday afternoon in late January 2002, a handful of people assembled on the long porch of Ye Kendall Inn, the historical hotel that serves as our company's flagship property, to see me off on the journey that would save my life. I shook hands with a few employees, hugged my family, and then wedged myself into the driver's seat of my Mercedes S500, one of the only cars into which I could still fit. As I pulled out of the parking lot, I was close to tears. In the rearview mirror I could see my wife, Elisa, and our children, Taylor and Ian, waving good-bye. It would be more than a month before I would be home again, and it was difficult to imagine being away so long. I had never even taken an entire week off from work, let alone a month.

I headed east on Interstate 10, dreading the long drive from Texas to Florida, but I needed to travel by car for many reasons. Flying had become an ordeal. I hurt too much to walk through the airport, plus I had to buy two seats and use a seat belt extension. And all the time I would have to ignore the stares of the other passengers.

There's no place for me in this world, I thought. *I simply don't fit.*

At my size, I did not fit physically. Not in airplane seats. Not in restaurant booths. Not in movie theater seats. Not in public restrooms. And never through a turnstile. Travel had become almost impossible, and family vacations were a thing of the past.

I did not fit socially, either. I was an embarrassment to my family and a terrible example to my employees and fellow church members. My size had isolated me from the things and the people I loved the most.

For several years I had prayerfully been asking God for relief somehow. I never thought of killing myself, not at all. It is just that the pain—physical, emotional, and spiritual—had become more than I could bear, and I craved release, even if that meant leaving this world and going to heaven.

1

I would often look in the mirror and ask myself, *When is enough, enough? When are you going to do something?*

I had come to the realization that I either had to make a drastic change, and make it soon, or I would die. I sensed the end was near. And even though I had prayed many times for the Lord to take me home, I still wanted to live—at least enough to make one last effort to do something about my tremendous weight problem and all the health conditions and emotional pain it had caused. My knees were crumbling under the burden of all the extra pounds, and I could barely walk. I relied on a cabinet full of medications to control high blood pressure, heart arrhythmia, depression, anxiety, and all my other ailments. My psoriasis was so bad that it had erupted into open, bleeding wounds on my skin, and because of sleep apnea, I had to sleep with a breathing machine.

So here I was, headed to Durham, North Carolina, to enter Structure House, a residential treatment center for obesity management and one of the few places equipped to deal with people as large as I was. But first I was stopping in Florida to see a new doctor, one who had been recommended by one of my employees, Chris Hagee. He was a last resort, if you will, but I was desperate enough to give this doctor a try.

When Chris had found out I was committing to spend four weeks, not to mention a small fortune, at a prestigious weight-loss clinic, he encouraged me to go see the doctor who had treated his brother. "You really should see Don Colbert," Chris told me. "He's helped my brother Matt lose more than 150 pounds."

"I recognize the name," I told Chris. "I saw Colbert on television once." I had been impressed by the striking man. He was very fit and very handsome, but what was so compelling about the doctor was the depth of his knowledge and passion. He was obviously a dynamic personality.

"If you are going away for a month to this program," Chris said, "why don't you at least meet Don? He might have the answer for you."

An answer. Was there really an answer for me? I was hoping the treatment center would give me some tools to help. They had told me I would probably lose fifteen to twenty pounds while I was there, but that was the proverbial drop in the bucket. I needed a serious plan if I was going to beat my weight problem once and for all.

When Chris offered to facilitate the contact with Dr. Colbert, I told him to go ahead. "But it will have to work out quickly," I said. "I'm leaving in less than a week."

When I finished talking to Chris, I was immediately absorbed in my work again. Work was my life. It was the one area where I felt in control. I had created the "world of Ed," a realm in which I was successful and confident: business. But outside of creating restaurants, hotel management contracts, and deal making, my life was a shambles.

Later that day I got a call from Diana Hagee. She and her husband, Pastor John Hagee of Cornerstone Church in San Antonio, were good friends with Don Colbert, who had been on their television program a number of times.

"I just got off the phone with Mary Colbert," she told me, referring to Don's wife. "I didn't think they'd be able to see you on such short notice because Don has more patients than he can handle."

"That's OK," I said. "It was worth a try, and I appreciate your making the call."

"But Mary said they can see you—Thursday morning, if you can get there." Diana spent a few minutes encouraging me to make the appointment, and I agreed.

What can it hurt? I thought. Perhaps this was a door God had opened for me. If so, I owed it to myself to take advantage of the opportunity to see Dr. Colbert. I moved my departure up a few days and decided to head to North Carolina by way of Orlando.

On Tuesday I loaded all my clothes and gear in the car, along with my new laptop computer—which I still didn't know how to use very well. My aide-de-camp, Charles Stallcup, had given me a brief demonstration of the basics. I would be able to send e-mail and read spreadsheets, if I could remember what he had showed me. Up until that time, I had arrogantly refused to learn how to use a computer. After all, I was king in the "world of Ed," and I had employees to do that kind of work for me.

But I was on my own now, at least for the next few weeks. I drove until midnight that first night and got back on the road early the next morning. From Baton Rouge to Tallahassee I was on the cell phone, changing out batteries every couple of hours, running my business from the car. It was an old pattern, and I kept at it nonstop, until I reached Orlando at around 10:00 p.m.

As scheduled, I arrived at Don Colbert's office at 9:00 sharp on Thursday morning. His office was in a residential area out in the suburbs. I looked at the one-story, red brick colonial building with its simple white shutters and less-than-imposing columns and thought, *I drove twelve hundred miles for this?* It certainly didn't look like a high-powered doctor's office. The other tenants in the complex were insurance and real estate agents and a few other small businesses. I almost turned the car around in the parking lot and left.

I had come too far to turn back, however. So I went inside. The waiting room was not fancy but very nice, furnished with cherry armchairs and benches covered in teal fabric and glass cases full of books Dr. Colbert had written. Christian music played softly in the background, and spelled out in gold letters on the wall was a verse from the Bible, John 10:10. I read the words of Jesus: "I have come that they may have life, and that they may have it more abundantly." I had been a Spirit-filled, Bible-quoting Christian for a long time, yet I knew I was not experiencing anything near abundant life.

After I filled out the typical medical history forms, the nurse called me into the examining room. When Dr. Colbert came in, he had me sit in a chair. He sat on a stool across from me, and we talked while he flipped through my chart. It was thicker than the usual chart because it included all the medical records and lab reports I had brought with me—copies of the extensive information the North Carolina treatment center had required for registration. I had already been through several physical exams, lab tests, and a treadmill stress test, and here I was talking to yet another doctor.

Dr. Colbert stopped at a couple of different points and asked questions, reading very quickly then talking very fast—it was almost like having a conversation with a computer, I thought. His brain could process a gigabyte of information in a matter of seconds, and then his mouth would spit out a question or comment that would zero straight in on a problem. I was fascinated.

Somehow it came out in the discussion that I had not been raised by my father. He was an alcoholic and so abusive that my mother—a precious Christian woman who did not believe in divorce—eventually ended the marriage. I had not seen or heard from my father from the time I was five until I was seventeen, but I spoke about it matter-of-factly; it didn't seem like such a big deal. Actually, I had never given it that much thought.

After we went through my medical history, I climbed up on the exam table, and Dr. Colbert began to look at my skin and briefly did some muscle testing. He paused and said, "You realize how close to death you are."

It wasn't a question as much as a statement, and I did recognize just how precarious my hold on life was. I also recognized that this was a moment of truth for me. I had been with Don Colbert for maybe fifteen minutes, yet I felt a connection with him and had the strong impression that God truly had sent me here for the answer Chris Hagee had alluded to a few days earlier.

Don's blue eyes bore into mine. "Actually, you could go at any time. You know that."

I nodded. "Yes, I know that." He had a very direct and truthful way of speaking, but it wasn't harsh. Instead, it had the effect of pulling a truthful response out of me.

It surprised me that I wasn't scared or embarrassed to admit it. No one had ever spoken to me like that before—not my family, not my friends, not my doctors—but I felt totally comfortable in the presence of this brilliant doctor who was talking to me like I was a real person, not just some anonymous patient he would never see again. That had been my previous experience with most doctors; many of them were detached, and a few had even treated me as if I were somehow invisible while sitting on their exam table.

"I talked to the Hagees about you," Dr. Colbert said, "and I know you are a strong man, a man of God." He acknowledged all the different medical conditions I was facing, but then he said, "The root of your problem is spiritual. The spirit of rejection is literally extinguishing your life. It goes back to your early childhood and your father. We have to deal with that deep-seated rejection before we can deal with the medical issues. Once we do that, the physical problems will not be all that difficult to fix."

I doubted it was the kind of thing he would usually say to a new patient, and I suppose such a spiritual diagnosis should have sounded strange or weird coming from a medical doctor, yet I sensed the presence of God in that room and readily accepted what Dr. Colbert said. I do not know how else to express it other than I felt as if I had entered into a time capsule. I was totally in the moment, and even though things were happening very fast, I knew this was something huge, that it would be a defining moment in my life.

"Your life is being stolen from you, Ed. But we can deal with this thing right now if you are ready. You have to decide if you want to live. It is up to you."

And I did. At that moment I knew, despite everything, I really did not want to go home to heaven now. I wanted to be around for my family.

"I'm ready," I told him.

"Then we're going to get down on our knees." Dr. Colbert turned the lone armchair around and repositioned it. "This will be our altar."

I climbed off the exam table and struggled to get down on my knees. I hadn't been able to kneel in church in years, and the linoleum floors of the examining room were cold and hard. My knees were so shot that I had already consulted an orthopedic surgeon about knee replacements. But I managed to kneel in front of our makeshift altar, and Don Colbert began to lead me through a prayer.

I cannot remember the words, even though I repeated them after Don. And I have no idea how long we prayed. All I can remember is that waves of peace swept over me. I felt completely safe and protected, and the tears I had been holding back for years began to spill over and flow down my cheeks.

After a while Don asked his wife, Mary, and his assistant to join us. I had taken my glasses off because I was crying hard, so I couldn't really see them. But when I heard these two godly women begin to petition heaven on my behalf, it seemed that something broke inside of me. They asked God to release me from the spirit of rejection that had defined my life. They prayed for my restoration—spirit, soul, and body. The more we prayed, the lighter I felt—not lighter in body, but lighter in spirit. Things that had weighed me down seemed to lift, and for the first time in decades, I felt a stirring of genuine hope. I have been in some anointed prayer meetings before, but I had never experienced anything as intense, and ultimately life changing, as I did kneeling on that hard linoleum floor in a rather nondescript doctor's office.

After we concluded the prayer, Dr. Colbert completed my physical exam. He talked about some of the previously diagnosed issues that were obvious, like the sleep apnea. But he rapidly pointed out other undiagnosed conditions. Where other doctors had written off some of my problems as stress—"Change jobs," they said. "You just have too much stress in your life."—Don identified certain physical problems that had contributed to my tremendous weight gain. And they were problems that could be reversed, he said.

"You have a systemic yeast infection," he told me. That surprised me; I thought yeast infections were something women contracted. But he explained that candidiasis, a serious yeast infection, can occur when the beneficial bacteria in our bodies can no longer keep *candida albicans*, a naturally occurring yeast organism, in check. The infection results from eating too many of the foods, like sugar, that allow the organism to flourish.

"Medications can cause the condition as well." Dr. Colbert pointed to my medical history. "When your appendix burst back in 1981, you were on antibiotics for six weeks. That destroyed the good bacteria in your intestines, and your digestive system has been impaired ever since. That is significant, and it helps explain why you continued to gain ten to fifteen pounds every year, no matter what you ate or how much you dieted."

He got my attention with that. I had tried every diet program that looked the least bit promising—from liquid diets to dehydrated food. I tried practically every major diet several times and had worked my way through the hit parade of diet plans, but nothing had seemed to work for me. After twenty years, that steady gain of weight had ballooned into an extra 200 pounds or more.

Dr. Colbert detailed other problems he had found. "Your adrenal glands are shot. You have been running on adrenaline for so long that your body is in a state of collapse, shutting down on itself. Nothing is functioning right. The candida and other toxins in your body are so pervasive that they are bursting out through your skin in psoriasis.

"I will run some blood tests to confirm it," he continued, "but I'm sure that your hormones are out of kilter, especially testosterone. That alone would make losing weight extremely difficult for you."

I listened in stunned silence. It was all making sense. He was not talking about new medications or treatments for depression or high blood pressure; he was getting to the root causes of all the health conditions I had been battling. It was not just stress. And I was not some weak-willed person who was out of control. Could it be that, for the first time, there really was an explanation? I just might have real, physical issues that could be reversed, or at least improved immensely, and Dr. Colbert had already identified the root of my emotional and spiritual battle: rejection.

The next thing he said surprised me even more. "Don't even think about losing weight right now," he told me. "You are not ready. Your body is so weak and depleted, you could die." He gave me samples of some supplements he wanted me to take and explained what each one would do.

"Keep reading the Word of God and praying," he instructed. "You have to get past the feelings of rejection. You have to learn to love yourself and at the same time build your body up so you are ready to fight. When you do that, the pounds will melt away."

By that time I was convinced I had the answer I had so desperately needed. But Dr. Colbert encouraged me to go ahead and spend the four weeks I'd signed up for at the treatment center in North Carolina. "It is a very reputable place," he said, "and you need to get away and let your body rest. It will do you good."

He concluded by giving me a food plan for battling candida. It was just a photocopied list of "don'ts" on a letter-sized sheet of paper. But that single piece of paper became a stepping stone to complete health.

When I left Dr. Colbert's office and got back in my car—five hours after I had arrived—I knew my life had changed forever. He had told me, "Ed, you are going to melt." And he was right. I dropped 200 pounds in the next twelve months, and the purpose of writing this book is to tell you how I did it.

✍

WHILE Ed's battle with weight and health was obvious to everyone, my problems with food were hidden. I may have looked healthy from outward appearances, but my body had turned against me. Almost everything I ate disagreed with me. I was always in pain, and my stomach stayed bloated. Some days I could not eat at all. When I did eat, I would be sick for two or three days.

We had access to excellent health care, so I went to several doctors about the problem. No one could find out what was wrong. Every test they ran came back "normal," yet I was getting worse.

I heard the same kind of reports Ed had: "There's nothing wrong with you. It is just stress. Your husband moves around a lot because of his career, and you are raising two children. You need to learn to cope with all the stress in your life."

Years later I realized that I was suffering from irritable bowel syndrome, but at the time I could not get a diagnosis, and I did not know what to do. I had always eaten a balanced diet; my mother had ingrained it into me. I still employed good food rules, following the USDA food pyramid and accepted nutritional principles. It turns out that was the very thing that was killing me. I had developed a sensitivity to wheat and some of the other foods, like lettuce, typically recommended for a healthy diet. As a result, my intestinal tract was so irritated that it got to where I couldn't eat anything without serious consequences.

Also, like Ed, travel became quite difficult for me because I always had to use the restroom. Long flights filled me with anxiety, and when we traveled by car, I had to make frequent stops. It was either that or not eat at all while traveling, which was sometimes my choice. But you can only go so long without eating.

In 1993 we started attending church regularly. Growing up in the Catholic church, I had taken my faith for granted. Now, however, I was developing a personal relationship with God, and I began to study Scripture seriously. I came to realize that God was interested in our daily lives. He was interested in whether we were healthy or not. When I heard the pastor refer to Jesus as the Great Physician, it made perfect sense to me. After all, God created our bodies, so he knows exactly how they are supposed to work. I began to meditate on God's Word and to pray that the Great Physician would heal my body and show me what foods to eat.

I continued to read and learn about nutrition. Cooking was my passion, and I read cookbooks the same way some people read novels. I devoured books on food and healthy living. Over the years I accumulated a great deal of knowledge, but I never found the right combination to unlock the key to healthy eating for me.

Then I began to pray over everything I ate. *Should I eat this or stay away from it?* I would pray silently at every meal. I didn't tell anybody what I was doing because I didn't want to hear people say, "Yeah, right. God tells you what to eat."

But he did. Every time I prayed over my food, I would know what to eat and what to avoid. What had been a hit-or-miss proposition, analyzing after the fact whether a particular food made me sick or not, became a sure thing. I had "inside information," if you will, straight from the Great Physician.

With God's help I developed a personalized food plan and began to improve. Much later Dr. Colbert would confirm that the program God had been guiding me through was exactly what doctors began using to treat irritable bowel syndrome—once they had pinned a label on the disorder and started figuring out what to do about it.

I had learned that certain foods would sit in my stomach forever; they just would not digest, and that was what left me bloated and in pain. It was not the quantity of food I was eating; it was what I was eating. Evidently my body did not have enough of the right enzymes to break down the food in my intestinal tract. I started taking digestive enzymes but found that some of them were very harsh, so I stopped.

Gradually, my body began to heal, but the complete reversal of my condition really started when one of Ed's doctors, a local physician he had seen for years, recommended a particular enzymatic supplement. This one contained only the enzymes our bodies actually produce. I noticed the difference immediately. This supplement gave my body the support it needed to restore my pancreatic function and allow my intestines to heal. Food no longer sat in my stomach causing pain and bloating; instead, I started to digest my food normally.

There were still some foods I had to stay away from because my body would not tolerate them. Lettuce, for example, was a big problem for me. It was not until we started working on this book, in fact, that I attempted to eat lettuce again.

Our writer, Connie Reece, had been talking with me about the book all afternoon, and we decided to take a dinner break. We got a table at the Limestone Grille, our restaurant inside Ye Kendall Inn, and studied the menu—which was not necessary for me; I knew the menu by heart because I had helped to create it. But I went through my usual routine of deciding what to eat, asking myself, *What am I hungry for? What will be good for my body?*

When I told the server I wanted the Salade Niçoise, I saw Connie's eyebrows shoot up. She had just learned that I had avoided lettuce for years, and here I was ordering a salad. But it was the only thing that sounded good to me at that moment, and somehow I knew that it would be OK; I had received the green light from the Great Physician.

"I believe my body has healed enough to eat salad again," I told Connie with a smile.

And I was right. I have never eaten a more delicious salad, and it did not cause me any digestive problems. It was yet another milestone on my journey to optimal health.

I still eat salads and some other foods judiciously, but I have trained my body to crave the foods that will benefit me the most. I love to cook and eat great food! And my desire for you is to show you how to customize a food plan for your particular needs, just as I learned to do.

In the following pages we will share the principles it took us many years to discover. But don't be discouraged: it will not take you nearly as long to start improving, because we are giving you the benefit of the knowledge we have accumulated by trial and error.

You will learn how we took that one sheet of paper about candida from Dr. Colbert, combined it with years of research on nutrition plus decades of experience in creating award-winning gourmet restaurants, added to the mix principles for spiritual and emotional healing, and came up with an entire weight-loss and health-management program of our own. It is a program that works equally well for those who want to lose ten pounds, one hundred pounds or more, or for those who simply want to improve their health. We will show you how to adopt a sustainable lifestyle of vitality and well-being and teach you, step by step, how to apply these principles to your life.

But first, let's take a brief look at the problem. How did we get here? How did so many Americans become so overweight and out of shape?

Chapter Two

America Supersized: Why We Are Getting Fatter and Sicker

WHEN we were children, soft drinks were an occasional treat, not a daily staple. They were sweetened with cane sugar and came in 6- to 8-ounce servings. A "Big Gulp" was free—it was something you took at the water fountain when you were hot and sweaty from playing outside.

Today, toddlers can recognize McDonald's golden arches before they are able to speak, and 7-Eleven's Big Gulp is 32 ounces—a full quart—of artificially flavored soda sweetened with cheap, high-fructose corn syrup. That one soft drink, completely devoid of nutritional benefit, provides more than 10 percent of a young person's daily calorie requirement and enough sugar (more than 80 grams) to insure bouncing-off-the-walls hyperactivity. Evidently, though, the Big Gulp does not quite satisfy our national obsession with supersizing; there's also a Super Big Gulp (44 ounces) and the 7-Eleven X-treme Gulp (52 ounces).[1]

Morgan Spurlock's hugely successful 2004 documentary, *Super Size Me*, vividly portrayed the perils of living on a supersized diet of fast food. In real life, no one eats at McDonald's, or any other fast-food restaurant, for three meals a day. But "heavy users," as they are referred to in the industry, visit twenty times a month and are likely to consume a day's worth of calories in a single meal.

In the last three decades the American diet has undergone a radical transformation, and the proliferation of junk food in restaurants and on grocery store shelves has triggered an epidemic of obesity in America—an epidemic that is spreading around the globe as more and more countries fall prey to the marketing ploys of the manufacturers of convenience food. Figures compiled by the American Obesity Association in 2000 show that 64.5 percent of American adults are overweight; almost half of those—over 30 percent of all adults—are classified as obese.[2] The number of children who are overweight or obese has doubled; about one-fourth of those nineteen and under now fall into that category.[3] Physicians are seeing an unprecedented number of young patients with type 2 diabetes—a disease previously seen only in adults.

Dr. Francine R. Kaufman, a professor of pediatrics and past president of the American Diabetes Association, has said that before the mid-1990s type 2 diabetes was so rare in children that cases were written up in medical journals. But by 1997 such cases were becoming so common that the ADA recommended that the term "adult-onset diabetes" be dropped. "Think of youngsters with type 2 diabetes," Kaufman says, "as the proverbial canaries in the coal mine: they signal that something is very wrong and endangers us all."[4]

The following chart demonstrates how obesity rates have ballooned over the last thirty years. Using body mass index (BMI) as an indicator, the first column shows the percentage of American adults who would be considered overweight (BMI > 25). Among those who are overweight, the next two columns show the percentage who are obese (BMI > 30) or severely obese (BMI > 40).[5]

INCREASE IN PREVALENCE OF OBESITY AMONG U.S. ADULTS			
	Total Overweight (BMI > 25)	Obese (BMI > 30)	Severely Obese (BMI > 40)
1999–2000	64.5	30.5	4.7
1988–1994	56.0	23.0	2.9
1976–1980	46.0	14.4	No data

"I'LL TAKE FOOD FACTS FOR $200, ALEX"

To show the underlying causes of these skyrocketing obesity numbers, allow me to describe briefly a bit of food history as it relates to perhaps the two most dramatic changes in the American diet over the last thirty years. Back in the 1970s, during an era of economic inflation, food prices hit an all-time high. To help farmers, the U.S. government relaxed trade barriers and ended mandatory grain storage. As a result, corn production soared—about the same time that Japanese scientists developed a cheap corn-based sweetener called high-fructose corn syrup (HFCS). This new sweetener was six times sweeter than cane sugar and would drastically reduce manufacturing costs for refined or highly sweetened products.

American food manufacturers soon put the corn surplus and the new technology to use. But, as author Greg Critser points out in his landmark book *Fat Land*, the use of HFCS was not limited to a few desserts or soft drinks. "Using it in frozen foods protected the product against freezer burn. Using it in products with a long shelf life—like those in vending machines—kept the product fresh tasting. Using it in bakery products (even in rolls and biscuits that normally contained no sugar) made those products look 'more natural'—as if they had just been browned in the oven."[6]

By the early 1980s agricultural prices were down, and there were no more food shortages. "In what would prove to be one of the single most important changes to the nation's food supply," Critser points out, "both Coke and Pepsi switched from a fifty-fifty blend of sugar and corn syrup to 100 percent high-fructose corn syrup. The move saved both companies 20 percent in sweetener costs, allowing them to boost portion sizes and still make substantial profits."[7]

Focused solely on economic issues, food researchers ignored the dietary implications of HFCS, even though it was known that the body metabolizes fructose in a much different manner than sucrose and dextrose, which undergo a complex breakdown process en route to the liver. By contrast, fructose short-circuits the normal digestive path and goes straight to the liver—a process called "metabolic shunting." It would be years before scientists fully comprehended the life-threatening consequences of the widespread use of high-fructose corn syrup in our food supply: the metabolic shunting of excess fructose is the leading cause of syndrome X and type 2 diabetes, two insulin-related disorders we will discuss in the next chapter.

The other food history fact I want to point out concerns cooking oils. In the inflationary 1970s American manufacturers began to rely on cheap imports such as palm oil from Malaysia, the world's largest producer. With its chemical similarity to beef tallow, palm oil was tastier than most vegetable oils, and new technologies had turned it into a viable commercial fat. It quickly became used for frying, baking, and making margarine; then it found its way into an endless variety of convenience foods. At the time, McDonald's used palm oil for their french fries, and they built an oil-processing plant in Malaysia as soon as trade restrictions were relaxed. McDonald's fries were considered better tasting than the competition and were cheaper to produce, and portion sizes began to grow.

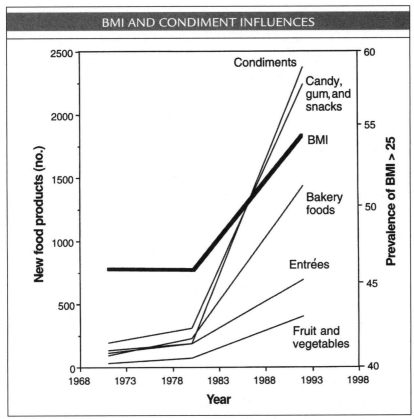

The number of new food products introduced into the U.S. food market annually, classified as condiments, candy, snacks, and bakery foods, parallels the increasing prevalence of obesity as measured by BMI and has increased strikingly out of proportion to new vegetable and fruit products.[8]

The use of these two new products, high-fructose corn syrup and commercial palm oil, revolutionized food production and, coincidentally or not, ushered in an era of obesity-related disorders. Where HFCS caused metabolic shunting and insulin resistance, overuse of refined palm oil had its own set of problems, leading to higher cholesterol levels and increases in cardiac disease. Not even hog lard had as much saturated fat as palm oil, which was 45 percent saturated.[9]

Today, health concerns have driven manufacturers away from refined palm oil, but the current substitutes are not much better. I will discuss the qualities of good and bad fats in a later chapter.

THE DANGEROUS FOUR Fs OF FOOD

For now, let's look at how we began to sink into this quagmire of obesity with its whole host of weight-related and nutrition-related health problems. In the weight-loss and health-management seminars we now give, we call this the Dangerous Four Fs of Food: fast food, fragmented foods, food additives, and family foods. If you are reading this book in order to get help for yourself or a loved one, I can guarantee that one or more of these four Fs have played a significant role in the problem you are facing.

Fast food

America has capitulated to convenience. Roughly one-fourth of all adults visit a fast-food restaurant on any given day.[10] The typical American eats three hamburgers and four orders of french fries every week.[11] In fact, we now spend *twenty times* the amount of money on fast food that we spent thirty years ago—more than $110 billion each year.

We are not only spending a lot more on fast food, but we are also eating much bigger portions. Without a doubt, we have been supersized. First, we were asked, "Would you like fries with that?" every time we ordered a burger. Then we were bombarded with "value meals" at every fast-food franchise. Restaurants made it cheaper to order a pre-packaged combo rather than individual items, and we quickly adopted the habit. Then we were not only presented with an array of combo meals, but we were also asked if we wanted to supersize them. For just a few cents extra, we could get *more* fries and *larger* soft drinks.

By the time Greg Critser wrote *Fat Land* and Morgan Spurlock filmed *Super Size Me*, portion sizes had become outrageous. Fast-food establishments, of course, aren't the only culprit when it comes to serving more-than-abundant portions; major chain restaurants offer entrées that will easily serve two people, but sharing is often discouraged. No wonder we keep getting fatter and fatter—we keep eating larger and larger portions of foods that are not nutritious to begin with.

Let's look at a single fast-food menu item: the beloved french fry. According to Critser, "A serving of McDonald's french fries…ballooned from 200 calories (1960) to 320 calories (late 1970s) to 450 calories (mid-1990s) to 540 calories (late 1990s) to the present 610 calories."[12] Recently, McDonald's—under pressure from consumer activists—has eliminated their largest serving of fries.

I don't mean to pick on McDonald's; other fast-food restaurants are equally responsible for super sizing portions. To give you a comparison, the chart below presents the latest nutrition statistics on McDonald's and Wendy's french fries.[13]

COMPARISON OF FAST-FOOD FRIES						
Serving Size		Calories	Total Fat	% Daily Value	Sodium	% Daily Value
McDonald's						
Small	2.6 oz.	230	11 g	16%	140 mg	6%
Medium	4.0 oz.	350	16 g	25%	220 mg	9%
Large	6.0 oz.	520	25 g	38%	330 mg	14%
Wendy's						
Kids' Meals	3.2 oz.	280	14 g	*	270 mg	*
Medium	5.0 oz.	440	21 g	*	430 mg	*
Biggie	5.6 oz.	490	24 g	*	480 mg	*
Great Biggie	6.7 oz.	590	29 g	*	570 mg	*

* Not listed in company information

What do all those numbers mean? Well, one large order of fries is equal to roughly one-fourth (or more) of the total calories you need for the day and will provide between 35 and 40 percent of the fat you should consume each day. That is only *one serving* of french fries; we haven't even mentioned the hamburger you are probably eating with those fries. You can see how easy it is to overconsume calories on a diet of fast food, and that is not even taking into consideration the nutritional quality of those calories, only the quantity.

Not only have the portion sizes increased, but so have the number of ingredients. The exalted french fry is not just a fried potato, you know. Here is the list of the ingredients in McDonald's fries: "Potatoes, partially hydrogenated soybean oil, natural flavor (beef source), dextrose, sodium acid pyrophosphate (to preserve natural color). Cooked in partially hydrogenated vegetable oils (may contain partially hydrogenated soybean oil and/or partially hydrogenated corn oil and/or partially hydrogenated canola oil and/or cottonseed oil and/or sunflower oil and/or corn oil)."[14]

And here is the ingredient list for Wendy's fries: "Potatoes, partially hydrogenated soybean oil, dextrose, and disodium dihydrogen pyrophosphate (color protector). Cooked in: partially hydrogenated corn and soybean oil. Seasoned with salt. Note: French fries may be cooked in same oil as Crispy Chicken Nuggets, Homestyle Chicken Strips, and Fish Fillets (where offered)."[15]

Now, you probably zoned out on me while struggling through that detailed list of ingredients, or perhaps you skipped over it altogether. I don't blame you; it is difficult reading. But let me point out a couple of things. First, the number-three item in each list of ingredients is dextrose. Also called *corn sugar* and *grape sugar*, dextrose is a naturally occurring form of glucose—chemically, a simple sugar. That is right; both McDonald's and Wendy's add sugar to their fries to enhance the flavor.

Also note that McDonald's fries contain a "natural flavor" noted to be from a "beef source." Although they are no longer fried in beef tallow or palm oil, McDonald's fries still contain that subtle beef flavor that first enticed consumers decades ago. (So do their Chicken McNuggets, for the record.[16] I will not bore you with the list of ingredients for those nuggets; it is three times longer than the ingredient list for the fries.)

Fragmented foods

With our increasingly busy lives, it is easy to get caught in the convenience trap. Even when we eat at home instead of a restaurant, we are likely to be using packaged or processed foods at every meal. Consuming the majority of our calories from such convenience foods, which are mostly "empty" calories, creates powerful cravings for real nutrition. Instead, we continue to overeat unhealthy foods, creating a downward spiral of weight gain and health problems. As you will see from our story and the information throughout this book, the health consequences of a diet based on processed foods are staggering.

Don Colbert refers to processed foods, which are "dead" foods given an artificially long shelf life through chemical engineering, as fragmented foods; by contrast, the whole, natural foods God designed for us are "living" foods. If I could give you only one word of advice about eating for maximum health, it would be this: "Eat your foods in the form God made them."

An orange is a good example of the way God packages foods. The orange has a natural protective cover, and inside is a delicious, sweet food that contains vitamins and nutrients. The orange also contains fiber, which makes the orange filling to eat and also helps move the nutrients through our digestive systems. What does man do with the orange? We squeeze it, strain it, process it, and box it. We strip the orange's natural nutrients and then "enrich" the juice by adding vitamins and minerals back to it, giving it the *appearance* of a healthy food.

Do you remember when a serving of fresh orange juice was around 2 ounces? Our grandmothers had very small juice glasses in their kitchen cabinets, and a highlight of summer would be hand-squeezing fresh oranges to make enough juice to fill the tiny glasses. Today we drink orange juice year-round. Furthermore, it is routinely served in an 8-ounce glass, which means it is likely to contain the equivalent of four or more oranges. It is like a powerful sugar bomb in your system—you might as well stir 8 to 10 tablespoons of sugar in a glass of water and drink that!

When I was growing up, my Italian family ate dinner at home every night, and my mother cooked everything from scratch. We enjoyed fresh vegetables from our garden and fruits in a rainbow of colors. There was beef, chicken, or seafood, and fresh pasta served with a homemade sauce that had simmered on the stove—no bottled sauces in our kitchen! Everyday meals were a social as well as culinary event, and the five Travisono (my maiden name) children grew up with a wonderful heritage of whole foods.

When young children eat at home these days, their meals are likely to come straight out of a box or a can or the freezer. Spaghetti-O's, Hamburger Helper, Kraft Macaroni and Cheese, frozen pizza, corn dogs, tater tots, fried fish sticks, burritos...you get the picture. And somewhere along the way we got the notion that between-meal snacking was absolutely essential. Hmmm. Could it be that the convenience food companies encouraged this idea? Absolutely.

This letter we received from the Sutton family says it all:

ZOE 8 TESTIMONY

My husband and I thought our children would "grow out of" their weight. Kayla was in sixth grade and weighed 150 pounds. Rachael was in kindergarten and weighed almost 100 pounds. Our youngest, Josiah, did not have a weight issue; however, he was addicted to sugar.

When we finally realized how bad the problem was, we felt hopeless. We didn't know how to change. After much prayer we met Ed and Elisa McClure, and they shared the ZOE W8 Loss Program with us. We knew we had the answer.

We started the program in June 2003, and within a month I noticed a big change in our children. Standing at the kitchen sink, I glanced out the window and saw all three of my children rolling and wrestling in the grass. They had never had that kind of energy before.

In just two months Kayla and Rachael each lost 20 pounds. Before school started we rewarded them with a new pair of regular-sized jeans. They were so thrilled to be able to wear the same style of clothes as their friends instead of having to wear stretch pants and big T-shirts....

Josiah started eating apples every day instead of his usual sugar fixes. Now six, he questions me when I make a snack. "Is it healthy?" he'll ask. Or, "Does it have sugar in it?"

Our daughters have so much self-esteem now. Kayla is a teenager, blossoming into a beautiful young woman, and she can run a mile or more with no problem. Rachael, now nine, says she can play on the monkey bars *at the playground with ease. "Before, I was too heavy to hold on," she told me. Now she can hold on all the way across. . . .*

Currently we are living and working in Paraguay. Our whole family is still following the ZOE 8 plan. We avoid the American fast-food chains that have been introduced here, and we eat the grilled meats and various fresh salads available. This has become a lifestyle for us.

We go walking in the park together, and Kayla will run her mile. We are raising our children with good habits for an abundant, zoe life—good eating habits, good exercise habits, and good memories of spending family time together.

—The Sutton Family
Rick, Kimberly, Kayla, Rachael, and Josiah

It is no wonder families like the Suttons find themselves struggling to break free from bad eating habits. Spurred by cheap sugar and fat prices, Big Food—my name for the major companies in the food processing industry—began to churn out more packaged sweets and snack products than ever. During the 1960s and 1970s the number of new candy and snack foods introduced every year remained stable at about 250. By the mid-1980s the number had jumped to 1,000, and by the end of the decade some *2,000* new snack foods were hitting grocery store shelves *every year.*[17]

Trying to give the appearance of nutritional excellence, many processed foods bear names like SnackWell's, Healthy Choice, Smart Ones, Lean Cuisine, and so on. Read the fine print on the Nutrition Facts panel on these foods, however, and you will find a long list of ingredients, many of which you cannot even pronounce. We'll tell you a lot more about label-reading later on, but I will state our simple rule about food labels here: "If you can't pronounce it, don't put it in your mouth."

Refined and processed foods are fragmented—less than God intended and less than you need. Man cannot improve what God has designed, yet food manufacturers feel compelled to try. And what you may not know is that most of the flavor appeal in the processed foods you have been eating every day come from chemicals created by food scientists working in huge refineries and chemical plants along the New Jersey Turnpike.

Food additives

Processed foods appeal to the five senses, and manufacturers spend billions of dollars researching how to add taste appeal to processed foods from which the nutrients have been stripped. While our taste buds can only detect five or six distinct tastes, our noses can perceive thousands of different smells. So the aroma of a food is of paramount importance to its flavor. In his remarkable book *Fast Food Nation,* Eric Schlosser says that what we perceive as flavor "is primarily the smell of gases being released by the chemicals you have just put in your mouth." Take that wonderfully enticing apple smell emanating from a packaged pastry…it is probably the chemical compound ethyl-2-methyl butyrate, which happens to smell just like a real apple. "The basic science behind the scent of your shaving cream is the same as that governing the flavor of your TV dinner."[18]

According to Schlosser, one manufacturing facility he toured in New Jersey produced flavor-enhancing aroma additives for all of the following: potato chips, corn chips, breads, crackers, breakfast cereals, pet food, ice cream, cookies, candies, toothpaste, mouthwash, antacids, soft drinks, sport drinks, bottled teas, wine coolers, "all-natural" juice drinks, organic soy drinks, beers, and malt liquors, as well as scents for household products such as deodorant, dishwashing detergent, bath soap, shampoo, furniture polish, and floor wax. "All of these aromas are made through the same basic process: the manipulation of volatile chemicals to create a particular smell."[19]

Unfortunately, the Big Food companies do not have to disclose the chemicals used in their products, as long as a flavor or fragrance additive is considered to be "generally recognized as safe" (GRAS). The Food and Drug Administration definition of GRAS states that "any substance that is intentionally added to food is a food additive, that is subject to premarket review and approval by FDA, *unless the substance is generally recognized, among qualified experts, as having been adequately shown to be safe under the conditions of its intended use,* or unless the use of the substance is otherwise excluded from the definition of a food additive."[20]

There are so many "generally recognized as safe" ingredients that the FDA has deemed it impractical to maintain an all-inclusive list. Furthermore, notification of the use of a GRAS ingredient is *optional;* it is up to the *manufacturer* to determine that an ingredient is GRAS, based on commonly accepted scientific information, and to choose whether to disclose its use.

This lack of labeling requirements for GRAS ingredients keeps the flavor industry highly secretive and disguises the fact that there may be far more additives than real food in a given product. (See the chart below for an example of a long list of ingredients for a single artificial flavor, strawberry.[21])

INGREDIENTS FOR TYPICAL STRAWBERRY-FLAVORED FAST-FOOD MILK SHAKE		
amyl acetate	amyl butyrate	amyl valerate
anethol	anisyl formate	benzyl acetate
benzyl isobutyrate	butyric acid	cinnamyl isobutyrate
cinnamyl valerate	cognac essential oil	diacetyl
dipropyl ketone	ethyl acetate	ethyl amylketone
ethyl butyrate	ethyl cinnamate	ethyl heptanoate
ethyl heptylate	ethyl lactate	ethyl methylphenylglycidate
ethyl nitrate	ethyl propionate	ethyl valerate
heliotropin	hydroxyphenyl-2-butanone (10% solution in alcohol)	α-ionone
isobutyl anthranilate	isobutyl butyrate	lemon essential oil
maltol	4-methylacetophenone	methyl anthranilate
methyl benzoate	methyl cinnamate	methyl heptine carbonate
methyl naphthyl ketone	methyl salicylate	mint essential oil
neroli essential oil	nerolin	neryl isobutyrate
orris butter	phenethyl alcohol	rose
rum ether	γ-undecalactone	vanillin
solvent		

When it comes to GRAS, I am not very comfortable with that word *generally*, are you? Would you buy gas for your car if there was a label that stated, "Warning: This gasoline is generally recognized as safe to use as fuel in your vehicle. In some cases, however, using this gasoline could result in engine failure…"? Would you buy that gas, or would you look for a better product? It is the same with our food. There are plenty of foods without additives, and we know they are good fuel for our "engines." Yet we continue to "fill our tanks" with fuel that is not only inferior and inefficient but also downright harmful to our bodies. There will never be a study to tell us that organically grown foods such as apples, onions, broccoli, or organic grass-fed lean beef, in their whole natural state, are bad for us.

In addition to GRAS, another designation allowed by the FDA can be very misleading. As long as an additive comes from a natural source—plant or animal—all you will see on the required Nutrition Facts panel is the label *natural flavor*. As we have already seen, McDonald's french fries contain the ingredient "natural flavor"; the company voluntarily discloses to its customers that the source of the natural flavor is beef. Other companies are not so conscientious (or perhaps they have simply not faced as much criticism as McDonald's), and they do not disclose the source of their natural flavors.

One ingredient that we know is harmful to us is monosodium glutamate (MSG). If a food product contains MSG, it must say so on the label, right? Well, yes and no. Food manufacturers have come up with a way to disguise MSG and slip it in under the "natural flavor" designation. Dr. Russell L. Blaylock, a board-certified neurosurgeon, writes extensively about the dangers of food additives in his book *Excitotoxins: The Taste That Kills.*

"MSG is a modified form of glutamic acid in which sodium is added to the molecule," Blaylock explains. "But the toxic portion is the glutamic acid, not the sodium." Food manufacturers often mix MSG with other substances, and it subsequently appears on a food label as "natural flavoring"—which may contain anywhere from 20 to 60 percent MSG.[22]

Low-fat foods are especially likely to have added ingredients posing as natural flavors; after all, something has to be added to these fragmented foods to give them a palatable taste. One of the ingredients you will frequently see listed on food labels is "hydrolyzed vegetable protein," which may simply be called vegetable protein or plant protein. It comes from plants, so it is bound to be safe, right?

You may rethink that conclusion once you understand how hydrolyzed vegetable protein is made. "This mixture is made from 'junk' vegetables that are unfit for sale. They are especially selected so as to have naturally high contents of glutamate. The extraction process of hydrolysis involves boiling these vegetables in a vat of acid. This is followed by a process of neutralization with caustic soda. The resulting product is a brown sludge that collects on the top. This is scraped off and allowed to dry. The end product is a brown powder" that is high in glutamate, aspartate, and cystoic acid—all of which are known to be harmful.[23]

I don't know about you, but adding acid-boiled "brown sludge" to my food is not something I would ever do. Ask yourself this: would you rather take a few extra minutes preparing fresh foods, or a few extra hours sitting in the doctor's waiting room? That is where a lifetime of eating additive-laden, fragmented foods will lead you.

While our diets are sadly lacking in essential vitamins, fats, and minerals, they abound in the artificially engineered taste that keeps us coming back for more while compromising our health. Big Food spends millions of dollars in research every year on additives, stabilizers, and preservatives. These foods do not preserve us; they are detrimental to our health.

Today most of the Big Food companies are owned by large corporations that also have interests in the alcohol and tobacco industry. It should not be surprising, then, that many processed foods are engineered not only to taste appealing but also to be addictive. A smoker can avoid cigarettes and a drug addict can avoid drugs, but everyone has to eat. The giant food corporations buy shelf space in grocery stores so that their products are always at eye-level, and they spend billions of advertising dollars targeted at consumers, especially young consumers. And as we will see next, children are particularly vulnerable when it comes to making food choices.

Family foods

Our taste preferences are formed during early childhood by eating the same foods as our families. Toddlers can learn to eat everything from bland to spicy foods, fast food to health food, depending on what they are fed from the family kitchen.

I grew up in an Italian family, so my taste preferences include pasta (a food I could *never* eliminate from my diet); seasonings like oregano, basil, and thyme; vegetables like eggplant and zucchini; and cheeses like parmigiano-reggiano. If you grow up along the Texas-Mexico border, your taste preferences will include pulled pork, refried beans, and seasonings like chili powder and hot peppers. If you come from Louisiana, you probably enjoy gumbo and spicy foods prepared with cayenne pepper. If you are from India, you have probably been eating curry ever since you switched from breast milk to solid food.

The importance of these early food preferences cannot be overstated. Under stress we turn to "comfort food"—these familiar foods from our childhood. In America, that is likely to include substantial portions of the three other dangerous Fs—fast food, fragmented foods, and food additives. We see so many parents feeding their toddlers a steady diet of chicken nuggets and fries, not knowing they are dooming these children to a lifetime of weight-related health problems.

While children are particularly vulnerable to their parents' poor food choices, there is solid evidence that children can learn good nutritional habits. A three-year study by the National Heart, Lung, and Blood Institute (NHLBI) showed that preadolescent children who attended a behaviorally oriented nutrition education program adopted significantly better dietary habits than the control group, which received only general nutritional information. After three years, children in the intervention group chose 67 percent of their foods from the heart-healthy category, which included foods that are low in saturated fat and dietary cholesterol, compared to less than 57 percent for the other group. Unfortunately, both groups of children consumed approximately one-third of their calories from snack foods, desserts, and pizza.[24] So there is plenty of room for improvement.

With the tremendous increase in childhood obesity and the concurrent rise of type 2 diabetes in young people, such intervention programs are critical. Of course, even more effective would be adapting the family diet to more healthy alternatives and teaching the principles of good nutrition at home. And it is not as difficult as you might think. This book includes the tools you will need to do just that.

One of the reasons most weight-loss programs are not successful is that they fail to address individuals' food preferences for the traditional, ethnic foods they grew up enjoying. That is where our program, however, excels. We teach people how to adapt the foods they love to be more compatible with a healthy lifestyle. By making a few substitutions, Italian food fans can still enjoy favorite pasta dishes, Mexican food lovers can enjoy tortillas and fajitas, and Asian food enthusiasts can dine on tandoori chicken, fried rice, and curries.

You will find specific information on making these changes in the following chapters. But first let's look at two other causes of the obesity epidemic. We call them "fat phobia" and "carb confusion." You might think that the government has the solution to our dietary dilemma, but the truth is that the cherished USDA Food Guide Pyramid is part of the problem, and here's why.

Chapter Three

The Fallacy of the Food Pyramid: Why the Government Has It Wrong

FOR twenty years diet-conscious consumers have suffered from fat phobia, making dietary fat Public Enemy Number One as far as health and nutrition are concerned. One evidence of this irrational fear is that the low-fat SnackWell's brand has likely surpassed the beloved Oreo as the number-one selling cookie in America. Our collective obsession with low-fat dieting, however, has actually resulted in dramatically expanding, rather than shrinking, waistlines.

In presidential elections the challenger will often ask voters, "Are you better off now than you were four years ago?" The implication is that if you are not, you should vote to boot the incumbent out of office. Let's apply that same question to health and nutrition: Americans, are we healthier now than we were twenty years ago?

The answer is a resounding *no*. After two decades of pursuing the fat-free dream, obesity rates have risen steeply, becoming a health problem with a staggering economic cost. "In the late 1990s obesity cost American companies $12.7 billion per year because of lost productivity and extra expenses for medical care and insurance."[1]

Why has the low-fat craze actually resulted in weight gain rather than weight loss? There is a simple scientific explanation. First of all, the amount of fat (within reason) in the diet is not as important as the type of fat. We've been hammered by governmental authorities such as the U.S. Department of Agriculture and medical authorities such as the American Heart Association to drastically reduce our fat intake. But according to Harvard professor of medicine Walter C. Willett, "Eating more good fats—and staying away from bad ones—is second only to weight control on the list of healthy nutritional strategies."[2]

Willett points to a number of surveys showing that "European women with the lowest fat intake are the most likely to be obese, while those with the highest fat intake are the least likely." By contrast, in the United States, "the gradual reduction in the fat content of the average diet, from 40 percent of calories to about 34 percent, has been accompanied by a gradual *increase* in the average weight and a dramatic increase in obesity."[3]

I will explain the different types of fat in detail when I explain the basics of the ZOE 8 food plan later on, but for now let's look at the second explanation for why low-fat diets actually wind up making you fatter. When food manufacturers create fat-free, low-fat, reduced-fat, or otherwise "lite" products, they add ingredients to enhance the taste, much of which is removed along with the fat. The most common ingredients to be added are sugar and salt, or artificial flavor enhancers—"extras" that are likely to promote fat storage and can be harmful to your health, as we saw in the last chapter.

In her latest book, *Eat Fat, Lose Weight*, nutritionist Ann Louise Gittleman cites the following statistics that demonstrate this unhealthy trend: "The U.S. Department of Agriculture has reported a 14-pound drop in red meat consumption between 1980 and 1990. In the past twenty years, butter intake has dropped by a whopping 25 percent, but, at the same time, the per capita ingestion of sugar has increased by 20 pounds per person, per year."[4] The source of all that extra sugar in our diets comes from fast foods or processed and packaged convenience foods. We've cut the fat but boosted the sugar, and now we're paying the price.

If you take time to read labels while you shop for groceries—and you should—you will see the faulty logic of the low-fat philosophy. Reduced-fat snack foods are especially enticing to dieters. But compare the regular and low-fat versions of the same cookie or cracker and you will find that while the number of fat grams has been slightly reduced, the amount of sugar will be around one to five grams higher in the low-fat version. The savings in calories is minimal (perhaps ten to thirty calories per serving), and it comes at the cost of the increased sugar content.

The irony is that, having succumbed to fat phobia, many Americans—regardless of their weight—are suffering from an essential fatty-acid deficiency. We are actually starved for the healthy fats our bodies need for metabolism. The clinical symptoms of fatty-acid deficiency can include "restlessness, short attention span, irritability, mood swings, and even panic attacks."[5]

Certain fatty acids are called *essential* because our bodies do not produce them on their own; therefore, we must obtain these essential fatty acids (EFAs) through the foods we eat. "There is no such thing as an essential carbohydrate or an essential sugar," Gittleman writes, "but there is essential fat. It is what our nutritional textbooks years ago called vitamin F."[6]

The most important EFAs are derived from the omega-3 and omega-6 fats and play a critical role in our body chemistry. Our brains are composed primarily of fat, and our neurotransmitters, the vital brain chemicals involved in cell communication, are regulated by hormonelike substances called prostaglandins. In fact, every cell in our bodies depends on prostaglandins for proper functioning, and we must have an adequate supply of EFAs in order to produce these prostaglandins. "Both the omega-3 and omega-6 essential fatty acids are components of the outer membrane of every cell in the body where they protect against viruses, bacteria, and allergens. The brain—and indeed the entire central nervous system—needs fats for nourishment and protection."[7]

Fat is also the satiety factor in our diets. In other words, fats not only provide flavor to our foods, but they are also satisfying. That is another reason that Americans have continued to gain weight while gripped by fat phobia: we constantly overeat because low-fat foods do not give us that pleasant feeling of fullness. Our bodies are trying to signal us that they have not received the nutrients they need—and one of those nutrients is a high-quality source of fat.

Fat also slows down the absorption of carbohydrates, another factor that results in feeling fuller longer, therefore reducing food cravings. And that brings me to another problem area with our diets. I call it "carb confusion."

CARB CONFUSION

The typical low-fat diet is high in carbohydrates, mostly simple sugars and refined carbohydrates. In fact, many calorie-restricted diet plans recommend that at least 60 percent of daily calories come from carbohydrate sources. "In the average American diet," Dr. Willett writes, "carbohydrates contribute about half of all calories. And half of these carbohydrate calories come from just seven sources: bread (15 percent), soft drinks and sodas (9 percent), cakes, cookies, quick breads, and doughnuts (7 percent), sugars, syrups, and jams (6 percent), white potatoes (5 percent), ready-to-eat cereals (5 percent), and milk (5 percent). In other words, most of our carbohydrate calories come from sugars or highly refined grains."[8]

Some nutritionists and doctors began to realize that not only were low-fat, high-carbohydrate diets not working for weight loss, but also they were not improving cardiovascular health in adherents, supposedly the great advantage of the low-fat diet. "Cutting back on all types of fat and eating extra carbohydrates will do little to protect against heart disease and will ultimately harm some people. Instead, replacing saturated fats with unsaturated fats is a safe, proven, and delicious way to cut the rates of heart disease."[9]

The pendulum began to swing in the opposite direction in the early 1970s with the publication of the popular high-protein, low-carbohydrate diet by Dr. Robert Atkins. Steaks, bacon, eggs, sausage, and cheese were staples on this diet, and the number of vegetables and fruits allowed was extremely low. The program fell out of favor rather quickly, but a revised Atkins Diet made a dramatic comeback a decade or so later and has spawned a number of similar food plans. In some circles, carbohydrates replaced fats as Public Enemy Number One for dieters.

It is confusing, isn't it? I believe the low-carb approach is misguided, for a number of reasons. First, recent studies have shown that while people may initially lose weight more rapidly on such a diet, over the long term it provides no advantage over other weight-loss plans. When too much protein is eaten at one meal—a common occurrence on a low-carb diet—insulin levels start to rise. The increased insulin levels actually tell our bodies to store fat, so the initial weight loss on such a diet is destined to slow down, and the program will ultimately be counterproductive. A high-protein diet can also leech calcium out of the bones, which would be problematic for anyone at risk of osteoporosis. I also do not think it is wise to eliminate or drastically reduce the consumption of an entire food group that contains valuable nutrients; the complex carbohydrates in fruits, vegetables, and legumes are more slowly digested than sugars and refined carbs.

In spite of the proliferation of low-carb fad diets, our bodies crave carbs, and for good reason. We need carbohydrates—sugars, starch, and cellulose in their natural forms. Rather than eliminating carbs, it is better to focus on which carbs are most beneficial for health. Nutritionists used to speak in terms of complex or simple carbohydrates, but it is more useful now to think in terms of low-glycemic and high-glycemic carbs.

The glycemic index (GI) is a ranking of foods based on their overall effect on blood sugar levels. During the digestive process, carbohydrates break down into a simple sugar, glucose. So your glucose, or blood sugar level, rises after a meal. Then the pancreas releases insulin in order to bring the blood sugar level back to normal.

High-glycemic foods are those carbohydrates that break down quickly during digestion. The resulting blood sugar response is fast and high. Low-glycemic foods are those carbohydrates that break down slowly, gradually releasing glucose into the blood stream. Low-glycemic foods help you avoid the drastic highs and lows of blood sugar fluctuation. Diabetics have been using the principles of the glycemic index for years because even small fluctuations in their blood sugar levels can cause problems that could quickly get out of control and lead to serious health consequences.

Our modern diet is too high in saturated fat (and too low in good fats) and too high in quick-release carbohydrates because most starchy foods— the staple of our diet—have a high glycemic index. One of the things we've done for you is to provide the Body Balance Food Chart as part of the ZOE 8 food plan. (See page 184.) This chart takes a lot of the guesswork out of meal planning and preparation: we have already eliminated high-glycemic foods in favor of lower-glycemic alternatives. Yet you will still find plenty of your favorite carbs, including pasta, rice, and potatoes—just in lower glycemic versions.

FROM METABOLIC SYNDROME TO DIABETES

The ZOE 8 food plan is designed to keep blood sugar levels balanced, so before we get into the specifics of the food plan, we need to look at metabolic disorders that can be caused by imbalances of blood sugar. As I mentioned earlier, the number of cases of diabetes has skyrocketed in recent years. The increase is primarily in type 2, formerly called adult-onset, diabetes. (Type 1 diabetes is an inherited autoimmune disorder in which the body attacks and destroys the beta cells, which produce insulin.)

There is a progression to the development of type 2 diabetes, and the disease may be building for years before any symptoms are noticeable. Doctors sometimes refer to this stage as "borderline diabetes" or "prediabetes." More than 41 million Americans are currently prediabetic, and many of them don't know it![10] The good news is that this condition is almost always reversible when blood sugar is brought under control.

ZOE 8 participants like Gil are living proof that you can change the course of your health by changing what you eat. He writes:

ZOE 8 TESTIMONY

Because of my high cholesterol and trigylcerides, the doctor was very concerned that I was headed for diabetes. But after fourteen weeks on the ZOE program, my cholesterol and triglycerides dropped to normal range, and I don't have to go back to the doctor for twelve months.

I've been on the program about a year now, and I've lost 45 pounds and 4 inches around my chest and waist. I even had to buy a smaller belt because I ran out of notches in the old one.

I'm also much happier and have more zest for getting involved in activities with my family, friends, and church. It used to be so hard to move around and I just didn't want to do much or go out with friends and family because of my weight. Those days are gone!

Now I take walks, go swimming, and can play more with my grandsons. To anybody thinking about trying the ZOE 8 Program, I would say, Do it! Save yourself and live longer by getting into this wonderful program.

Cholesterol	Triglycerides
Before: 240	Before: 150
After: 185	After: 101

— Gil L.

In the spectrum of disorders leading to full-blown diabetes is a condition known as metabolic syndrome, which has also been called syndrome X or insulin-resistance syndrome. Approximately one-third of obese adults, and perhaps as many overweight teenagers, suffer from this metabolic disorder, which refers to "a cluster of risk factors for diabetes and cardiovascular disease: high blood sugar, high waist circumference, high blood pressure, high levels of triglycerides, and low levels of high-density lipoprotein (the good cholesterol)."[11]

This condition results in insulin resistance, which means that the beta cells in the pancreas still produce insulin, but the cells throughout the body no longer respond to the insulin properly. In an attempt to restore normal blood sugar levels, the pancreas pumps out more and more insulin. According to Dr. Francine Kaufman, former president of the American Diabetic Association, "This works temporarily: the extra insulin compensates for the cells' insensitivity, so blood sugar remains normal. That is why the condition is silent.

"Over time, the beta cells become exhausted and can no longer sustain their abnormally high insulin production rate."[12] Exactly how and why it happens is not completely understood, but it is likely that fat itself plays a critical role.

"Metabolic syndrome is in large part caused by visceral fat. A key mechanism involves chemical signals from our fat cells that trigger inflammation.... When we have too much fat, we also have a chronic overabundance of the inflammation-triggering chemical signals."[13] This link between fat cells and inflammation helps explain the connection between obesity, diabetes, heart disease, and stroke.

THE FALLACY OF THE FOOD PYRAMID

So, what does a person do who rejects fad diets and wants to "eat right" in order to control blood sugar and avoid "diabesity" with all its complications? Surely the answer lies in the food pyramid we all learned in school, right? After all, the government promotes good nutrition, and they should know best.

Unfortunately, that is not the case when it comes to the traditional food pyramid promulgated by the U.S. Department of Agriculture. Whoa—wait a minute! There is a problem right there: it is the *Agriculture* Department, not an agency like the Food and Drug Administration or Health and Human Services, that writes the nutritional rules for our nation's health. According to Dr. Walter Willett, chairman of the Department of Nutrition at Harvard, that is "the root of the problem—what is good for some agricultural interests isn't necessarily good for the people who eat their products."[14] Compounding

that is what Willett calls "the overproduction problem. U.S. farmers produce 3,800 calories' worth of food a day for every man, woman, and child in
America. That is almost double what the average person needs."[15]

One of the most informative and highly readable books on nutrition in
the last few years is Dr. Willett's book *Eat, Drink, and Be Healthy*. It is a valuable resource if you want to go beyond the basics presented in this book.[16]

ARGUMENTS AGAINST THE USDA FOOD PYRAMID

It assumes that all fats are bad. The pyramid's recommendation to "use fats
sparingly" ignores our need for an adequate supply of good fats—the monounsaturated and polyunsaturated fats found in olive oil, nuts, whole grains,
and fish. The only kind of fat that should be "used sparingly" is saturated
fat, and trans fat should be eliminated altogether.

It assumes that all "complex" carbohydrates are good. Carbohydrates
play the starring role in the food pyramid, which recommends up to eleven
daily servings of bread, cereal, rice, and pasta. All of these are high-glycemic
foods. Willett points out that "your digestive system turns white bread, a
baked potato, or white rice into glucose and pumps this sugar into the bloodstream almost as fast as it delivers the sugar in a cocktail of pure glucose."[17]
When your blood sugar levels spike after eating these foods, and then suddenly plummet, it triggers hunger signals—not to mention increasing the
risk of diabetes or insulin resistance, as we've just seen.

The types of carbohydrates we should be eating are whole grains, like
brown rice and oats, or whole-grain pasta or bread, or beans. These are low-
glycemic foods that do not produce surges in blood sugar levels; they also
keep you feeling fuller longer and are an important source of fiber.

It doesn't distinguish between sources of protein. Red meat, poultry, fish,
eggs, beans, and nuts are all good sources of protein. But red meat, which is
high in saturated fat, should play a lesser role in your diet than other forms
of protein. Poultry has less saturated fat, and fish also provides important
unsaturated fats. Beans and nuts not only provide protein, but they also contain fiber and vital nutrients we need.

It states that dairy products are essential. There is no calcium emergency, as milk producers would have us believe; Americans get more calcium
than almost any other country in the world. Whole milk has saturated fat,
the kind that can raise cholesterol levels, and it also has a fairly high sugar

content in the form of lactose. (People who are sensitive to milk products are said to be lactose-intolerant.) If you need extra calcium, supplements are cheaper and healthier than dairy products.

It recommends potatoes. The average American eats 140 pounds of potatoes a year—140 pounds! According to Dr. Willett, "It is one of the few vegetables to be mentioned by name in the Dietary Guidelines—except it shouldn't be classified as a vegetable. Potatoes are mostly starch—easily digested starch at that—and so should be part of the carbohydrate group.... While eating potatoes on a daily basis may be fine for lean people who exercise a lot or who do regular manual labor, for everyone else potatoes should be an occasional food consumed in modest amounts, not a daily vegetable. The venerable baked potato increases levels of blood sugar and insulin more quickly and to higher levels than an equal amount of calories from pure table sugar."[18]

If you are one of those "meat and potatoes" people who shun other forms of protein and the incredible array of naturally healthy vegetables and fruits, you are putting your health at risk!

THE MEDITERRANEAN DIET

When it comes to eating healthy, Americans could learn a lesson from our neighbors across the ocean. Perhaps you have heard of the Mediterranean Diet. It is not a weight-loss program; it is a term used to describe the way people in the countries located around the Mediterranean Sea customarily eat—both the types of food and the way these foods are prepared. In other words, the Mediterranean people have a heritage of healthy cuisine, and there is plenty of scientific evidence to prove the benefits of their traditional diet.

When asked to describe the "ultimate diet," Dr. Willett says it "would be one that controls hunger, is pleasing and satisfying, meets the body's needs for energy and nutrients, and minimizes the risk of chronic disease."[19] Like many nutrition experts, he points to the positive example of the Mediterranean Diet and the clinical studies that have examined it. The first significant study was conducted in the 1950s and '60s. Called the Seven Countries Study, it investigated the link between diet and heart disease and found that people living in Crete, parts of Greece, and southern Italy had longer life expectancies and very low rates of heart disease and cancer. Their traditional diet was plant-based, with plenty of fruits, vegetables, coarsely ground grains and breads, beans, nuts, and seeds. Fish, poultry, and meat were prepared for special, not everyday, occasions. People often drank wine with their meals, and olive oil was the main source of dietary fat.

In 1988 a five-year study in Lyon, France, was launched to test whether a diet patterned after the Mediterranean example could reduce the risk of a second heart attack or cardiac-related death in a large group of men and women who had already survived an initial heart attack. Half of the group followed a typical American Heart Association low-fat diet, and the other half ate a modified Mediterranean diet. The study's ethics and safety committee stopped the trial less than halfway through "because the benefits of the Mediterranean diet were so compelling—a 70 percent reduction in deaths from all causes. When the investigators checked in on the study participants several years later, the benefits—including a reduced risk of cancer—seen after two and a half years were still in evidence."[20]

Most of the participants had continued to eat a Mediterranean diet long after the study was over. Why? I believe they had found that it met Dr. Willett's criteria for the "ultimate diet": it not only had tremendous health benefits, but it was also enjoyable, satisfying, and controlled hunger.

So, it is time to throw out the old Food Guide Pyramid. In mid-2005 the government revised the pyramid, but it still doesn't measure up to the best scientific evidence as far as a healthy diet is concerned. Dr. Willett has proposed a new Healthy Eating Pyramid based on the Mediterranean model and enhanced by his many years of research.[21] I recommend it as a helpful resource if you want more information. Our Body Balance Food Chart (page 184) incorporates the same principles, and, in fact, the ZOE 8 Weight Management Program takes them a step further: we teach you how to completely personalize these principles for healthy eating into your individual lifestyle.

Before we move to that topic, however, it is time for Ed to tell you more about his story and how he put these principles to work in his life—with dramatic results, to say the least. The first step was learning that his self-worth could not be measured on the bathroom scale.

Chapter Four

You Are More Than a Number on the Scale

THE intake nurse at Structure House smiled fleetingly as the electronic scale reset and motioned me forward. Her attitude was professional yet somewhat detached. I suppose for her these weigh-ins were so routine that she performed them on autopilot. But for me this was a significant milestone, a moment I had been dreading for months. I had originally been scheduled to arrive the previous September, but the upheaval from the 9-11 tragedies hit the hotel and restaurant business hard, so I had postponed my trip. Since then, however, I had been dieting seriously. It may seem silly now, but I was trying to shape up before I had to step on the scales or exercise in public. Elisa said it was like straightening up the house on the day before the housekeeper comes.

Once I had moved past 350 pounds, I was unable to weigh myself on a regular scale, so I'd had no idea how much I actually weighed. Over the last few months I had surely lost ten or fifteen pounds, but I knew they were not going to make much difference when I hauled my massive frame onto the dieter's archenemy: the doctor's scale.

The previous evening, when I had arrived at the weight-loss clinic, I'd learned that I would have to weigh in every morning before breakfast. The system worked like this: You entered a computer ID card into the electronic scale, and it recorded the date and your weight. If you tried to use your ID card in the dining room without the daily weight scan, your card—and you—would be ejected. Now it was time for my first weigh-in. For a moment I felt as if my feet were glued to the floor, but I took a deep breath, said a silent prayer, and stepped on the scale, hearing a drum roll in my mind.

I tried to prepare myself, remembering what Dr. Colbert had said about the pounds melting away once I got my intestinal tract in balance and my emotional and spiritual issues, especially rejection, resolved. But my heart still sank when I saw the number on the scale: *457.* That meant I must have weighed about 470 pounds, maybe more, at my heaviest. I knew I was in terrible shape—Dr. Colbert had verified that I could die very soon—but a sense of dismay overtook me at seeing such a large number written on my chart. I had not only ballooned past 400 pounds; I was closer to 500!

My self-esteem was at an all-time low. I had loathed my body for a long time. I had even prayed for release in order to escape the pain and shame of my deplorable physical condition. Obviously that wasn't God's will or my true desire because here I was—on my fiftieth birthday—taking steps toward healing. Although I was tempted to drop out of the program, I stuck it out all four weeks. And during that time I made some friends, learned a lot about myself, and dropped twenty pounds or so. At the rate I was paying, I later figured it had cost me over five hundred dollars a pound, but at least I was losing weight and starting to make the lifestyle changes that would, indeed, start melting the pounds away.

MEASURING SELF-ESTEEM ON THE BATHROOM SCALE

Most people who are overweight, even if they're carrying only ten or fifteen extra pounds, suffer with self-esteem problems. It certainly doesn't help that the $40 billion diet industry is fueled by Hollywood and Madison Avenue images of an impossible ideal. The average woman, for example, is 5'4" tall and weighs 140 pounds, which is a healthy weight according to accepted medical standards. Yet the average American model is 5'11" tall and weighs 117 pounds—an unhealthy, and potentially dangerous, weight.

Television viewers and magazine readers are bombarded with images of impossibly thin, supremely attractive models and actors promoting every product imaginable, including low-fat, low-carb, high-protein, high-whatever diet products, foods, and snacks. "Eat this," the ads imply, "and you'll look like me." Striving for an impossible ideal, millions of people buy these products, and the majority of them probably wind up *gaining* weight, or perhaps losing a few pounds only to regain them. Why? One reason is the feelings of disappointment and even despair that come from comparing yourself with this false ideal. We seldom stop to consider that looking good is a full-time job for movie stars and models; it is their business.

"Bombardment" is an accurate description of what the media do to us—we cannot escape the ever-present images of beauty and perfection.

According to Mary Pipher, PhD, a therapist who specializes in eating disorders, the average person sees between four hundred and six hundred ads daily. "Most of these ads show women who are pencil-thin, even anorexic. Sometimes the images are not even of real women. Instead, the photos in the ads are composites that combine the head of an adult woman, the torso of a young girl, and the legs of a boy."[1]

While much more attention has been focused on women and eating disorders, the problem now affects both genders. Men are becoming more body-conscious as today's advertisers shamelessly objectify the male physique. As a result, more and more men are becoming fat-phobic and obsessive about dieting and working out. In fact, researchers have now defined a body-image distortion disorder they liken to "reverse anorexia." They call the disorder "muscle dysmorphia," and it afflicts both men and women, usually athletes, who are convinced that they are too small, even though they are fit and muscular. "Imagine a bodybuilder—250 pounds, 20-inch biceps, 6 percent body fat—horrified to take his shirt off for fear he looks out of shape."[2]

More common eating disorders such as anorexia and bulimia also plague men these days. Approximately seven million women and one million men are currently being treated for eating disorders, but the men may be underrepresented in these numbers since it is usually more difficult for a man to seek help for what has so often been considered a female disorder. It is understandable, therefore—but tragic, nonetheless—that men and women alike wind up judging their self-worth solely by the number on the bathroom scale. And that is especially unfortunate when you consider that the bathroom scale is not a very reliable indicator of health or even weight loss.

THE INADEQUACY OF THE SCALE

Most of us who have struggled with the burden of excess pounds develop a ritual when it comes to weighing ourselves. Now it is true confession time. Have you ever gotten off the scale and then gotten back on to see if you liked the second reading better than the first? Have you shifted from one foot to the other or leaned forward to see if the reading changes? Does your mood go up or down depending on that all-important number?

Here's an example of one woman's weighing ritual, and while she writes with a humorous tone, it is obvious that she is quite serious about the trepidation with which she views her bathroom scale.

I don't know why the number on any of those stupid scales matters so much to me.... It makes no sense that in one moment I feel like I have got the world by the tail and the next I feel like my tail is the size of the world. That is an awful lot of power to give a stupid electronic device....

Once I'm naked, I pull the scale out of the bathroom closet and turn it on. Then I check myself to be sure I haven't absentmindedly tossed a wet towel or cat over my shoulder. I check to be sure I don't have to pee again. I check to be sure I didn't sweat in my sleep, because if I did and my hair is even slightly damp, I will blow-dry it. (Sadly, I'm not kidding.) I step on the scale and stare straight ahead, counting to ten. Then I step off the scale and look down to see what the Bad Scale claims I weigh. I weigh myself twice more, because although Bad Scale is always rock-solid and gives me the same number repeatedly, it can't hurt to triple-check.[3]

This woman is not alone when it comes to letting the scale dictate the way she sees herself. But what if, as fitness expert Bob Greene suggests, the "process of weighing yourself was one big practical joke"?[4]

There is some truth to Greene's assertion. While it is important to track your weight to determine long-term trends, the bathroom scale cannot measure what *type* of weight you have lost or gained: water weight, fat, or lean muscle mass. Add to that the fact that your weight naturally fluctuates from day to day and even from hour to hour, and just how reliable is the number on the scale?

When we set out to lose weight, we want to lose fat. But what shows up as a loss on the scale may be something else entirely. Greene describes the fallacy of the scale by giving two different examples.

In the first scenario, let's say you lost four pounds of water, gained three pounds of fat, and lost a pound of muscle. When you jumped on the scale, it would read that you lost two pounds. The chances are that you felt pretty good about yourself, even though the reality is that you *gained three pounds of fat*. You just didn't know it. In the second scenario, you have lost four pounds of fat and gained five pounds of water. The scale reads that you gained a pound, when the truth is that you *lost four pounds of unwanted body fat.* Your reaction would probably be one of disappointment.[5]

So the scale does not give you the whole picture, and overreliance on the bathroom scale as a measurement of progress can be self-defeating, especially if that magic number on the scale defines your self-worth.

It seems that society has made a value judgment about weight: skinny equals beautiful equals good, while overweight equals ugly equals bad. Listen to what one writer says about the impact this has had on her struggle with weight:

> My self-esteem and my body image are fused together. They are not supposed to be. You are supposed to be able to separate how you feel about your body and how you feel about yourself as a person. You are supposed to be able to be overweight and not let it affect your mood or your personality. It doesn't work that way for me.
>
> Thin equals beautiful and beautiful equals perfection. I have grown up with this imbedded in me....I don't know who I am outside my weight.[6]

How sad that so many people define themselves solely by their weight. And how sad that society reinforces that concept. It is as if, in Dr. Pipher's words, society deems weight to be "the ultimate moral determinant": fat people are bad and thin people are good. "Society's rejection of the obese is unusually thorough," she writes. "Generally, most of us can separate an alcoholic's behavior from his or her personhood. Smokers may find their behavior is criticized, but they are still valued as people. Obese people are condemned not just for their overeating (a behavior that is not necessarily present). Their entire character—from their IQ to their work habits and their sexuality—is imagined, judged, and found wanting."[7]

Now, I am not on a crusade to change the way society views being overweight, but I am on a crusade to help people quit judging themselves solely by the number on the scale. Our friend Oliver comes to mind as I share this. In a recent statement, he shared how he struggled with self-worth because of his weight.

ZOE 8 TESTIMONY

"I'm not worthy." Those were my words to Ed and Elisa McClure when they decided to make a significant investment, personally and professionally, to help me become the man God intended me to be.

You see, I had been out of work for eight months. My credentials as an executive chef were outstanding—every interviewer who read my résumé felt they had found the grand prize in the cereal box. Until they saw me in person, that is. I'm certain they felt I would probably not be around very long.

They were right. At 528 pounds I was barely functioning physically, able to walk maybe fifty yards at a time. I was emotionally shut down as well. I suppose I had lost my self-confidence a hundred or so pounds earlier, and I was in massive denial about the consequences of my tremendous weight gain.

Somehow Ed and Elisa looked beyond my weight—and all my problems—and saw my potential. I was more than a number on the scale to them, and they helped me see my true worth. I was never suicidal, even at 528 pounds (one of the "supertankers," as Ed calls us) and very, very sick. But I had no quality of life anymore and no self-esteem at all. I truly thought I wasn't "worthy." I was wrong.

Although I've lost 70 pounds in the last year, I still have a long, long way to go. But I can honestly say that this program has become a way of life for me—a way to save my life. I might not be alive today if I hadn't adopted the ZOE 8 way of life.

—Oliver V.*

Just as we were able to show Oliver, each one of us must start to see ourselves differently before we can make permanent changes with regard to our weight or health. So, while we encourage people to set specific goals for their weight loss, we advocate an integrated approach to the matter, an approach that honors who we are as God's creation.

---

*Read more of Oliver's story in chapters five and eight.

IDEAL WEIGHT VS. ZOE W8

The foundational concept of ZOE 8 is that true success in weight loss and health management (or any other endeavor of life) can only come through an integrated approach that fully addresses body, mind, and spirit. God created each of us as one-of-a-kind individuals, giving every person particular talents and abilities as well as unique fingerprints, eye and hair color, and body shape.

When we were looking for a name for our weight-loss program, we wanted something that described life in all its fullness. One of our key principles has always been the pursuit of not just weight loss or health management but abundance of life. *Zoe* is a Greek word the Bible uses to express this abundant life God created us to enjoy, and eight is the number of new beginnings or regeneration. Jesus said, "I have come that they may have life [*zoe*], and that they may have it more abundantly" (John 10:10, NKJV). Our program teaches people how to discover the zoe life of God, especially as it applies to health and weight loss.

Everyone who starts a weight-loss program has a goal in mind, and usually it is a specific number because the notion of ideal weight is so ingrained. As I have studied this subject—and as I have *lived* it over the past few years—I have come to a somewhat contrarian viewpoint of ideal weight. I no longer believe there *is* such a thing, at least not as it has traditionally been measured. Let me share with you how I arrived at this conclusion.

First of all, *ideal* is a concept that by definition is not achievable. Ideal refers to an idea, an image, or an archetype that represents beauty, excellence, or perfection. While perfection may be a noble goal, I do not ever expect to arrive at perfection, do you? Instead, my goal is to glorify God and honor my family by becoming the absolute best I can be, with God's help, in all areas of my life and to be a good example for others. And you know what? That simply is not measurable by achieving a number that someone else has defined for me.

Second, my personal experience is that after losing 200 pounds, I still have not attained the so-called ideal weight as it has typically been measured by the insurance companies' height-weight charts or the newer measurement of body mass index (BMI). I may fall outside the norm weight-wise, yet I am extremely fit, able to lift over 20,000 pounds in one training session, and capable of intense aerobic workouts with great cardiopulmonary function.

And remember, I used to suffer from heart arrhythmia and high blood pressure, as well as a whole host of medical problems, including chronic oxygen deprivation due to sleep apnea. Now, however, I take no prescription drugs for my heart or my blood pressure or anything else. Every single lab report comes back in the normal range, I feel great, and I have tons of energy.

WHAT'S IN A NAME?

Zoe = Life

Several Greek words are translated *life* in the Bible:

Bios is limited to the natural order.

Psyche is self-conscious physical existence.

Zoe is life as the possession of God and as his gift to mankind; it is the only term for life with which the adjective *eternal* is used.

8 = New Beginnings

The number eight signifies a new beginning, regeneration, or resurrection.

Consider these examples from Scripture:

- The number seven represents perfection or completion; therefore, the number eight signifies a new beginning.
- Eight people, Noah and his family, were saved on the ark in order to repopulate the world.
- Male children are circumcised on the eighth day, signifying their entrance into a covenant with God.
- The eighth day, the day following the end of a seven-day feast, signaled the beginning of a new cycle.
- In ancient Israel, the land was to lie fallow in the seventh year, and replanting began in the eighth year.
- When a person was healed of leprosy, he presented himself to the Levitical officials for certification on the eighth day and then made a burnt offering; that day became the start of his new, disease-free life.
- Christ arose on the eighth day, the new "first day of the week."

From every standpoint except the "magic number," I am the picture of health. In fact, I carry approximately six million dollars'worth of life insurance. Just three years ago I had the highest possible rating for my premium—any higher and I would have been uninsurable. Now I have no adverse health conditions that would affect my life span. The insurance company required comprehensive physical exams for the new policy because of my previous conditions, and I'd say you are undeniably healthy when a major insurer is willing to gamble *six million dollars* that you are not going to die for at least twenty more years.

So, what about the standard height-weight charts? How did they become enshrined as the be-all and end-all of weight management? Did you know these charts are not even based on medical evidence? The most famous, and indeed the chart that became the gold standard of measurement, was formulated in the 1940s by a biologist working for the Metropolitan Life Insurance Company. The data used to compile these charts included heights and weights of people who had purchased life insurance policies. Things like smoking, drinking, exercise, or lifestyle were not taken into consideration, and the resulting actuarial tables considered only mortality (life span), not morbidity (the incidence of disease or illness). The real purpose of the chart was to justify charging higher premiums for policies.

The original chart referred to the weights listed as "desirable," but that description soon gave way to "ideal." Most people don't know that the heights listed assume a person is wearing street shoes, with a one- to two-inch heel. That can change the results significantly. Also, the reference to frame size (small, medium, and large) is entirely subjective. The Met Life height-weight chart also assumed that people maintained the same weight after age thirty, which we know is not normal; people naturally gain a few pounds as they grow older.

Other mortality studies, particularly the four-decade long study of the population of Framingham, Massachusetts, show that as far as longevity is concerned, the best weight is actually above the average for both men and women. Another long-term study, by Dr. John Andres of Johns Hopkins University, "found that the lowest mortality occurs in adults who would normally be considered 24 to 38 percent overweight."[8]

More popular now for measuring "ideal weight" is the concept of body mass index, or BMI, which does not measure but does correlate with body fat (a much more reliable indicator of good health than total weight). The newer BMI charts take into consideration age and gender, which greatly affect body composition. Even here, though, the measurement is subject to interpretation and is only one indicator of health status.

A recent study, for example, showed that half of all NFL and NBA players are overweight according to their BMI. In fact, basketball superstar Shaquille O'Neal even met the criteria for obesity with his BMI of 31.6.[9] Of course, the BMI calculation is based only on height and weight, not fitness, so an athlete with lots of lean muscle mass will have a higher than normal BMI.

So, for all these reasons, we have quit referring to "ideal weight" in our program. Instead, we encourage people to seek what we call their ZOE W8 (weight), and we define this as the optimal weight at which a person enjoys all the health benefits God desires for his children. Now, let me help you wrap your mind around this concept. Think about your own children or the people you love most in the world. Don't you want the very best for them? Wouldn't you do everything in your power to help them succeed and be happy? Imagine, then, how much more our heavenly Father wants us to be healthy and happy, and to what extent he will go to help us achieve and maintain a healthy weight that will allow us to live long and well and to be active and productive. ZOE W8 is *God's* ideal weight for the bodies he gave us.

For some people, ZOE W8 may even mean gaining weight. A great number of our program participants have appeared trim and fit, without an ounce of extra fat on their bodies. Yet they were struggling with serious health issues that could be improved through dietary and behavior changes. What good is it to achieve an "ideal" weight according to traditional standards, yet have high blood pressure, high cholesterol, or severe heartburn?

Now, how do you know when you have achieved your ZOE W8? The number on the scale is one—but only one—measure of your progress. Even better indicators of progress are your overall health and fitness level. As I mentioned earlier, I'm feeling very "zoe" these days, even though I'm still carrying a few extra pounds according to traditional height-weight measurements. But my health is excellent, and my fitness level allows me to do anything I want to do—I no longer have any limitations. Unless I wanted to become a body builder, there's not much else I could do to improve my physical conditioning.

There is one final reason we encourage people to seek their ZOE W8 rather than some arbitrary number: to break people of the dangerous habit of chronic dieting.

WHY DIETING BECOMES BONDAGE

You have to realize that dieting inevitably results in bondage. It is an unending endeavor, because once you stop the "diet," the excess weight returns. What is the typical response at that point? Try a different diet. And another one...and another one. Some fad diets are even more dangerous than the obesity they are trying to reverse.

In fact, dieting can actually *cause* obesity. Why? Perhaps you learned Newton's Third Law of Physics in school: for every action there is an equal and opposite reaction. Now, apply that to dieting; it is equally true. Every period of deprivation is followed by an equal and opposite binge. After days or weeks or months of depriving the body of the quality and quantity of food it needs, a person will inevitably start to eat the kinds of food or amounts of food they have been avoiding. That is why so many people go through repeated cycles of losing and gaining weight, usually achieving an even greater increase of total weight on each up cycle.

Chronic dieting is now recognized as an eating disorder in itself. In its extreme form, chronic dieting leads to anorexia or bulimia. The problem is that dieters learn to be what doctors and therapists call "externally controlled eaters." In other words, they rely on external cues for eating rather than relying on internal cues such as true physical hunger. "Externally controlled eaters grow fat when food cues are abundant. And in our society, food cues are everywhere....The junk food industry and its twin, the diet industry, both profit from our impulse eating and subsequent guilt and shame."[10]

The last thing I want to do is to enslave people with another diet. Quite the opposite is true: I want people to find *freedom* and to enjoy the abundant, zoe life God planned for us. That can never be accomplished with a diet; instead, it requires a lifestyle change. But the good news is that Elisa and I can show you how to gradually make small lifestyle changes that will produce big results.

That is what happened to me. I had to learn to lose weight from the inside out, and you can too. Turn the page, and I will explain what I mean by that.

Chapter Five

How to Lose Weight From the Inside Out

IN 1998 I spent most of the Christmas holidays in bed with near pneumonia. While Elisa and the kids were out shopping and having fun, I was laid up in a hotel room in Newport, Rhode Island, running a high fever and feeling miserable. I missed out on exchanging gifts and feasting with the Travisono family—and I do mean *feasting*. Holiday dinners with Elisa's large Italian family are a joyous occasion, and Diana, Elisa's mom, is an excellent cook. I had been adopted into the family as an "Italian-in-law" and always enjoyed my visits there, other than the ever-present guilt of feeling inadequate as a husband and father.

But there was no Christmas joy for me that year. I was so sick that the holiday passed in a blur. Yet it turned out to be one of the most significant weeks of my life, for two reasons.

First, I didn't realize that it would be my last trip with my family for a long time; for the next few years I stayed home and tended to business during Christmas. When you are in the hotel and restaurant business, holidays are for guests, not staff; we often have to celebrate on other days or at odd hours. But staying home for business reasons was really an excuse. The simple truth was that I had gotten too big to travel anymore.

The second reason that Christmas trip was significant is that it turned into a powerful encounter with God. I had been raised in a Christian home and had a personal relationship with God that began at a young age. But for many years I had put that relationship on hold. God was always real to me, but just as I did with everything else in my life, I dealt with God on my own terms. I put him in a box and said, "This is where you belong—over here. I will get back to you when I need you."

My method of survival was to force the rest of the world to adapt to my priorities, and my number one priority was work. I wouldn't have admitted it at the time, but it was true. "You are like a machine," Elisa once told me. "You have a one-dimensional life, and that dimension is work." As I said earlier, I had created the "world of Ed," a corporate cocoon where I was seemingly in control. Anything that tried to intrude into my domain soon got shut down. As I look back on it now, I can see that even those—or perhaps especially those—who love me best have experienced my ability to drive through obstacles. At the time it was what I thought I needed to do to survive.

While my workaholic ways had not changed, I had renewed my relationship with God in a very real and deep way a few years prior to that 1998 trip. Elisa and I had started attending church regularly and had recommitted our lives to Christ. I had been through a discipleship program and gotten involved with missions, something I have a heart for to this day. I had even started integrating my faith into my business, initiating prayer at meetings. And even though I tried to keep God first in my life, there was always an unspoken question lurking in the back of my mind: *What is wrong with you, Ed? What is wrong with you spiritually?*

Stuck in that hotel bed by myself, isolated from the myriad of distractions from running my business, I spent extended time in prayer and contemplation, reading the Bible when I felt up to it, then lying in bed and meditating on what I had read. My fever was high, and I would drift in and out of sleep. And I am not even sure whether I was awake, asleep, or somewhere in between when God began to show me some things about myself. For years I'd had tunnel vision, but now my spiritual horizon began to expand, and I got a glimpse of things as they *really* were, not how I had convinced myself to see them.

In those long hours of fever-induced reflection, God showed me five areas where I had fallen short and needed to submit to his will and his control, not mine. One of them was my weight. I had never considered my size as a spiritual problem before; perhaps I simply didn't want to. But there on my sickbed, I knew that I would have to get my weight under control if I wanted to become the man I desired to be.

It also became clear to me that I had developed an unhealthy relationship with food, and it had started at an early age. I remembered things from my childhood, and I recalled how my mother—like most parents—started rewarding me with food. If I had to go to the doctor and get a shot, she would take me out for ice cream afterward.

I had even chosen food and wine as a career! As a teenager I began working in the restaurant business, and by the time I was nineteen, I was managing a restaurant. From there I went into the hotel business, and for the next decade I climbed the corporate ladder, becoming food and beverage director over North America for one of the world's largest hotel chains. I opened gourmet restaurants, hiring the chefs, creating the menus and the décor, and managing every aspect of the operation. At one point I oversaw a $250-million annual budget.

As part of my business—and my pleasure—I regularly enjoyed gourmet meals accompanied by fine wines. It became my way of life, and while I was not a glutton or a drunkard, I was definitely a *gourmand:* "one who is heartily interested in good food and drink."

Yet I never connected my weight to an unhealthy relationship to food. I ate well but did not overeat. Elisa had commented to my doctors that she didn't understand how I had gained so much weight when I didn't eat much more than she did. "We eat the same things," she told him. And it was true. But it was also true that I had built my life around food. I had become deeply, passionately involved with food. It was my work, and work was my life, so food played a huge role in the "world of Ed."

After that encounter with God, I recorded in my diary the five problem areas I had identified, using shorthand abbreviations so no one else would know what they were. I promised God that I would conquer all five of those shortcomings. On four of the things I needed to deal with, I had clarity. I could see the problem and identify what to do. But the fifth thing, my weight, I still didn't understand. I wrestled with the notion that my weight was a spiritual matter.

Perhaps God was ready to show me then, but I simply wasn't ready to see it. By that time I'd gotten so big that it was scary, and I was running away from the truth. My way of dealing with it was to avoid it. My way wasn't working, of course, but I did not know what else to do.

☙

LIKE Ed, I did not know what to do, either. I had watched him decline physically and withdraw emotionally for years. It is difficult to put into words, but I had reached a point where I had to ignore the situation and get on with life; that was the only way I could survive. We lived in the same household and occupied the same space, but Ed lived in his own world while I lived in mine.

Complete independence was his natural inclination. He had been on his own—mentally, anyway—since he was six or seven years old. "I am an island, and I take care of myself" was always Ed's philosophy of life. I was the total opposite. I had a really great childhood with a happy, fun family. The worst thing that ever happened to me was moving during my senior year of high school. Ed had been through much, much more as a child, and those things had shaped his character.

I knew when I married Ed that he was not the kind to stop and smell the roses. He has always been a workaholic and, it goes without saying, a great provider for his family. He was very successful in his hotel career and won a number of awards while he was climbing the corporate ladder. One of the things that drove Ed to establish his own company was his inability to do anything about his increasing size. And he definitely did try—even as he continued to gain weight he was aggressive about exercise. He swam laps in the pool every day and walked up to an hour on the treadmill. He even worked with a personal trainer. But nothing seemed to make any difference. Finally, we realized that because of his size Ed would have faced discrimination to the point of being unemployable. So he started his own business and continued to make his mark on the hotel and restaurant management industry.

From the beginning of our marriage, Ed experienced some major depressive episodes. But he was somehow always able to pull himself together enough to work. He has an incredible mind and a strong will. So even as he got worse and worse, he was able to keep things together, at least on the outside.

I understood the business he was in, so I was never upset when he did not come home at five o'clock every afternoon. I was so capable of taking care of the kids that I really did not need him. I needed him at a higher level, of course, but not for the daily functioning of the family. I was brought up in an Italian culture where a woman took care of the house. I watched my mother raise five children and take care of the family and household. That was second nature to me because I had grown up with such a good example.

So as I watched Ed decline, I simply did what I had to do. I spent time with the kids and tried to make sure they had as normal a life as possible. I didn't deal with Ed's situation because he didn't let me. He shut me out of that aspect of his life, and, right or wrong, I let him. Sometimes people would say to me, "Why don't you do something to help Ed?" And I would think, *But what am I supposed to do?*

We rarely talked about his weight, and when we did, the conversations were brief. We mainly talked about business because that was what we had in common. Years earlier, we had met at work and later became not only husband and wife but also business partners, and we had—and still have—a great partnership. Looking back on it now, I don't remember a whole lot about Ed's increasing withdrawal as his weight ballooned. It was just life, and we somehow lived from day to day. I do remember telling him one time, "You only live half a life. You exist solely in the mind. You're just a mind that ignores its body." But that is how he was able to handle it; he ignored his body.

It may sound harsh, but at some level Ed was already dead to me—or, rather, those parts of him that I now realize were just too painful to share. He was not used to failing; he was trying, but having no success. The kids and I did what we could, but it wasn't much.

I was actually prepared to receive the phone call telling me that Ed had passed away. It would not have surprised me; I was ready for it. The kids and I often wondered, *When is he going to die?* We did not say that to him, but we thought about it. And while they did not talk to their father about the subject, Taylor and Ian both came to me on more than one occasion and asked, "Is Dad going to die?"

Serious illness never affects just the sick person; it changes the entire family. Our son, Ian, was especially affected because he had become the caretaker when Ed traveled. When he got to where business trips became extremely difficult because of his physical limitations, Ian started traveling with him. If they flew, Ian would carry the luggage and help Ed navigate through the airport. If they drove, Ian would make sure Ed stayed awake, poking him when he would doze off at the wheel because of severe sleep apnea.

It became a hopeless situation for all of us. I thought about leaving Ed, but I knew that was not really the answer. Perhaps it was a coping mechanism, but I felt that he was handicapped. I asked myself, *Would I leave Ed if he had been crippled in a terrible car accident?* The answer was no. Even though it was tough, really tough, I decided I couldn't leave him. He had gotten in this condition in spite of his best efforts. Over the years he had truly tried to do something about his weight and health, and I respected that. I rationalized that he was not an alcoholic, he was not abusive, he was just handicapped. Since his recovery I have asked myself whether Ed would have changed sooner had I done something drastic such as leaving. I simply do not know, and it is fruitless to second-guess now.

My hopelessness was compounded by the fact that I was having problems mentally for the first time. I was feeling very alone and depressed—not just about Ed, but about the way our business situation had transformed our personal lives. We had renovated a phenomenal property called the Guadalupe River Ranch, and running the place had largely been my responsibility. We had over sixty employees, who had become our extended family. When the relationship with one of our business partners went completely sour, we made the difficult decision to sell our share. I not only felt a responsibility for the welfare of our employees, but I also lost some deep personal relationships and a place that I had loved. We had lived on the property, intending to make it our home for the rest of our lives. So I lost a cherished dream as well, and it was a very emotional time for me.

We didn't take the advice that our friend (and now ZOE 8 counselor) Dr. Mark Jones had given us at the time of that tremendous upheaval in our lives. "Take six months off," he said. "Kick back, go to the beach, rest." But we didn't. Instead, we immediately opened a new restaurant and within a few months had bought another hotel property.

Ed and I grew farther apart, and while I still cared what happened to him and took care of things as I always had, I made the decision that I was no longer going to enable him. Losing weight and getting healthy had to be something he decided to do. I prayed for him, and many of our Christian friends prayed for him. But I knew that in his own spiritual walk, Ed had to learn that to get an uncommon result, you need to do something uncommon.

And as you have seen, it was only when Ed finally made a spiritual decision to get control of his weight and health that true change was possible—for all of us.

❧

Ed

AFTER my bout with pneumonia and my encounter with God, it would be another four years before I really understood my fifth problem area—weight—and how to deal with it as a spiritual condition. When I first met with Don Colbert, he quickly identified the root cause of my weight problem as a spiritual issue, and he started dealing with me as a whole person—spirit, mind, and body. It was a revelation to me, because no doctor I'd ever known had approached treatment in that way.

Yet it made perfect sense, once I thought about it, because such an approach dovetails with the way God created us. We are created with three parts to our nature: spirit, mind, and body. That is the way God designed us, and any treatment program—for weight loss, physical or mental health, or anything else—that does not address all three elements of our existence cannot bring lasting success.

ALL ISSUES ARE SPIRITUAL ISSUES

This three-part nature of man is a biblical concept, yet it is increasingly recognized by more and more doctors and health practitioners, especially those involved in what is called alternative or complementary medicine. We have people from all walks of life who attend seminars we put on to teach the principles of the ZOE 8 Weight Management Program, and some of them have no religious or spiritual background at all. They often seem a bit nervous when I start referring to Scripture, but I assure them I am not trying to be preachy. It is just that the Bible is a storehouse of practical wisdom, and everyone can benefit from examining what it has to say.

A number of Scriptures demonstrate the three-part nature of man. Here is one of the key verses we often use: "May God himself, the God of peace, sanctify you through and through. May your whole *spirit, soul* and *body* be kept blameless" (1 Thessalonians 5:23, emphasis added). *Soul* is another word for *mind.*

When we started teaching this concept in our seminars, Elisa would draw a figure on the chalkboard that really helped people understand it quickly. (See below.) This symbol, composed of three interlocking circles, illustrates the three-part nature of man, which we also refer to as the three elements of our existence. Note that the spirit is the topmost circle in this diagram. That is because it is the enduring element. At death our bodies and minds will cease existing, but our spirit will continue: it is the invisible, eternal aspect of our existence.

I sometimes state it this way: I *am* a spirit, I *have* a mind, and I *live* in a body.

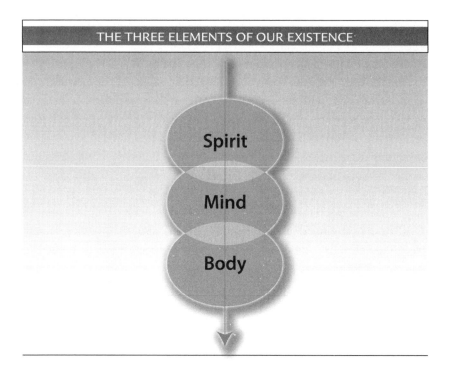

THE THREE ELEMENTS OF OUR EXISTENCE

Spirit

Mind

Body

Uppermost is the spirit—the invisible, immortal aspect of our existence. At ZOE 8 we believe all things are spiritual and that things happen in the spirit realm first. Neglect or lack of awareness of our spiritual nature leaves us vulnerable to being controlled by our emotions.

The mind (or soul) is the realm of our thoughts and emotions. Ideally, the spirit directs the mind, which in turn controls the body. Unfortunately, most of us carry around emotional "baggage" from the past that unconsciously influences our bodies to do unhealthy things.

The third element of our existence, purposely placed at the bottom, is the body. Frankly, it only does what it is told to do by the mind. If your body or physical being is not what you want it to be, you need to look up—to your mind and spirit.

I think you can see now why we say that all issues are spiritual issues. For years I tried to keep God in the box where I had placed him. I let him go to church with me—isn't that where God belongs?—but locked him out of the rest of my life. But God wants to be involved in every area of our lives because that is why he created us. In fact, he is the Lord of all creation. It is *man* who always tries to separate the universe into spiritual and secular realms, relegating God to only one aspect of life. But God is the Lord of all.

Consider how that applies to our weight and health. Our physical bodies are the "temple of the Holy Spirit [God]" (1 Corinthians 6:19), and God cannot separate himself from his temple. That is why we cannot separate God from our weight-loss efforts or our struggles to deal with certain health problems. He created our bodies, and he still has ownership rights, whether we acknowledge that or not.

SYMPTOMS VERSUS CAUSES

When I fully comprehended that my weight *problem* was a spiritual issue, I knew the *solution* would also have to be spiritual. Oh, I would need a food plan and exercise program, but those would only be a part of the equation. As Don Colbert told me on my initial visit, I had to attack the spiritual root of my problem first, and then the pounds would melt.

The way our health-care system works today, most medical practitioners simply treat individual symptoms in isolation without looking for underlying causes. Take the "common cold." We treat the symptoms (runny nose, sneezing, cough, fever), but the cause is something you can't see: a virus or bacterial infection. While an untreated cold may not have serious consequences, leaving more serious illnesses untreated can lead to serious long-term health problems. To complicate things further, we go to one doctor to treat one symptom and another doctor to treat something else—and sometimes the second symptom is caused by the treatment prescribed to control the first symptom! What is needed, as Dr. Colbert demonstrated, is an integrated approach, but it has been my experience that many doctors never consider the emotional and spiritual aspects of disease. Of course, I don't know what they think personally or believe, and certainly our current health-care system inhibits doctors in many ways.

Most weight-loss programs are limited by the same mind-set; they only address the physical aspect, offering diet and exercise regimens. Some programs address the emotional aspects of overeating, and a few programs approach weight loss from a spiritual standpoint. Those programs, however, are generally weak when it comes to nutritional research. That is why we designed the ZOE 8 Weight Management Program to fully address all the elements of your life. A true cure can be found only when you discover the causes of weight gain and illness, not just treat symptoms.

Many people suffer physical problems because of underlying spiritual and emotional issues. That was my situation, and things only began to change for me when I delved deep inside myself and made the decision—a spiritual decision—to change my life from the inside out. As we read Oliver's continuing story, we see that the same was true for him:

ZOE 8 TESTIMONY

When I first started the ZOE 8 program I didn't quite get the spiritual aspect; I thought it was all about food. But I soon learned that the emotional and spiritual aspects were every bit as important as the physical part of the program. If you try to focus on just one aspect, you may find limited success, but you will be missing the opportunity for a truly zoe life—life in all its abundance.

Faith was a part of my upbringing, but I had put it on the back burner as I pursued my career. So it was an incredibly painful and humbling experience to finally come out of my denial and realize just how ill I had become. For someone as independent as I had always been, it was no small realization to admit I needed help—God's help—to dig out of the pit I was in. But then there was nothing small about me; I had passed the 500-pound mark and kept on going.

Through Ed and Elisa McClure, Dr. Don Colbert, and the members of the ZOE Plus group, I came to understand the love God has for me as his child. I have accepted Christ and asked God to forgive me for what I have done to my body—his temple.

I can't even begin to describe the changes since then. It's not just the fact that I've lost 70 pounds and two shirt sizes. It's not just that I'm able to do so much more than I could before. More than that, I am a new person. Doubts may come sometimes, but I have seen God work in this program, in me, and in my family.

I'm so much happier and healthier now, and making progress on my journey. And it is a journey. Dr. Stephen Covey says that it only takes an *instant to decide to change, but it takes a lifetime to maintain that change. That's where I am now, and I thank God for ZOE 8 and for my future.*

— Oliver V.*

TAKE INVENTORY

My inside-out change began by taking time to assess my current spiritual, mental, and physical condition. The same was true for Oliver, and the same is true for you. The first step is to ask yourself: *Where am I now?* If you don't know where you are, how can you know where you are going?

Make a written inventory of where you are now from the inside out—spiritually, emotionally, and physically—in order to determine your starting point on the journey to optimum health. We feel so strongly about this that we made it step number one in our ZOE 8 Weight Management Program. Why? Because it really is the starting place. Everything I went through in the first chapter of this book brought me to the place where I took the first step: acknowledging where I was. We provided information in chapters two and three to help you understand the facts and realize some of the eating habits that may have led you to your current condition. Now it is time to grab a pen and paper, be honest with yourself, and acknowledge where you are.

Your spiritual inventory will include your personal beliefs about God, your purpose in life, and God's design for your health. Have you ever considered your weight or health concerns as a spiritual issue?

Your emotional inventory will include looking at unresolved issues from the past that still trouble you today. In what way are these issues related to your weight or health problems? What is your outlook on life? What is missing in your life? Answering these questions is an important part of getting started on the program.

Your physical inventory is like a medical history you fill out at the doctor's office. You should list any health problems you are currently experiencing, as well as health issues you have had in the past. If you haven't had a checkup in a while, please get a comprehensive physical exam. You need a qualified health practitioner as part of your support team, preferably one who will treat you as a whole person and who is open to the use of nutritional therapies and supplements as part of your health management program.

---

*Read more of Oliver's story in chapters four and eight.

Make a note of any lab results you have received, such as blood pressure, cholesterol levels, blood sugar levels, triglycerides, and so forth. This will be helpful baseline information you can refer to later on to see how far you have come. Don't just leave your results at the doctor's office—use them, and understand them. If you have questions about the results, don't be afraid to ask. And if your health-care practitioner is not open to questions, then find one who is. You are putting together a team for your success, and the star player is you!

Don't just take my word for it. Listen to Judy's story of how taking an inventory got her started on the path to wholeness:

ZOE 8 TESTIMONY

For the last twelve years I have battled depression and obesity. But the knowledge I have gleaned from this program has freed me from depression and given me hope that I will be at my ZOE W8.

I had never taken a personal inventory before, and I was amazed by how much self-awareness I gained through the process. When I saw my answers in writing, the truth popped out at me and helped me discover how much I really did not know about myself. As a result, I have new dreams and goals, and I'm excited as I see them come true one by one.

So far I have lost 30 pounds and two dress sizes! I have already updated my inventory and goals and plan to do this on a regular basis. . . .

Now I have moved forward not just physically but emotionally and spiritually. I have grown closer to the Lord, and I've been freed from deadly emotions that had caused great battles in the past. I am truly beginning to experience the abundant, zoe life, and it is rewarding to be able to introduce others to the ZOE 8 concept.

—Judy R.*

I cannot overemphasize the importance of taking time to write out your inventory. Remember, it was my medical and social history—my inventory, if

---

*Read more of Judy's story in chapter seven.

you will—that Dr. Colbert used to unravel the mystery of Ed. If I had not been able to present him with all this information, I might very well be dead today.

SET GOALS

Now that you know where you are, ask yourself this question: *Where am I going?* If you don't know where you are going, you will not be able to get there!

Setting goals is not just a mental exercise; it is an integral part of the process. That is why we made it the second step of the ZOE 8 Weight Management Program. It is important that you fully understand why you are doing this program and that you have a clear vision of what you want to accomplish. Be bold in setting your goals. Stretch. Dream. Imagine. Visualize a new you.

Some of your goals may be so big you cannot quite comprehend ever achieving them. So it is a good idea to break bigger goals into smaller ones. Take "little bites" at first, then you can revise your goals as you go along. Long-distance runners never start with a marathon; they begin a few yards at a time.

Be sure to include spiritual and emotional goals as well as physical ones. Where do you want to be a year from now, spiritually and emotionally? What attitudes do you need to change? What about your relationships?

Here are examples of physical goals you may want to set: to lose weight; to improve your health; to look and feel better; to reduce or eliminate the need for prescription drugs; to enjoy a healthier lifestyle. In setting your own goals, you may want to include other things, such as being able to travel comfortably or just being able to walk without pain.

Some of my goals included being able to walk without having knee replacements. I also wanted to be able to fly again, in one seat and without a belt extension, and to enjoy rides at the amusement park with my family—things I had not been able to do for a long time. I have done all of those things, and many more. One of my goals was to hold hands with my wife and walk on the beach. At the time I wrote down that goal, I could barely walk on concrete, let alone sand. Now we have a house at the beach, walk one to three miles a day, and that is a story in itself.

As I was gathering my thoughts for this book, I remembered a particular motivational exercise we did in a class at Structure House. We closed our eyes and listened to the instructor lead us in visualizing a favorite place, somewhere we felt safe and secure and happy. I have always loved the beach, so that is where I pictured myself. Once we had a vivid picture of that in our minds, the instructor told us to build a house at that location. We all imagined our houses, and then the instructor told us to open our eyes and draw a sketch of our own personal, "special" room in our imaginary house.

If I could put my hands on that sketch (I stashed it somewhere for safekeeping), I would reproduce it here, along with a picture of our "great room" at the beach house we purchased last year. I had forgotten all about that visualization exercise when we were remodeling the house, and yet as I think about it now, I realize that subconsciously I had re-created that room I had imagined several years earlier—down to the picture window overlooking the beach, the fireplace, the recliner, and yes, the big-screen TV.

What is it you can't do now (because of your weight or health) that you want to be able to do in the future? You can make it happen if you set goals and work toward them.

Break your goals into small, achievable steps. For example, if you have a lot of weight to lose, set your initial goal at losing 10 percent of your body weight. This is a benchmark number: the major benefits of weight loss occur at the point you drop 10 percent of your weight, no matter where you begin.

Another very important step in setting your goals is to write down in your own words a personal commitment to change. Think calmly, purposefully, and honestly about your inventory and goals. What do you need? What do you want to change? Make a written commitment to yourself that you can refer back to over time. You will likely want to expand your commitment statement as you proceed through the eight steps of the ZOE 8 program and gain knowledge about what specifics you may need to change to achieve all of your goals.

You may think that taking an inventory and setting goals is something you can do lightly, but if you want lasting changes to take place, you must take an honest look at what has been going on. This type of evaluation may require you to put certain areas of your life under a microscope, including some issues you may be trying to avoid. As you will see from the next two chapters, taking an inventory of my life required some heavy-duty soul-searching to get to the root of the problem and begin to heal it.

Chapter Six

"Ed, You Are Not a Candidate for Change"

DOCTORS, nurses, nutritionists, and psychologists—I saw them all the first few days of my stay at Structure House. The three-day intake process was rigorous for someone in my shape, with numerous interviews, evaluations, and testing. How far could I bend over? How much could I lift?

When I received my initial fitness assessment, I was at the lowest possible level. Because I was so completely deconditioned, I was not allowed on the treadmill or other exercise equipment. Even at the lowest level, some of the activities were too intense for me. Therefore, I was cleared for two activities only: water exercise and seated resistance training using long stretch bands (and, of course, walking—to the extent that I could). That was OK, though. They were wisely protecting me from overstressing my body by trying to do more than I was physically able.

Problem number one for me was with the nutritionist. For the three days prior to my arrival, I had been following Don Colbert's written instructions—the list of foods to avoid because they would stimulate candida growth. After my remarkable session at his office, and after several days immersed in prayer and reflection on where I had been and where I was going, I was convinced that he had answers for me. So I handed Dr. Colbert's dietary recommendations to the Structure House nutritionist upon my first visit.

"I'd like to eat this way while I'm here," I told her.

She glanced at the sheet briefly and was less than receptive. "We follow these guidelines," handing me some articles from professional medical journals endorsing a typical low-fat, low-calorie regimen and other articles stating that the candida diagnosis was just a fad at best and quackery at worst.

"We are not able to make modifications or exceptions for each attendee," the nutritionist informed me. She made it quite clear that I would either eat their way, or I would leave. I had to endure a lecture on how many thousands of people they had helped over twenty-five years and how successful their program was. I understood where she was coming from, but I didn't like her attitude. Besides, I had already been convinced that I had found my answer.

When I had left Dr. Colbert's office on Thursday, I hadn't known where to go. I had three days before I was due to report to Structure House and no hotel reservation because the trip to Florida had been a last-minute addition to my schedule. I called Elisa from the car, but we talked only briefly because I could not really articulate what had happened to me. It was just too powerful, and I was still basking in an afterglow from experiencing God's presence and love in Don Colbert's office.

With the CD player turned up full blast, I listened to the group Delirious sing about how Jesus was closer than a brother. Over and over I listened to "What a Friend I Have Found," weeping all the way to the East Coast. I played the music so loud, it is a wonder I didn't blow out the car windows.

When I saw the exit for Amelia Island, I turned in that direction. I knew where I was going now. I had always wanted to stay at one of the beautiful resorts there, and since it was off-season, I was able to book a beachfront condo without a reservation. I gave the clerk my credit card, then went to my condo—and didn't leave for three days.

The February wind cut like a knife, and it was too cold to walk on the beach. So I stayed inside, ordering my meals from room service. The only person I talked to was Elisa, but I still hadn't absorbed the experience enough to fully communicate it to her. I didn't turn on the TV. I did work a little, but mostly I watched the waves and thought about my life. I prayed, cried, and prayed some more. I studied the material Don had given me, and I clung to the hope he had offered.

I have a chance for a fresh start, I thought. *I can change my life.*

Now, here I was at the so-called "Fat Center of the United States," and the nutritional expert was as much as telling me that Dr. Colbert was a nutcase. She did not use those words, but I felt that was what she meant. I also felt that some of what the clinic would be feeding me would be poison to my system—the menu included almost everything on the "don't list"—artificial sweeteners, margarine, white rice, refined bread, sugar-free Jell-O. Their food plan was in many ways diametrically opposed to what I had learned from Dr. Colbert, and it presented me with an internal conflict: should I stay, or should I leave?

Before I could dwell on that dilemma, however, I received the results of my psychological assessment. And that frustrated me even more than my meeting with the nutritionist. I had undergone a battery of tests and interviews, and the entire process culminated in this terse pronouncement by the intake counselor: "Ed, you are not a good candidate for change."

Just how did they reach this conclusion? I was told, "You use God as a coping mechanism." The counselor went on to explain that I rationalized everything around God or his will, and that as a result, I likely would not benefit from much of what they had to offer as far as behavior modification was concerned, which was certainly a specialty of theirs. It would be beneficial if I attended classes, she said, but I may be excluded from group therapy sessions.

It is not that the people running the program were hostile to my faith; they simply concluded that because of the infusion of my personal faith into the answers I gave on the intake reports, I likely would not fit with their program. It was clear by my answers that if I participated in group therapy sessions, I would naturally inject God into my conversation. I think they felt that I was close-minded, which was true on that subject. Not that I would ever try to force my faith upon anyone else, but they did have a point: it would be impossible for me to open up and share what was on my mind *without* talking about God in some way or another. That is just who I am.

Now I was totally disoriented. What should I do? The food tasted awful, I was convinced it was not right for me, I could do only two kinds of exercise, and my "God" coping mechanism negated much of the benefit one may get from psychotherapy activities. I had just had one of the greatest spiritual experiences of my life, and now it seemed that everyone and everything in this place was intent on undermining that top-of-the-mountain feeling and my conviction that I had found an answer.

Two things helped to settle me down and give me direction. First, I talked to Elisa, and she encouraged me to stay. "You are already there," she said. "You wanted to get away, to be isolated. And this seems like a place you can do it. You can use the pool, and you can get some physical therapy, which you need.

"Go to the classes, or skip them," she continued "It is up to you to participate or not. Just do things your way."

Don Colbert echoed what my wife said. "Stay there," he told me. "They'll teach you a lot."

They had both reminded me of my purpose for being there, which was to get away from all the distractions of life. In the few days I had been there, I had already started a pattern of beginning and ending each day with prayer and Bible study. In her wisdom, my wife pointed out that I was not really there for those people or for the program; I was there for *me*. It was *my* time.

The second thing that helped me feel comfortable about staying at the clinic was finding a staff member who did not make me feel like such an outsider. God has a way of planting people where they will be used to bless others, and Cassie was just such a person. She was the assistant head of physical training, and while talking to her during the intake process, I discovered that she was also a Spirit-filled Christian. So amid the sea of psychologists, Cassie became my secret ally. I could talk to her and not feel out of place. She went out of her way to encourage me, and I do not know if I could have hung in there without her.

Cassie also introduced me to a trainer and massage therapist named Debbie, who really had a heart for broken-down people like me. Debbie showed me how to exercise in the pool, and she worked for hours on the atrophied muscles that had caused my body to be in such awful pain. When I arrived, my entire body hurt anywhere you touched me. But after four weeks, I was able to have a full body massage without extreme pain. I also got to where I could walk the short distance from my apartment to the clinic instead of driving, although I had to make several "sit-down" stops along the way.

I attended many of the classes, and I took copious notes. Some of it seemed like psychobabble to me, but other topics—such as *volumetrics,* a weight-loss concept pioneered in recent years by Barbara J. Rolls—helped give me a fresh perspective. And because I was spending time in prayer, things really began to open up for me. I got in touch with the reality of my life, and the four weeks I spent there wound up being very productive—physically, because I lost about twenty pounds, decreased my pain, and increased my mobility; spiritually, because I spent a lot of time in prayer and Bible study; and emotionally, because I began the process of exploring feelings that I had kept locked up for years.

If I had it to do over again, I would go to Structure House for help. I don't know of a better place, and in fact, I have recommended it to others. It is rare indeed to find a facility that excels in making a person of my size feel comfortable and accepted. Perhaps one day their food plan will evolve beyond the "food is fuel" and standard American diet approach and embrace sound, sustainable principles. Nonetheless, they taught me a great many things, some of which we utilize in ZOE 8.

THE PHYSICAL IMPACT OF NEGATIVE EMOTIONS

As Don Colbert had noted during my initial visit, my life had been defined by rejection. That sense of rejection, compounded by other negative emotions I had stuffed deep inside, had resulted in actual, physical consequences. When I would see a doctor about my physical symptoms, I was often told they were due to too much stress. I know now that stress was a part of what ailed me, but it was only a part. And nobody ever looked at the "big picture of Ed"—not until Dr. Colbert, that is. He was the first doctor I ever met who treated me wholistically, giving equal attention to spirit, soul, and body.

Dr. Colbert's recent books *Deadly Emotions* and *Stress Less* explore the link between the mind and the body in great depth. He explains that we do not simply experience emotions in our hearts or minds. "Rather," he says, "a person experiences an emotion in the form of chemical reactions in the *body* and the *brain*. These chemical reactions occur at both the organ level—stomach, heart, large muscles, and so forth—and at the *cellular* level."[1]

Let that soak in for a minute. Your emotions—what you feel and think—can produce physical changes not just in your organs, but right down to the microscopic cells of your body.

Remember how I suffered with psoriasis so severe that it would bleed? One of Dr. Colbert's professors in medical school was a psychiatrist who had started his career as a dermatologist. Dr. Colbert inquired as to why his professor had changed fields and relates his surprise at the response: "Treating so many people suffering from skin disorders led him to the conclusion that people were actually 'weeping through their skin.' That is what prompted him to go back to residency training in psychiatry. He knew the skin disorder was just a superficial sign of a much deeper problem."[2]

So I had not one, but two root causes for my bleeding psoriasis: the overgrowth of candida and toxins in my bloodstream, and painful emotions I had never acknowledged. No wonder I was suffering so miserably!

Negative emotions produce stress. This stress triggers physical responses that can have serious effects on your body when left unchecked for prolonged periods of time. The more negative emotion you have, and the longer you hold onto it, the more damaging the consequences to your health. Your brain can create a stress response when you experience emotions such as anger, guilt, shame, rejection, worry, fear, bitterness, and resentment. This mind-body link is amazingly powerful. For example, just one emotion—fear—"triggers more than fourteen hundred known physical and chemical stress reactions and activates more than thirty different hormones and neurotransmitters."[3]

Now you can understand why I couldn't heal physically until I dealt with some difficult emotional issues that began early in my life. My tendency to bury myself in work, for example, actually started when I was a child. As I mentioned earlier, my father had been an alcoholic, and my mother divorced him when I was five. I got my first newspaper route when I was six or seven years old. It was just a twice-weekly job, and my family had to help me roll the papers and drive the route while I threw the papers. But from the moment I got that very first job, I was driven to be financially independent. I didn't realize it at the time, of course, but I was unconsciously competing with my new stepfather to be the provider for my family. Perhaps it was a primal instinct.

I started saving my money, and before long I bought myself a bike. Later on I bought a TV, and by the time I was fifteen and old enough to get a driver's license, I had purchased a motorcycle to drive to school and work. By that time I was already learning the restaurant business, and by the time I was twenty I was a manager of a steak house in Scottsdale, Arizona.

While those early work experiences may have fostered some unhealthy habits—unbalanced priorities, working long hours, running on adrenaline—they were not nearly as devastating emotionally or physically as my battles with fear and rejection.

After my mother remarried, I had a stable family life. But I was already scarred from the abusive environment my biological father had created during my early years. Many evenings, at an hour when most children would be getting ready for bed, he would take my sister or me with him while he went out drinking. I can recall sitting in a dimly lit bar with him. Other times he would leave us locked in the car while he went inside and got sloshed. I remember being afraid and so hungry that I ate cigarette butts out of the ashtray and chewed the heads off of matches.

Those are my earliest memories, but I never made any connection between those formative experiences and my physical or mental condition until I had a nervous breakdown at the ripe old age of twenty-eight. I was managing food and beverage operations for the Hyatt Corporation at the time, and one day in the spring of 1980 I collapsed in the lobby of the Houston Hyatt. That was before my weight gain, and I had been in great health up until then. I was about to be engaged to Elisa, was successful in my career—winning top awards in the hotel industry—and seemingly had the world by the tail. Then, boom!

I began having anxiety attacks, and they increased in frequency and severity until I started having spells where I almost blacked out. That is what happened that day at the Hyatt, when I wound up facedown on the cold brick floor. An ambulance carted me off to the hospital, but the doctor could not find anything wrong with me physically, so he sent me to the psychology department. I had a few therapy sessions, and I started taking Elavil, one of the early tricyclic antidepressants. They called it a "mood elevator."

In a few weeks I had stabilized, but nothing really changed. Anxiety was now a dominant, ever-present part of my life. I lived in a state of terror. I did not deal with my emotions, and the use of a psychiatric drug was one of the factors that started me on the cycle of a gradual, but steady, weight gain. I stayed in that cycle for more than twenty years, and that is a long, long time.

MOVING PAST THE PAST

Time does *not* heal all wounds, as the old saying goes. But time does give *you* the opportunity to heal those old wounds or to continue living in denial, never being free from the past. That is where I was for so many years.

If my own story is not enough, meet Linda, a ZOE 8 participant. Like me, she discovered that some deeply rooted issues were at the heart of her weight problem. Here's what she wrote about it:

ZOE 8 TESTIMONY

For years I focused on diets in my ongoing struggle with weight. I have lost weight with almost every type of diet on the market—including over 100 pounds using liquid protein drinks—only to watch it all creep back once I returned to my old eating habits. I never allowed myself to make the connection between short-term dieting and permanent lifestyle changes. I just kept searching for the "perfect" diet or the next quick-fix miracle. Like so many others, I wanted to reach the goal while trying to bargain my way out of doing the work.

But recently, the Lord has shown me that the real problem consists of a spiritual battle and that I have been using food to mask deeper issues. Funny how answers come your way when the time is right, isn't it? You have addressed the very things I need to face, just when I am ready to face them....

I thank you for the love you have shown for those of us just beginning to deal with the deep-seated issues in our lives. You have given me the tools I need to launch myself down this path. I still have some fear because of past failures, but I need to lay those at the feet of our Lord and trust him to see me through this.

—Linda J.

We all carry around unresolved issues from our past: rejection, abandonment, hurts, loss, anger, fear. At the subconscious level, events that should be in the past tense continue to affect us in the present. When I talk about moving beyond these old issues, I like to say, "It is time to let your past be the past at last."

I learned the process of "moving past your past" from Mark Jones, a licensed marriage and family therapist and a dear Christian friend. In the months following my return from Structure House, I had lunch with Mark a number of times. He generously shared many insights with me, and although I have had only one official counseling session with him, I have learned more than I could ever begin to share here.

So, how do you move beyond the past and get free from emotional baggage? You have to understand how the brain works. "Thoughts produce emotions," Mark taught me. "So with each thought, your brain sends signals to the central nervous system, telling it to produce corresponding feelings and emotions."

This can happen completely at the subconscious level, and it can happen even after you have resolved a past issue. For example, someone says something to you and you respond completely out of proportion, as if you are answering a question they did not even ask. "We refer to that as a triggering mechanism," Dr. Jones says. Without conscious thought on your part, the trigger stimulated your central nervous system to produce old feelings and emotions. "It is a programmed response, a cycle of learned behavior."

Let me give you an example of that. Suppose I ask my son, Ian, to get the newspaper for me and he says no or shrugs off my request. The old Ed, mired in the fear of rejection, would have immediately thought, *He doesn't love me.* I would have felt personally rejected because my son did not respond the way I expected. I do not react that way anymore, however. *Maybe he's too busy to do it at the moment,* I would think now. *Or maybe too lazy.* My point is that I would no longer make the leap all the way to *He doesn't love me.* I have broken that cycle of learned behavior.

Consider how this works in weight loss. Many people fail at losing weight because they have programmed their brains to respond to different situations or perceived threats by eating. Wake up in a blue mood? *Response: let's eat.* Feeling anxious about the new job? *Response: let's eat.* Had a shouting match with a friend or family member? *Response: let's eat.* Snubbed by someone you love? *Response: let's eat.*

People try to stop that kind of behavior pattern but find it nearly impossible. "That is because," Mark Jones explains, "you can't stop something without replacing it with something else. Removing a destructive behavior requires replacing it with a positive one. If not, you will simply replace one negative behavior with another one."

How do you reeducate your brain and start making positive changes? According to Dr. Jones, you must first identify and correctly label the negative behavior you want to change. Next, identify the positive behavior you want to put in its place. You also need to resolve the past issues that encourage the negative behavior. Identify a particular past traumatic event, and say aloud: "I let it go, and I will stop rehearsing it in my mind."

Practiced behavior will become a habit in about twenty-one days. But habit is still in the realm of the conscious mind. We all know how easy it is to give up a new habit and fall back into our old ways. But when you practice a new behavior long enough, it will become part of your subconscious, and that is when you will enjoy lasting results.

According to Dr. Jones, it takes about six months of continuing to practice the new positive behavior in order to move beyond habit (conscious behavior) to character (unconscious behavior). When you begin to practice the new behavior without conscious thought, it has become a lifestyle.

That is why we always say that ZOE 8 is not a diet but a change in lifestyle. With the ZOE 8 food plan, you will be teaching your mind and your body to eat in a new way. If the food plan simply becomes a habit, you will have changed for the better, yet you may not experience all the results you want to achieve. When you follow the food plan long enough, however, it will become not just your normal way of eating but part of your character. It becomes who you are—you will not even give conscious thought to the foods you eat but will naturally make healthy choices.

When it comes to replacing negative behavior patterns with positive ones, results are the only accurate measuring tool. Sincerity is good, but it does not insure long-term success, and therefore it is not an accurate measuring tool for change. Convincing words or emotions do not guarantee change. How do you know when you are changing permanently? One word: *results.*

Results, you see, are not accidental. There is a universal law that governs results, and this law always works. The best example of this law is the agricultural metaphor of sowing and reaping. As every farmer knows, if a seed is planted into soil and watered, that seed is going to burst through the ground and grow. In other words, what you plant is what you will reap.

The Bible uses this same analogy of sowing and reaping; it also refers to results as *fruit.* For example, when Scripture talks about the "fruit of the Spirit," it is referring to the results that God's Spirit can produce in your life if you live according to his principles.

"Let us not become weary in doing good," Galatians 6:9 says, "for at the proper time we will reap a harvest if we do not give up." This universal law applies to any desired results. You cannot plant beans and grow carrots;

you cannot apply godly principles and receive ungodly results. You will always reap what you sow.

When you do the right thing, and continue to do it, you cannot stop good results from happening. Conversely, if you do the wrong thing, and continue to do it, you will reap a harvest of bad results. It is a law of nature.

THE HEART OF THE MATTER

While working on this chapter, another agricultural metaphor came to mind. Artichokes are one of my favorite foods, and Elisa is a master at preparing them in different ways. The process of confronting and changing behavior patterns that stem from deadly emotions is a lot like cooking and eating an artichoke.

Artichokes are not a convenience food; there is no quick way to prepare these rich, nutty-tasting buds of the thistle plant. They are best when steamed, and it is a slow process. Artichokes cannot be eaten quickly either because of their thorny outer covering, which can be very prickly if not trimmed correctly. With your fingers, you remove a single petal, then pull it between your teeth to extract the delicious flesh of the petal. When all the leaves have been removed, you finally get to the heart of the matter: the tender, succulent, almost buttery center. Artichoke hearts are a true delicacy, as much for the difficulty in reaching them as for their delicate flavor.

That is the way we work through difficult emotional issues as well. We tackle them one at a time, removing them from the stem and pulling them apart slowly, until we reach the tender heart of the matter. I started with rejection and kept stripping off layers of past hurts and emotional wounds until, like an artichoke, I was plucked bare.

Almost bare, that is. There was one final "petal" that kept me from reaching my heart, and I chewed on that one a long time. That petal is forgiveness.

Chapter Seven

The "F" Word: Forgiveness

WHEN I share my story with people, I try not to give too many specifics because it is really not about me. You see, everybody has their own story—some of them are PG-rated, some are R-rated or even X-rated. The point is simply that by the time I was a teenager, a couple of major events, in addition to the rejection of my alcoholic father, had begun to define my life.

Looking back, I can see that my teenage years were the point at which I began to withdraw from life. Outwardly, I appeared fine. I continued to make good grades in school. I performed in plays at the Phoenix Children's Theater, even stepping in at the last minute for another boy who had been paralyzed by stage fright. But something inside me had been crushed—almost extinguished—and it left me feeling unlovable, unworthy, and unsure of myself and my place in the world.

Most of the wounds I received had been minor, but a couple were very traumatic. Even the most emotionally resilient of people can be gradually destroyed by the cumulative effect of hurtful experiences. It conjures up pictures in my mind of bringing down a wooly mammoth with a bow and arrow. The first arrow is never fatal, but it leaves an opening. And after being struck by arrow after arrow in the area of the original wound, the massive beast finally falls. The repetitive nature of the injuries takes the ultimate toll.

Gradually, I dropped out of most extracurricular activities. Naturally athletic, I excelled in sports. I played football through my freshman year in high school, and then played tennis for a while after that. My confidence had been shattered, though, and when conflict arose I handled it by withdrawing. The fear of rejection kept me burrowing deeper and deeper inside the cocoon I was spinning for myself. That cocoon was my ability to earn a paycheck; it was my shelter from the world around me. I spent my adolescence putting up walls and reinforcing the facade that became the "world of Ed."

When I finally began to deal with these old issues from the past, I realized that, for my own sake, I needed to forgive, but I just could not do it in all cases. I could forgive others and even, after a long struggle, myself. It was easy to forgive Elisa for anything she had or had not done; I believed I was the one who had failed and had inflicted so much pain on her. I also forgave my father. He was a flawed human being who had allowed alcohol to dominate his life and destroy his relationships.

But some things were different. Some of those long-ago experiences had made an invisible, but very real, scar on my psyche that had festered like a wound. Author John Eldredge powerfully described this kind of wound in *Wild at Heart,* which I read long after I had recovered. I have read it several times and have given away dozens of copies, because it so precisely puts into words the painful process I had been through.

> Every man carries a wound. I have never met a man without one.... And every wound, whether it is assaultive or passive, delivers with it a *message*. The message feels final and true, absolutely true, because it is delivered with such force. Our reaction to it shapes our personality in very significant ways. From that flows the false self. Most of the men you meet are living out a false self, a pose, which is directly related to his wound....
>
> For years I was a very driven man, a perfectionist, a hard-charger, and a fiercely independent man. The world rewards that kind of drivenness.... But behind me was a string of casualties—people I had hurt, or dismissed—including my own father. There was the near casualty of my marriage and there was certainly the casualty of my own heart. For to live a driven life you have to literally shove your heart down, or drive it with whips. You can never admit need, never admit brokenness.[1]

Eldredge could have been writing that about my life. For years I had been a wounded man who could not face just how broken and damaged I was.

THE KIDNEYS HOLD THE KEY

In the previous chapter I compared the emotional recovery process to stripping off the leaves of an artichoke before getting to the heart of the matter. I started that process in February 2002, and by November I was

160 pounds lighter in body and indescribably lighter in spirit. That was the point at which I reached the tender heart of the artichoke of Ed, that unthinkable, unutterable "F" word: *forgiveness.*

Elisa and I understood that health was becoming the focus of our lives and that we wanted to share the blessing of reclaimed health with others. She suggested we attend a conference in Oklahoma conducted by Bill Gothard's Institute in Basic Life Principles. The subject of the conference was biblical perspectives on medical issues.

The keynote speaker was a medical doctor who talked at length about the renal system and how our kidneys function to purify the blood by eliminating toxins in our body. My mind wandered as he described the biochemical processes in intricate detail, but when he began comparing the renal system to our spiritual state, he grabbed my attention. He talked about forgiveness as a means of getting rid of emotional and spiritual toxins, and he emphasized one point in particular: "You must forgive the object of your suffering." By *object,* he meant the person or thing that had caused your suffering.

I forget now the seven-step process he outlined and the scriptures he used to back up each step. But I remember very clearly his statement that forgiveness is necessary to survival. When the kidneys fail, when they can no longer eliminate the waste from your body, you can't survive. "And if you don't forgive," the speaker warned, "you will not survive."

If God had shined a spotlight on me and audibly announced, "Ed McClure, this is all about you," it could not have been any clearer. I knew without a doubt that I had to forgive "the object of my suffering" if I wanted to be completely free and healthy in body, mind, and spirit. But I had harbored such anger and resentment toward a couple of people that I didn't know if forgiveness could ever be possible.

Within a few weeks of returning from the conference in Oklahoma, I decided to begin the process of forgiving these individuals. It took a great deal of prayer just to show up on their doorsteps for the purpose I had in mind.

It was obvious I had lost a lot of weight by then, so I would start by telling them about the healing journey I'd been on, how I'd been able to lose so much weight, and how I was learning to let go of the past. After that brief preamble I would say something like, "I came here to clear the record. I want you to know that I forgive you. God is changing my life, and this is an important part of my healing." I didn't elaborate more than that.

After the last such visit, I got in my car feeling numb. All I could think was, *I did it. I finally did it.*

At home, when the numbness wore off, all the pent-up hurt and anger exploded out of me. I screamed, I kicked, I cried, I punched my fist through the wall. I kept venting my emotions for over an hour. Elisa was visibly upset by my outburst, perhaps fearing that I'd had a relapse into one of the severe depressive episodes I'd had after the nervous breakdown years earlier. During those dark days, I was so depressed and anxious that I would occasionally hallucinate, seeing blood ooze out of the walls and cover everything. She was the only one who ever knew the extent of my mental suffering during that time, and she certainly did not want to see me break down again.

But this was no breakdown or depressive episode. It was simply an emotional release, a dramatic letting go of decades of toxic emotions I had stored inside my heart and soul.

I was "emptying the glass," as my friend Pastor Jimmy Sewell calls it. He is the one who taught me the concept of capacity. Our ability to contain thoughts and emotions is finite, just like a glass of water. When the glass is full, you cannot pour any more liquid into the glass without it spilling over. If you want the glass to hold anything new, you have to first empty some of its contents.

When we continually fill our hearts and minds with negative thoughts and emotions, we have no capacity for anything positive and healthy. Forgiving, letting go of hurts, will empty the glass so God can refill us with his love, joy, and peace. Only then can we be well—emotionally, spiritually, and physically.

WHAT IS *YOUR* STORY?

In this book I have shared parts of my life story with you for one purpose: to help you discover what may be holding you back and keeping you from complete wholeness and health in body, mind, and spirit. Your story will be different from mine, but the point is that everybody has a story. We all receive wounds and hurts that affect us deeply, and until we deal with those wounds, we lack the capacity to go forward. Take it from Judy:

ZOE 8 TESTIMONY

My battle with weight gain and depression escalated after the death of my mother. While I grew up in a stable, Christian home and was showered with lots of love, I suffered extreme shame from the circumstances of my birth. My biological father had "taken advantage" of my mother, and I was the result. He would bring me gifts sometimes, but I saw how much it hurt my grandfather when my father came around. So while I was still a very young child, I told my father I didn't want to see him anymore, and he never contacted me or my mother again.

Deep down, though, I resented him for not coming to my rescue and being a real father. And after my mother died, those painful emotions I had buried began to gnaw at me. It was only after I started the ZOE 8 program that I began to get in touch with my feelings about my father and the overwhelming sense of abandonment I had always felt.

I decided to see Dr. Mark Jones, a professional counselor and member of the ZOE 8 team, and I had a tremendous breakthrough during my visits with him. Dr. Mark helped me through the process of forgiving my father. He also helped me see how I had been holding on to the rejection I'd felt from my father. The rejection was actually the only bond I had with him, so I was afraid to let it go. None of these feelings had been at a conscious level, of course.

Also, because of my intense hatred of the image of my father, I did not want to identify with him in any way. Putting on weight was one of the ways I made sure I bore no resemblance to the face I so despised. Letting go of the shame and rejection has helped me see myself in a completely different way. I may have some of my father's features, but I have learned—and believe—that I am beautiful, inside and out.

Forgiving has brought me freedom from depression. I am not the same person I was before, and I know this lightness of mind and spirit will result in a corresponding "lightness" in my body—30 pounds gone so far! For the first time I feel I truly can achieve, and maintain, my ZOE W8.

—Judy R.*

---

*Read more of Judy's story in chapter five.

Whatever your story is, you must forgive "the object of your suffering." As a Christian, it is not optional: we have a biblical mandate to forgive. Regardless of your faith, however, forgiveness is vital to a healthy lifestyle. In fact, forgiveness has proven medical benefits.

Once confined to the realm of religion, the study of forgiveness is now one of the hottest fields of research in psychology, with more than twelve hundred published studies. A recent article in the *Harvard Women's Health Watch* outlined five benefits of learning how to forgive: (1) reduced stress; (2) lowered risk of heart disease; (3) stronger relationships; (4) relief from pain and chronic illness; and (5) greater happiness.[2]

Three of those benefits produce measurable physical improvements. Replaying old hurts or anger creates a stress response that produces higher levels of the stress hormone cortisol, as well as increased blood pressure and heart rate, and even immune suppression. Conversely, reducing stress through forgiveness and letting go of hurts results in improvements in the physical symptoms caused by chronic stress.

Researchers investigating what happens in the brain when we forgive have discovered that "different parts of the brain are activated when we contemplate forgiveness rather than revenge or retaliation."[3] A study conducted by the International Forgiveness Institute of the University of Wisconsin showed that cardiac patients at the Veterans Administration hospital experienced significant improvements in heart functioning three months after finishing a twelve-week forgiveness program.[4]

In this context the purpose of forgiveness is not so much to help the person who hurt you as it is to help *you*. You should be quick to practice forgiveness because *you* have the most to gain. If that sounds selfish—well, it is. According to *Newsweek*, Dr. Dean Ornish, "America's all-purpose lifestyle guru, regards forgiveness as the tofu of the soul, a healthful alternative to the red meat of anger and vengeance. 'In a way,' Ornish says, 'the most selfish thing you can do for yourself is to forgive other people.'"[5]

Now, I'm not into tofu, and we certainly include red meat in the ZOE 8 food plan, so I have to strongly disagree with Dr. Ornish's interpretation of "health food." But he does make a valid point: forgiveness is for *our* benefit, and it is a vital part of taking care of ourselves mentally and physically. To understand how forgiveness works, we need to look at what forgiveness is and what it is not.

WHAT FORGIVENESS IS NOT

First of all, forgiveness is not denial or repression, which is usually unconscious. Neither is it pretending that something bad did not happen or turning a blind eye to a painful situation; those are conscious choices to ignore an offense or injury, always to our detriment.

When I talk about forgiveness in our seminars, I stress that you must first come to grips with the fact that, whatever it is, "it is real, and it happened." In other words, you have to acknowledge past hurts before you can move beyond them. Many people get stuck at this very first point, blocking out or refusing to acknowledge what has happened to them. But if it did not happen, you cannot fix it!

In no way does forgiveness equal approval of what someone has done. R. T. Kendall's book *Total Forgiveness* presents an in-depth view of what forgiveness is and what it is not, and I like what he says: "Just as God forgives people without approving of their sin, we also must learn that forgiving people does not imply an endorsement of their evil deeds. We can forgive what we don't approve of because that is the way God has dealt with each of us."[6]

Even those of other faiths, or those who have no faith at all, have an understanding of this concept whether or not they realize that it comes from the Bible. "Let him who is without sin cast the first stone" has become part of our vernacular. The saying comes from the Scripture passage that records Jesus' response to a woman who had committed adultery and faced being stoned to death. Jesus recognized that the hypocrites who had set up the woman were really trying to trap him in a theological dispute. After he ran all her accusers off, Jesus spoke to the woman. "Neither do I condemn you," he said. "Go now and leave your life of sin" (John 8:11). He neither condoned her sin nor condemned her for it.

Furthermore, forgiveness does not necessarily mean reconciliation, which implies a restoration of a relationship. It takes two people to reconcile, so unless both parties are willing to repair the breach, it cannot happen. Reconciliation may not even be possible, for example, if one person has passed away since the injury to the relationship occurred. And in some situations, reconciliation may not be desirable. Kendall gives the example of adultery, which can sometimes destroy a relationship beyond repair.

If your spouse is unfaithful and sleeps with your best friend, both your marriage and your friendship will probably never be the same, no matter how genuine the forgiveness that is offered.

An injured person can forgive an offender without reconciliation. It is wonderful if the relationship can be restored, but this must not be pressed in most cases. Some things can never be the same again.[7]

When reconciliation is possible, however, the repaired relationship may be stronger than ever. A broken bone takes a long time to heal, but when mended it is even stronger than it was before it was broken.

Forgiveness, then, does not mean denial, approval, excuse, pardon, justification, or even reconciliation. So what exactly does it mean to forgive?

WHAT FORGIVENESS IS

Forgiveness is a choice. It is not a feeling; it is an act of the will. Feelings will eventually follow—remember, thoughts produce corresponding emotions and feelings, not the other way around. So you cannot wait until you feel forgiving toward someone before you make the choice to forgive that person.

Like love, forgiveness "keeps no record of wrongs" (1 Corinthians 13:5). R. T. Kendall says that forgiveness "is the choice to tear up the record of wrongs we have been keeping. We clearly see and acknowledge the evil that was done to us, but we erase it—or destroy the record—before it becomes lodged in our hearts. This way resentment does not have a chance to grow. When we develop a lifestyle of total forgiveness, we learn to erase the wrong rather than file it away in our mental computer. When we do this all the time—as a lifestyle—we not only avoid bitterness, but we also eventually experience total forgiveness as a feeling—and it is a good feeling."[8]

Bitterness is one of the deadly emotions we looked at in the previous chapter. It is a state of mind that harbors an injury and feeds on resentment and a desire for revenge. Like a malignant tumor, bitterness spreads its tentacles, choking the life out of its host. If you allow bitterness to continue unchecked, it will destroy not only you but also those around you. "See to it that no one misses the grace of God," Scripture says, "and that no bitter root grows up to cause trouble and *defile many*" (Hebrews 12:15, emphasis added). If you have allowed the weeds of bitterness to grow in your life, it is time to do some pruning!

Not only is forgiveness a choice, but it is also an act of obedience to God. Consider these biblical admonitions to forgive:

> Be kind and compassionate to one another, forgiving each other, just as in Christ God forgave you.
>
> —EPHESIANS 4:32

> Bear with each other and forgive whatever grievances you may have against one another. Forgive as the Lord forgave you.
>
> —COLOSSIANS 3:13

> Forgive us our debts, as we also have forgiven our debtors.
>
> —MATTHEW 6:12

> And when you stand praying, if you hold anything against anyone, forgive him, so that your Father in heaven may forgive you your sins.
>
> —MARK 11:25

My friend, those are steep consequences for refusing to forgive! If you live in a state of unforgiveness, your relationship with God will suffer. There are different schools of thought on whether our salvation is conditional or unconditional, and I am not here to argue the issue. But I know for certain that I do not want to do *anything* that would jeopardize my relationship with God. I also know that God's blessings are conditional, and you can block God's blessings in your life by your refusal to forgive others. An unwillingness to forgive signals your ignorance, indifference, or ingratitude for what God has done for you through the cross of Christ.

When we turn to God in repentance, he forgives our sins—and he wants us to extend that forgiveness to others. *But you can't give away what you don't have.*

THE CHICKEN OR THE EGG

Which came first—the chicken or the egg? Forgiveness presents a similar dilemma, expressed this way by R. T. Kendall: "It is almost impossible to say which comes first—forgiving others so you will be able to forgive yourself, or forgiving yourself so you will be able to forgive others."[9] Whichever comes first, it is not true forgiveness until both are equally true.

Why do we find it so hard to forgive ourselves? It is something I worked on for many months, and there are times even today when guilt and shame again sprout in my soul, and I have to repeat the process of forgiving myself. That is why I described forgiveness as the last petal I pulled off the artichoke, the one I had to chew on for a long time before my heart was finally revealed.

Let's look at what the Bible says about forgiveness. God is our example. When God forgives us, he puts away all remembrance of our sin, wiping the slate clean:

- He puts our sins behind his back (Isaiah 38:17).

- He casts our sins into the depths of the sea (Micah 7:19).

- He blots out our sins and remembers them no more (Isaiah 43:25).

- "As far as the east is from the west, so far has he removed our transgressions from us" (Psalm 103:12).

If God refuses to remember our sins, then we must release the memory of them and forgive ourselves. "Therefore, if anyone is in Christ, he is a new creation; the old has gone, the new has come!" (2 Corinthians 5:17).

I had to learn that even though I was a "new creation" in Christ, I had a lot of "old baggage" to get rid of, and one piece of that baggage I had not even known I was carrying around: I was angry at God. I had forgiven others, I had forgiven myself, and then all of a sudden I discovered I had to forgive God. I know that sounds strange because most of us never consider the possibility that we are harboring resentment toward God for what has happened to us. But that is often the case.

It was certainly a surprise to me; I only discovered this buried anger after I had the great emotional release that stemmed from confronting "the object of my suffering." Elisa was so worried afterward that she encouraged me to see Mark Jones—not as a friend but as a client. That is how my one official counseling session with Mark came about, and it was an eye-opener.

I told Mark what had happened and that I knew the confrontation had been an essential part of getting well. During our lunches he had taught me a lot of the principles that form integral parts of our ZOE 8 program, but in a one-hour session that day he moved me beyond the theoretical and into the practical—and it changed my life.

Mark confirmed that I had done the right thing by forgiving those who had wounded me. "Now you need to stay away from them," he continued, "because they are not healthy for you. I want you to identify that you are not them, and they are not you. You can love them, pray for them, help them if they need it. But don't get involved in their day-to-day life. And stop thinking you can be the one to 'fix' them."

I realized that what Mark was saying was true, and I readily accepted his advice. But I wasn't quite prepared for what he told me next.

"You have usurped God." Mark paused briefly to let that sink it. "You have put yourself in God's place, thinking you have the responsibility for fixing everything that is out of kilter in your life and the lives of those around you. You don't, and you can't. It is time to ask God to forgive you for trying to walk in his shoes. And most important," he said, "you need to forgive God."

Forgive God? What is he talking about? My mind couldn't quite wrap itself around the thought.

"Ed, you must come to the realization that you are angry with God. The root of all your issues is your anger at God."

I found my voice. "No way," I protested. "I'm not angry at God. I love the Lord, I trust him. I'm relying on him—"

"How can you?" Mark interrupted. "How can you say you are trusting God when he commands us to love one another and you don't even love yourself? Your own body was almost destroyed because you didn't love yourself. In fact, you were angry with yourself, angry with those who hurt you, and when you carry around that kind of anger and unforgiveness, you are pitting yourself against God. That is the real issue."

I was stunned, but I listened to Mark and considered carefully what he was saying. "You have to forgive *God* for your father leaving, forgive *God* for the painful things others did to you, forgive *God* for everything you have had to forgive someone else for. Because at the subconscious level, your reality is that if God was really God—if he was your loving heavenly Father—then he wouldn't have let all these things happen to you. It is time to let go of your anger toward God."

Before I left his office, we prayed together. Mark led me in repenting of my anger and forgiving God. It was a truly liberating experience—humbling, but freeing.

GOD'S GRACE CONQUERS GUILT AND SHAME

As I mentioned earlier, I still have occasions when old feelings of guilt and shame crop up, but I know how to deal with them now. My friend and mentor Dr. Don Colbert wrote about this in his book *Deadly Emotions.* What he says is so helpful that it is worth quoting at some length here:

> Guilt and shame are both rooted in what should *not* have occurred as much as in what *did* occur. Guilt is a state of having done something wrong or having committed an offense, legal or ethical. Guilt is a painful feeling of self-reproach for having done something that we recognize as being immoral, wrong, a crime, or sin. Shame generally arises from what *another* person has done, something that society widely recognizes as immoral, wrong, a crime, or sin—shame is the reflection onto the victim of an abuser's bad behavior.
>
> Guilt and shame evoke different responses in us. Shame tends to create feelings of deep sorrow and sadness, as well as a lack of self-worth. Guilt produces a certain amount of anger because we feel trapped at being caught or at having fallen victim to our own weaknesses. In both emotions, however, a feeling of being worthless, hopeless, or helpless may result.[10]

The antidote to guilt and shame is forgiving and letting the past be the past. One of the things that will help us accomplish that is to understand God's grace and its effect on our lives.

What, exactly, is the grace of God? It is *unmerited favor.* In other words, we can do nothing to earn it; grace is his divine gift to us. Feelings of unworthiness cannot change the fact that we are recipients of God's grace.

As R. T. Kendall points out, there is a difference between grace and mercy.

> Mercy is not getting what we do deserve (justice); grace is getting what we don't deserve (total forgiveness). Grace isn't grace if we have to be good enough for it to apply to us....We cast our care

on God and rely on Him to restore the wasted years and to cause everything to turn out for good. We find ourselves, almost miraculously, accepting ourselves as we are (just as God does) with all our failures (just as God does), knowing all the while our potential to make more mistakes. God never becomes disillusioned with us. He loves us and knows us inside out.[11]

On my own, I could never conquer my weight and health problems—all of the conventional approaches had failed. But I learned that while my strength is not sufficient, God's grace is. The apostle Paul expressed this concept so clearly. Plagued by a physical ailment—a "thorn" in his flesh—Paul pleaded with God to take it away. But God said to him, "My grace is sufficient for you, for my power is made perfect in weakness" (2 Corinthians 12:9).

When we acknowledge our weakness and submit to God, we begin to operate outside of our own strength, relying on the strength of our almighty, all-knowing, all-powerful God, and he will see us through every roadblock on our journey to health.

We've looked at the emotional and spiritual roadblocks; now let's look at the physical roadblocks you need to plow through.

How to Break Through
Your Weight-Loss Barriers

WHY is losing weight so difficult? Why is it even more difficult to keep it off? Studies indicate that most people who lose weight gain back some or all of the weight they lost. The popular consensus is that most people regain about two-thirds of their weight within a year, and that over a three-year period only 5 percent will have maintained their original weight loss. In many cases, including me for a twenty-year period, a significant weight loss is followed by an even greater gain.

The statistics do not have to be quite so grim, however. The National Weight Control Registry[1] tracks some four thousand people who have lost thirty pounds or more and kept it off for at least one year. I am one of the registry statistics now, having kept off approximately 200 pounds for three years. When we were putting together the ZOE 8 program, Elisa and I studied the published reports on what helped the people in the registry achieve their objectives. Whatever their background or circumstances, the successful people were the ones who identified and developed strategies for overcoming the roadblocks they encountered during their weight-loss journey. That is why we made identifying roadblocks the third step in the ZOE 8 Weight Management Program.

Have you ever been driving along in your car and suddenly hit a pothole you could not see? It is easy to wrack up a major repair bill because of an obstacle you would have avoided if only you had been able to identify it in advance. It is the same way when you are attempting to lose weight or improve your health: you are going to face certain roadblocks that will delay or derail your progress, and many of these roadblocks are hidden. These hidden roadblocks are a very big part of the reason why almost all people regain after a weight loss, and some cannot even lose weight in the first place.

EIGHT ROADBLOCKS TO HEALTH AND WEIGHT LOSS

Although each person has individual health problems and nutritional needs, we have found that most of our ZOE 8 participants seem to face the same roadblocks over and over. Below, Elisa and I have outlined eight common roadblocks that may be causing you or someone you know to stumble. Frequently, as was the case with me, one roadblock led to another, trapping me in a complex web of weight gain, illness, disease, and—ultimately—a death trap. Once you identify your roadblocks, however, you can blast right through them to reach your goals.

> PLEASE NOTE: Never stop taking a prescription drug without first consulting your doctor. Sudden withdrawal of a medication could be dangerous.

Roadblock #1: Prescription medications

The first roadblock you may encounter is the myriad of side effects that can occur when you are taking prescription medications. Many medications either cause weight gain or can hinder you from losing weight; read the fine print on the circular included with your prescription for information on possible side effects.

When I first started taking prescription drugs for high blood pressure, anxiety, and depression, it coincided with and contributed to a spiral of weight gain and deteriorating health. While each drug worked to control a particular symptom, the overall effect was not the restoration of my health. Instead, I got progressively worse and continued to gain ten to fifteen pounds every year, even while trying different diets and clocking thousands of miles on a treadmill. Three particular drug types made losing weight almost impossible for me: antidepressants, antibiotics, and drugs to regulate blood pressure.

A common side effect of many antidepressants is weight gain. While it may often be necessary to treat a chemical imbalance with prescription medications (and thank God such drugs are available when we need them), a long-term plan for health should address the whole person, including emotional and nutritional counseling as well as the interaction of different medications and supplements.

Upon my first visit to Dr. Colbert, he pinpointed another side effect of medication that had wreaked havoc in my life: the extended use of antibiotics following my emergency appendectomy in the early 1980s had created an internal environment that led to a steady weight gain and left me unable to lose the extra weight. Antibiotics change the balance of beneficial and harmful bacteria in the intestine. These drugs wipe out the "bad bugs," but they also destroy the beneficial bacteria, leaving the body deficient and disrupting the normal digestive process.

To counteract the antibiotics—and thank God again for life-saving antibiotics—a high-quality probiotic supplement with combinations of friendly bacteria like acidophilus and bifidobacterium can help restore the balance of the intestinal tract. My failure to do this (of course, neither my doctors nor I had a clue) facilitated what Dr. Colbert eventually diagnosed—twenty years and 240 pounds later—as candida overgrowth.

In 1981 my blood pressure was noted as "slightly elevated." I was prescribed a mild hypertension-controlling drug. For the next twenty years my blood pressure and weight steadily increased, as did the strength and complexity of the drugs to "control" my hypertension. I developed a heart arrhythmia, which required further medication. Obviously, my increasing weight negatively affected my hypertension and heart issues. Not so obviously, the medications also affected my metabolism, weight, and who knows what else.

Another exasperating example from my personal experience involved another common disease, psoriasis, which I developed in 1995. It quickly became serious. Open, weeping wounds and scaly gray calluses covered my hands, calves, elbows, and forearms. There was no medical solution, I was told; it would never go away. The best and only treatment available was topically applied cortisone cream, which somewhat alleviated the symptoms. Surprise, surprise! We now know that for someone in my condition, corticosteroid drugs lead to more weight gain. I exploded another hundred pounds from 1995 to 2002.

Since eliminating all my roadblocks through what is now the ZOE 8 program, I have been off all of the prescription drugs I was taking. I have been "drug free" since April 2003. When Pat Robertson's The 700 Club and CBN News aired a story about my healing of hypertension through diet and faith, they copiously checked my medical records to confirm both my history and current status.

Again, we do not recommend any changes in your current use of prescription drugs. We are in no way opposed to taking medications; we simply want you to be informed of the possible side effects and to know how to overcome any roadblocks you may be facing. We implore you to work with a physician to identify the impact of drugs on your total health, and we encourage you to believe that a life without prescription medications may be possible for you. But that decision is between you and your personal physician.

Roadblock #2: Candida

I have already shared how Dr. Colbert diagnosed me with candidiasis, usually called candida for short. *Candida albicans* is a type of yeast, a single-celled organism abundant in our environment. In *The Bible Cure for Candida and Yeast Infections,* Dr. Don Colbert says, "Under normal conditions yeast lives in our bodies without causing us any problems. Nearly three pounds of friendly bacteria help to keep it in check."[2]

But a number of things—antibiotics, prednisone, hormones, stress, diabetes, or eating too much sugar and processed foods—can change the intestinal balance and cause an overgrowth of yeast. If this happens when your immune system is weakened, the harmless yeast can transform into an invasive fungus.

Are you bothered by any of the following symptoms, which might indicate a problem with candida?

- Fatigue or lethargy, feeling drained
- Depression, attacks of anxiety, or crying spells
- Poor memory, confusion, or inability to make decisions
- Muscle aches or weakness, numbness or tingling
- Abdominal pain, bloating, belching, or intestinal gas
- Constipation and/or diarrhea
- Men: prostatitis or impotence
- Women: vaginal burning, itching, or discharge
- Women: endometriosis or infertility
- Women: premenstrual tension or menstrual irregularities
- Cold hands or feet and/or chilliness

The Yeast Connection, by William G. Crook, MD, contains a comprehensive self-test for candida, as does Dr. Colbert's Bible Cure series. We encourage you to learn more about your risk of candida, and if you have many of the above symptoms, we recommend you undergo food sensitivity testing. Simple muscle testing can reveal which foods are feeding the yeast overgrowth in your body and tell how severe your candida condition may be.

Even without testing, if you know or suspect you have problems with candida, the ZOE 8 food plan will help you bring it under control. The foods on the Body Balance Food Chart (page 184) have been carefully selected because they do not stimulate yeast overgrowth.

My weight loss began as I addressed and eliminated my candida problem over a nine-month period. During this time, I consistently dropped 4.2 pounds a week. In our ZOE 8 program, approximately 50 percent of those who have at least 20 pounds to lose appear "puffed up," for lack of a better word; they almost always have a candida issue. A typical trait of these people is a craving for car-bohydrates and sweets, which feed the candida. As the candida comes under control, cravings for these health-destroying foods disappear, and they are able to lose weight.

Roadblock #3: Stress

Stress is a huge roadblock for many people. In fact, stress—all by itself—can make you fat!

Stress is another thing I know all about from personal experience. I have been a workaholic since my youth. Both insiders and outsiders have described my working style as "organized chaos," and the way I managed my professional life resulted in serious consequences for my health.

Dr. Colbert defines stress as "mental or physical tension, strain or pres-sure."[3] The scientific link between stress and both physical and emotional disease has been well documented. Stress triggers a significant physi-ological response—what is sometimes referred to as the "fight-or-flight" response—by the release of certain hormones, especially adrenaline (also called epinephrine). A short burst of adrenaline can be beneficial. But too much adrenaline over a prolonged period of time, such as occurs when the body is under chronic stress, will eventually cause depletion of the adrenal glands. When that happens, the adrenal glands quit functioning properly, a condition known as adrenal insufficiency or adrenal exhaustion. Excess adrenaline can produce symptoms such as headaches, high blood pressure, panic attacks, muscle tension, fatigue, and irritable bowel syndrome.

Certain people become addicted to stress; you will often hear them referred to as "adrenaline junkies." In his book *Deadly Emotions,* Dr. Colbert writes: "Adrenaline is a stress hormone that produces a high as powerful as that of any drug. Elevated levels of adrenaline can make a person feel *great.* The person who has adrenaline pumping through his body has a lot of energy, needs less sleep, and tends to feel very excited about life in general. Many professionals who enjoy the high-stress demands of their professions can become addicted to stress—actually, they are addicted to their own flow of adrenaline."[4]

There is absolutely no question that I fueled my workaholic lifestyle with adrenaline, unknowingly "medicating" myself with a self-induced high. As a bona fide stress junkie, I definitely suffered the consequences of this hidden roadblock.

Cortisol is another hormone released in response to stress, and it plays an important role in fat storage, especially around the abdomen. When you do not manage stress well, you are literally expanding your waistline! Chronically elevated cortisol levels can lead not only to high blood pressure, but also high cholesterol or triglycerides, insulin resistance, and increased risk of diabetes.

Our bodies process the hormones adrenaline and cortisone at night, while our body recuperates during sleep. Lack of sleep compounds the problem of high cortisol levels, interrupting the body's natural rhythms and leading to further overstimulation of cortisol. So high stress levels accompanied by inadequate rest can trap you in a vicious cycle of weight gain. Every morning you wake up tired and hungry, with aches and pains magnified, and unable to concentrate.

Stress can also result in a decrease in serotonin, a brain chemical that regulates mood and helps promote restful sleep. So a drop in serotonin levels will also interfere with sleep and aggravate cortisol-induced feelings like crankiness and irritability. Even worse, low serotonin causes hunger, especially cravings for sweets and refined carbohydrates—the foods most likely to pile on the pounds.

Gaining weight itself is a stressor that affects all of your body systems. According to Dr. Elizabeth Vliet, author of *Women, Weight and Hormones,*

"This sequence of physical changes is very real, and when it occurs day after day, it contributes to your getting fatter....It takes only about fifty extra calories each day to add ten pounds of body fat in a year. Do this for a few years, and you see why you 'suddenly' have an extra fifty pounds to lose."[5]

I believe you can see now why stress management and cortisol reduction are critical components of a successful weight-loss program. To suggest it is possible to eliminate stress is, of course, absurd. However, many great tools are available to assist you in reducing stress in a healthy way, including faith-based or other support groups. In my case, stress had a deep underlying source, which frequently happens at a subconscious level. Don't ignore the spiritual and emotional aspects of your stressful situation. Help is here—now.

Roadblock #4: Lack of sleep

Everyone knows that getting enough sleep is important, but few people realize just how important sleep is and how severe the consequences of too little sleep can be—it can kill you, quite literally. You have read about our friend Oliver's success in previous chapters of the book. Now I want to share what he had to say about his struggle with lack of sleep and other roadblocks:

ZOE 8 TESTIMONY

When I started ZOE 8, I discovered that I had just about every roadblock mentioned in the program. At 528 pounds, I was barely able to function and could walk maybe fifty yards at a time.

I was always drowsy, even nodding off in meetings. Always sleepy, yet every night was a sleepless night. It got so bad that on the way to work one morning, I fell asleep at the wheel and ran off the road. I wasn't hurt, and fortunately, no one else was either.

But it was definitely a wake-up call. I went in for a sleep test and was diagnosed with sleep apnea. I began using a CPAP (continuous positive airway pressure) machine, and I felt like a completely different person the first time I got a good night's sleep. I felt better than I had in years!

I was also battling candida, something I'd never heard of before. Cutting out the foods that were feeding the candida and taking appropriate supplements enabled me to start losing weight.

Another huge problem for me was stress. I work in a high-pressure profession, and the stress of trying to carry around my "supertanker" frame contributed significantly to my weight gain and health problems. I suffered from very high blood pressure. It's still on the high side, and I still take medication, but my blood pressure has lowered significantly since being on the ZOE 8 program.

Discovering my roadblocks has helped me drop 70 pounds and two shirt sizes in a year. My doctor is so pleased that he has quit suggesting I have gastric bypass surgery. He sees my commitment to lose weight and regain my health.

Now I am able to work, think, sleep, and carry my weight around. A year ago I was only walking about 300 steps a day. Now I can easily do 1,500 steps a day, and I get much more done at work. I also enjoy interacting a lot more with my family.

—Oliver V.*

Oliver's story illustrates how lack of sleep can affect our health and weight. We have already mentioned the relationship of the stress hormone cortisol and the lack of sleep; now let's look at the relationship between lack of sleep and weight gain. Back in 1960, a study of over one million people found that participants slept an average of eight to nine hours each night.[6] These days you would be hard-pressed to find anyone still getting eight hours of sleep. Studies conducted from 2000 to 2002 show that average sleep duration is now under seven hours, and many people are in bed only five to six hours on a regular basis.[7]

Chronic sleep deprivation can produce a number of negative results, and among them is weight gain. Without adequate sleep the pituitary gland—our "master" endocrine organ that controls the secretion of hormones from other glands—is unable to perform efficiently. Our autonomic nervous system also depends on sleep to regulate endocrine activity. In a person with a normal sleep pattern, levels of the stress hormone cortisol begin to

---

*Read more of Oliver's story in chapters four and five.

decline in the early evening in order to reach minimal levels shortly before the usual bedtime. But in people who have undergone as little as six days of restricted sleep, cortisol levels take six times longer to decrease—and that has serious consequences for weight gain. "Elevations of evening cortisol levels in chronic sleep loss are likely to promote the development of insulin resistance, a risk factor for obesity and diabetes."[8]

Disturbances in sleep patterns can also reduce the nighttime levels of thyroid-stimulating hormone by up to 30 percent and increase blood glucose levels by approximately the same amount. *It takes less than one week of sleep restriction to induce a prediabetic state in young, healthy subjects.*[9]

One of the surprising effects of a chronic lack of sleep is an increased appetite due to interference with the appetite-regulating hormones leptin and ghrelin. "Sleeping and feeding are intricately related. Animals faced with food shortage or starvation sleep less; conversely, animals subjected to total sleep deprivation for prolonged periods of time increase their food intake markedly. Recent studies in humans have shown that the levels of hormones that regulate appetite are profoundly influenced by sleep duration. Sleep loss is associated with an increase in appetite."[10]

Leptin is a hormone that signals your brain when it is time to eat as well as when satiety, or fullness, has been reached. Sleep deprivation markedly interferes with leptin levels, particularly during nighttime. Making matters worse is the fact that ghrelin, a peptide secreted by the stomach that stimulates appetite, is elevated significantly when sleep is inadequate. So it is a double-edged sword: if you do not get enough sleep, the ability to reach a feeling of fullness is blunted at the same time your appetite increases—especially for foods with high-carbohydrate contents. Both daytime and nighttime studies show the correlation between lack of sleep and increased appetite.

The bottom line is that your body needs an adequate amount of sleep each night. Going without sleep is a risk factor for major diseases, including obesity and diabetes, and will hamper your ability to lose weight and keep it off. Many things can cause you to get inadequate rest. Some, like sleep apnea and heartburn, are physical; other causes of insomnia may be emotional, like depression and anxiety. If you are having difficulty sleeping, start keeping track of your nighttime activities and sleep patterns, and see your doctor if you need help. He may recommend a sleep study to test you for sleep apnea.

As I mentioned, lack of sleep can actually be a killer. I suffered from the severest of sleep conditions, sleep apnea, and it almost killed me. This condition strikes men and women alike and is a spiraling disease that slowly but steadily increases in intensity and severity of effects as the body is deprived of essential sleep and oxygen. Early signs of the disease are unusually loud snoring and intermittent choking, gagging, or gasping while sleeping. If you find yourself gaining weight, losing energy, and falling asleep behind the wheel or while sitting in church or at a meeting, that is a wake-up call that you need medical attention.

At my worst, I had to travel with my young son so he could punch me in the arm as I nodded off while driving. It happened every day. It was tragic and almost deadly to me, my family, and countless others sharing the highway with me. Again, adequate sleep is a significant factor in managing stress and being able to cope with the physical and emotional rigors of life. With sleep apnea, you never get adequate sleep, and you become a walking zombie, unable to deal with the realities of life in a meaningful way.

Sleep is also essential for maintaining a metabolic rate that works for you, not against you. The body is amazing in the way it regulates and protects itself. Inadequate sleep will result in a drastic slowdown of physical and mental function.

We may all be created equal, but each of us has an individual need for sleep. Elisa requires more sleep than I do—sometimes two hours more per day. That has nothing to do with her character or my drive; it is simply what she needs in order to be productive and stay healthy. It is an example of how unique each of us is as God's creation. Learn how much sleep is adequate for you, and respect that need. Also respect the individual needs of your family members as well.

Roadblock #5: Hormones

The subject of the relationship between weight and hormones is not just for women anymore; it applies to both sexes. But while women are comfortable talking about hormones, most of us men are not. Well, men, it is time to get over it. We need to know about our hormones, too.

Our bodies have both male and female hormones, primarily testosterone and estrogen, and maintaining a hormonal balance appropriate to our physical requirements is important for health and weight management. Men, of course, have a predominance of testosterone while women have far more estrogen than men. There are other sex hormones, but these are the two most important.

It is obvious that as a woman hits the premenopausal years, estrogen levels begin to drop in relation to progesterone, and various symptoms ensue: dry skin and hair, weight gain, hot flashes, mood swings, and disruption of the normal menstrual cycle. Hormone replacement therapy is an area of great controversy right now and is definitely something you should discuss with your physician. Do not try to diagnose or treat yourself based on what you read in the popular press. Good alternatives are available, but they may not be right for your particular situation, but do ask your physician about natural hormone replacement therapy or NHRT. After all, we are individuals, and we each require a personalized approach.

The equivalent period of a man's life is called andropause. When most men hit middle age, their testosterone levels begin to decline about 1 percent per year. What usually follows is a gradual loss of muscle mass and a change in body composition with a tendency toward accumulation of belly fat. Men may also experience hair loss, depression, increased anxiety, irritability, or mood swings, in addition to a loss of sex drive.

At any stage of life, if your hormones are out of balance, you will have a problem with weight control. Too much estrogen leads to increased fat storage and interference with insulin regulation; too much insulin leads to more fat storage, insulin resistance, and blood sugar irregularities; too little testosterone makes it extremely difficult to build muscle mass and metabolize fat. In addition to unexplained weight gain or inability to lose weight, symptoms of hormone imbalance may include increased irritability, mood swings, memory loss, difficulty concentrating or "brain fog," increased facial or body hair (women), loss of hair (men or women), depression, anxiety, increased chemical sensitivity, and increased sugar cravings.

You see why I have used the description "spiraling weight gain and deteriorating health." Once you are in the spiral, it is hard to get out without a comprehensive plan for reversing obesity and other health conditions.

This is a huge potential roadblock, and we highly recommend that you have your hormone levels tested. Ask your physician to order a blood test or a saliva test. Once you have an accurate measurement of your hormone levels, then your doctor can help you plan a course of treatment using prescription medications or natural hormone replacements prepared by a compounding pharmacy.

I experienced andropause myself, and for many years it was undiagnosed, unexplained, and devastating. Women's mood swings and other health issues stemming from hormonal imbalance are equally devastating. Be sure your physician tests your *complete* hormonal profile, and not just one or two hormones. Unfortunately, insurance companies often inhibit our health-care professionals, and hormone testing may not be covered. In that case, it may cost you more out of pocket, but it is worth it to uncover your roadblocks.

❧

Roadblock #6: Food sensitivities and intolerances

Like Ed, I had developed a number of food sensitivities and did not know it. As I shared in chapter one, I had no idea why my insides were always in turmoil. Traditional medicine had no answers. I had taken every test and had been looked at inside and out, but there seemed to be no answer to why everything I ate made me sick almost immediately. Stress seemed to be the catch-all cause. "Just relax and you should be fine," I was told more than once.

Eating was no longer a pleasure but a tenuous experience of experimentation and intricate food combining. I did find some relief when I ate a simple diet of one food at a time, nothing complicated. When traveling or dining, my first thought was not of having a good time but of locating the nearest bathroom.

Was I thin and anorexic looking? No, I was bloated, puffy, in pain, and hungry. With no answers available, I turned to God and literally asked at each meal, "Should I eat this, or should I eat that?" The answers always came, and my healing began. It was not until my first appointment with Dr. Colbert that I had an answer: irritable bowel syndrome (IBS), brought on by years of food sensitivities.

How can that be? I wondered. I had been a healthy eater, for the most part, nearly all of my life. Dr. Colbert explained that even if people eat wholesome foods—a Mediterranean diet, in fact—we can actually become sensitive to good foods that can continually irritate our digestive systems.

These sensitivities can create a list of miserable symptoms and, if untreated, disease.

Well, at least I had an answer after having no answers for so long!

In *The Bible Cure for Irritable Bowel Syndrome,* Dr. Colbert writes: "IBS is a functional gastrointestinal disorder, which means that its symptoms cannot be explained by any anatomical, physiological or biochemical abnormality. In other words, after performing a battery of tests including X-rays, blood tests and endoscopic exams of the GI tract, no biological cause for the symptoms can be found. Therefore, IBS is diagnosed from its symptoms, not by any medical exam or test."[11]

In his book *Your Hidden Food Allergies Are Making You Fat,* Dr. Rudy Rivera states that "no drug, no medical therapy, and no diet alone can improve your health or help you lose weight if you continue to bombard your body with your own personal poison."[12]

My personal poisons were lettuces, wheat, dairy, yeast, and sugar. My miserable food existence was forever changed when I eliminated these foods from my diet. Relief at last, with an added benefit that I lost twelve pounds of bloating!

Margie, another ZOE 8 participant, also discovered that food sensitivities were at the root of her problems. Here's what she shared with us in a recent letter:

ZOE 8 TESTIMONY

My mother suffered from food allergies for a long time, and I suspected that might be my problem as well. Every morning and night I had to take a prescription allergy medication to cope with the nasal congestion. I was also taking Lipitor to lower my cholesterol, but even with the medication my cholesterol level still hovered just above 200.

Halfway through Phase 1, my nasal congestion disappeared, and by the end of the three-week period I no longer had to take my allergy medication in order to breathe normally.

Less than a month after starting the program, I had my annual checkup. My cholesterol had come down to 186, but my blood sugar was 113. (No telling how high it had been before I started the program.) My doctor told me I was prediabetic and might have to go on medication. But after I shared the ZOE 8 food plan with the doctor, we made arrangements to test me in another month.

I worked with the ZOE 8 team to fine-tune my food plan to get better control of my blood sugar levels. I had already made the switch to lower-glycemic starches like brown rice pasta and millet bread, but I was relying too heavily on them. And for me, that was a problem because of my blood sugar levels. When I modified my starch intake and made sure that I included adequate protein and beneficial fats to each meal, the results were dramatic. In thirty days my blood sugar dropped 27 points, down to a perfectly normal 86. The doctor also took me off cholesterol medication at that point.

And I surprised myself by losing 30 pounds, without really focusing on the weight. My motivation for starting the ZOE 8 program had been to get healthy. But as I got my health problems under control, the weight just naturally came off. It was the upper abdominal area where I had carried the extra pounds, which was primarily from bloating due to food sensitivities. That weight dropped off first, and much faster than I would have ever thought.

I feel so much better now. If I start eating foods I know aren't good for me, my body lets me know. The nasal congestion comes back after two or three days of being off-program.

Cholesterol	Blood Sugar
Before: 200+ (with medication)	Before: 113 (prediabetic)
After: 186 (no medication)	After: 86 (normal)

—Margie S.

The way people respond to different foods is similar to a bee sting. For some people, a bee sting is painful but not serious. You might experience redness, itching, and swelling of the immediate area, all of which will go away in a few days. For those who are highly allergic to bees, however, a sting can result in a fatal reaction; you carry an EpiPen and get to the nearest hospital ASAP!

Most people know when they are allergic to a particular food because the consequences of eating that food are so obvious. But sometimes certain foods cause problems that are much more subtle and hard to detect. In this case, a person may have developed a food sensitivity or intolerance. If you are interested in your food sensitivities, ask your physician for an ALCAT test or any ELISA/ACT test. With your personal profile you will be able to target your food intolerance and blast through one of the major roadblocks to a healthy body.

Now we will look at the most common foods that are likely to become hindrances to your health or weight. To become more familiar with these foods and their derivatives, carefully read the Nutrition Facts panel and ingredient lists on all food products.

Corn

In the digestive tract, corn quickly converts to glucose, affecting blood sugar levels. Eaten in moderation by those who have stabilized their weight and health, fresh corn is delicious and not at all harmful.

When it comes to sensitivity to corn, one of the problems is the prevalence of corn in our food supply. (See chapter two.) When corn crops began to be heavily subsidized by the federal government about thirty years ago, overproduction became common. Then came the discovery of how to turn cheap corn into a sweetener—high-fructose corn syrup (HFCS). This provided a way to utilize the increased production of corn; however, it created a nightmare for the unsuspecting consumer. HFCS is six times sweeter than cane sugar and is used as a stabilizer in processed foods as well as a sweetener. It is difficult now to find a packaged food that does *not* contain some form of corn or corn by-product.

Processed foods are not the only source of excess corn in our diets. Highly marbled "corn-fed beef," for example, tastes delicious because of its high fat content. Until a few decades ago, grass-fed beef was the norm, and it took up to four years to fatten a steer. When the beef industry changed to corn, it speeded up the process dramatically. Now calves are routinely sent to a feedlot when they are about six months old. Just eight months later a corn-fed steer weighs enough for slaughter.

The bottom line is that high corn consumption promotes fat storage in humans as effectively as in cattle or hogs.

Yeast

Brewer's yeast and baker's yeast must be eliminated from the diet of those battling candida (discussed in the next chapter). But these substances are prone to cause sensitivities in other people as well, because of their abundant use in processed foods. Removing yeast from the diet can be difficult because of its prevalence and the different names for yeast-derived food additives. The FDA database lists the following additives that contain yeast: dried irradiated yeast, autolyzed yeast extract, malt sprout extract, phaffia yeast, baker's yeast extract, baker's yeast glycan, baker's yeast protein, and yeast autolysate. If you find any of these additives on a food label, you know that food product contains yeast.

Sugar and sweeteners

Sugar is not what it used to be. Derived from sugar cane or sugar beets, sugar is really a natural substance, but on its way to your table it undergoes refinement, just as whole wheat does on its way to becoming white flour. Now the sweet stuff not only comes from natural sources but also from man-made sources straight out of laboratories. Artificial sweeteners are the new sugar. The pervasive sweeteners of today are disguised in many different ways, derived from many different sources, and listed under many different names on Nutrition Facts panels and ingredient lists.

Are we against sweets at ZOE 8? No, but we are against artificial, processed, refined, bleached, and altered sweeteners.

As a matter of fact, a small serving of a wholesome dessert after a well-balanced meal is a pleasurable experience and should be part of your food plan. The problem with desserts, of course, is that our society has gone sugar-happy. Old-fashioned apple pie, made with crisp apples, fresh butter, whole-grain piecrust, and a moderate amount of cane sugar, has disappeared. Instead, we have huge desserts laden with refined and bleached flour, partially hydrogenated oils, and high-calorie artificial sweeteners. And not only desserts—almost all packaged foods contain sugar or sweeteners in some form. Just read the labels.

Overconsumption of sugar and sweeteners causes a host of problems, the most obvious including weight gain and the risk of diabetes. And the more sweets you eat, by any name, the more you crave. It is tough to break out of the cycle, especially when food manufacturers use dozens of different terms for sugars and sweeteners on product labels. Not only are there dozens of terms for sweeteners, but some are listed on the Nutrition Facts panel under carbohydrates while others are under sugar. It takes a bit of detective work to decipher food labels. For a long list of alternative names for sugar, see "Identifying Sugar" in Appendix 5.

One of the reasons people crave sweets is that sugar temporarily raises serotonin levels. Serotonin is a neurotransmitter that plays an important role in mood stabilization. That is why eating a candy bar or a piece of pie leaves us feeling pleasant and satisfied—for a while. When our blood sugar and serotonin levels plummet afterward, that pleasant feeling flees and leaves us wanting another sugar "fix."

The solution is not found in artificial sweeteners. While they have no calories, they also have no nutritional value. Furthermore, the brain perceives these artificial sweeteners in the same way as sugar, which means that using the artificial sweeteners continues to stimulate the craving for sugar. They also negatively impact blood sugar levels.

Dairy products

Many people are sensitive to lactose, the sugar found in milk and dairy products. These people are often said to be "lactose intolerant," meaning that they suffer digestive problems such as bloating, gas, or diarrhea when they consume milk products. Other common side effects from dairy products are nasal congestion and ear and bronchial infections. Look for these dairy derivatives on food labels: whey, casein, caseinate, lactalbumin, lactase.

Wheat

For centuries humans did not eat a lot of wheat, relying instead on many different grains for their "daily bread." But with the advent of the refining process, wheat became the staple of choice, and now we are addicted to nutrition-poor white bread. As a result, sensitivity to wheat has become quite common.

Many people, especially those with celiac disease, cannot tolerate gluten grains, and wheat is the chief offender. Because wheat has been so over-refined, and because it is so prevalent in processed foods, we recommend using gluten-free grains instead of wheat. Although spelt and oats contain gluten, many people with wheat allergies are able to tolerate these alternative grains.

Wheat and wheat derivatives are difficult to discern. To be sure no wheat products are in a food, look for the words *gluten-free* on the label.

Peanuts

Nuts are a wonderful, nutritious part of our food plan. They are high in magnesium and vitamin E and contain a beneficial form of fat. Peanuts are actually not tree nuts at all; they are a legume like peas and beans. With the exception of peanuts grown in extremely arid climates, we recommend avoiding them for two reasons. First, they are one of the most common—and potentially deadly—food allergies. And second, when these nuts are stored they come in contact with aflatoxin (a by-product of a type of fungus).

Labeling common food allergens

In 2004 the U.S. government passed legislation that calls for clear, consistent labeling of the most common food allergens. This law, which goes into effect on January 1, 2006, will require food manufacturers and restaurants to disclose, in plain language, the presence of any of the following eight major food allergens:

- Milk
- Eggs
- Peanuts
- Tree nuts (walnut, pecan, etc.)
- Fish
- Shellfish
- Wheat
- Soy

According to the advocacy group Food Allergy and Anaphylaxis Network (FAAN) (www.foodallergy.org), these eight foods account for 90 percent of all allergic reactions to food in the United States. FAAN estimates that 30,000 people make trips to the emergency room each year because of food allergy reactions, and between 150 and 200 people die annually from food-induced anaphylaxis (a severe, and potentially fatal, allergic reaction).

The new food labeling will make it much easier for the approximately eleven million Americans who suffer from food allergies. Some people are so sensitive to peanuts, for example, that they cannot eat foods that have been processed on machines that have handled peanuts, even if the food product itself does not contain peanuts. Again, you must read food labels carefully.

❧

Roadblock #7: Sabotage

Before we take an in-depth look at Elisa's ZOE 8 food plan, I want to give you two final things to consider. Even when you have figured out your hidden roadblocks and discovered your food sensitivities, there are two more obstacles you are likely to face, and I would be remiss if I did not warn you about them.

The first is sabotage. You would not think that someone would deliberately sabotage your efforts to lose weight and improve your health, but it happens all the time. Sometimes it is an unconscious reaction from those around you, and sometimes you can even sabotage yourself without knowing it. Whatever the case, you need to identify any saboteurs who will try to block your weight loss.

I never knowingly worked against myself, but I did suffer from subconscious emotionally and spiritually rooted issues that led to, or aggravated, my weight gain and resulting health issues. At no time did anyone in my family work against me. I did suffer a bit from "passive" third parties, but it was pretty benign.

As we have worked with many people from all walks of life, the issue of sabotage has become a significant part of our ZOE 8 program because we see it over and over. Sabotage is real, and it can be present in one or more of the following three ways.

1. The enemy within

In the words of Walt Kelly's comic strip character Pogo, "We have met the enemy, and he is us." Many people, knowingly or unknowingly, sabotage their own efforts—whether they are trying to lose weight or working toward some other goal. In almost every case, they are suffering from some form of emotional distress underpinned by fear, which can be manifested in many ways. Fear of rejection, intimacy, relationships, or just about anything can cause one to make choices that prevent the achievement of their health objectives.

I want to make a very important point here. The Bible says, "My people are destroyed for lack of knowledge" (Hosea 4:6). *Conscious* sabotage only occurs after you have the knowledge necessary to make right choices. I was dying due to lack of knowledge. If I make bad choices today—not exercising, eating processed food—I am sabotaging myself consciously. That is not good.

Many more people sabotage themselves unconsciously by engaging in self-destructive behaviors without being aware of what they are doing to themselves. Why? I believe there are destructive spiritual strongholds and resultant emotional issues involved when someone is completely unaware that they are their own worst enemy. In most cases these people don't love themselves or they don't fully appreciate or understand the power, purpose, or potential of their lives. Many have suffered abuse or some other negative circumstance that is causing them to feel unworthy or unloved.

In all cases of self-sabotage, knowing or unknowing, the individual needs professional counseling from, in my opinion, both the medical realm—psychiatrists, psychologists, or licensed therapists—and the spiritual realm—churches, synagogues, or even twelve-step groups. Another biblical thought: "You shall know the truth, and the truth shall make you free" (John 8:32, NKJV). It is important that you be honest with yourself. If, once you have the knowledge of right choices, you still struggle, be honest with yourself and seek professional help.

2. Sleeping with the enemy

As surprising as it sounds, your own family—the very people who love you most—might be sabotaging your success. Have you ever said to yourself, *Finally, I'm getting rid of those unsightly or even deadly pounds,* yet you can't quite seem to get there? Have you ever thought, *Finally, I'm going to get off insulin for my type 2 diabetes,* but something always seems to prevent you? Is it possible that someone very close to you is actually keeping you from your goal?

It is not only possible, but I have come to accept that it is also *probable,* and it is not because they do not love you. The bottom line is that when you change, you force everyone around you, or connected to you, to change. Guess what? All those other people might not want to change. Perhaps they do not need to change. When you change what you eat, what you spend, how you spend your time, and so on, those closest to you are affected. Frequently they will not change with you, at least not until they see the benefits of your "new" lifestyle and are convinced that this is not just another half-hearted or doomed-to-fail attempt to cure what ails you.

This is a very tough issue, and I find myself counseling on this subject weekly. It takes true love and understanding between family members to give up popcorn, for example. Or for you, if you are sensitive to corn, not to feel personally attacked when your family members eat it in front of your face.

I have already said that Elisa and my children never, not once, worked against me. I am blessed on that count. However, it is true that I turned their world upside down, particularly Elisa's. My health issues and the resulting behaviors and circumstances forced her to cope. That coping involved many emotional, physical, and ultimately spiritual difficulties and hardships. It wasn't fair. To survive, she did to the best of her ability what she needed to do. My "resurrection," if you will, forced her to cope with new and frankly shocking—and perhaps in some ways unwanted—circumstances that once again involved physical, emotional, and spiritual issues.

I think the world of Elisa and our relationship, but believe me, we are as human as humans get. It has been an amazing three years, and we are still learning and growing, individually and together. But it has not been easy. So, I have no sabotage experience, but I do understand how and why it happens. Depending on the case, counseling may be helpful individually or as a couple. It has been my experience that consistency and results bring people who love one another together. It does take time and understanding, though. Be prepared, be patient, and lead by example.

3. Passive third parties

These outside saboteurs are not nearly as important or threatening, but just like your family members, those you work for, work with, and socialize with are used to the old you. If you stop hitting happy hour to help manage your blood sugar while peeling off a few pounds, those "good" friends might not be as good as you thought. Once again, it is not that they don't wish you well; they just like their *lives* the way they are and will not go out of their way to help you do what is best for *you.*

I experienced a reasonable amount of this sort of sabotage, and on a few occasions it hurt. I had people say to me, "I miss the old Ed," or "I liked you better before." That hurt, but these professional or social relationships are not part of the fabric of our lives like our family.

Roadblock #8: Compartmentalization

Are you familiar with the concept of synergy? It has become a buzz-word in the business world, and it refers to the idea that "the sum of the parts is greater than the whole." That philosophy has led to the breaking apart, spinning off, and disposition of many once healthy companies like AT&T, which spun off Lucent Technologies. Unfortunately, the sum of our parts—spiritual, emotional, and physical—in no way approaches the value, potential, and reality of us as a whole.

Our physical bodies marvelously illustrate the point. While our organs and limbs may have a value on their own, only when all our organs and systems are working well together is the human body at its best; only then is it whole. Olympic gold-medal winners or the unmatched Tour de France winner Lance Armstrong exemplifies the potential of the human body when focused on maximizing health and performance. Yet the physical, or what is seen, mirrors the unseen. Our minds and spirits also need to be whole and healthy and working together for us to have zoe, abundant life. I may not be Lance Armstrong, but I am a pretty good example of someone focused on maximum health and enjoying my own zoe lifestyle.

Compartmentalization is a part of our evolving society, and nowhere is this more evident than in our health-care system. Now, I am very glad to be an American. I love our country and am blessed to live here. I also love and respect just about every member of the medical community I know; many of our best friends are medical professionals. However, the compartmentaliza-tion of our health-care system has created a lot of room for improvement.

We grew up with a family doctor, commonly known as a general prac-titioner, or GP, who managed our health. The role of this quarterback of health care has been severely impaired, primarily by the medical insurance system. Primary-care physicians are now known as "gatekeepers." They are under onerous pressure to manage expenses, which limits the quality of care they can offer. The situation is exacerbated by the degree of medical special-ization. Our GPs pass us off to a variety of specialists, supreme experts in their field. Unfortunately, a psychiatrist or dermatologist or other specialist may not understand or be aware of the consequence of other aspects of a patient's health. The interactivity of treatments and symptoms can cause real problems.

This was so much a part of my health debacle. None of it was done to me negligently or maliciously. I was a victim of many things, including parts of our health-care system. All my doctors, then and now, I respect and appreciate. But as compartmentalization progresses, our GPs know less and less about the parts that make up the whole. Many are also unduly influenced by the pharmaceutical companies, who sell drugs as a primary business and who are often the primary source of information on new treatments for overworked physicians with no time to keep up with the latest research.

And finally, "New Age" or "natural" treatments, which are usually very old-world herbs or nutrition, are generally discouraged by the medical world. Frankly, I would be dead by now if Dr. Don Colbert had not made the courageous decision to treat all—as in the whole body, mind, and spirit—of his patients, employing every technique known to heal God's children.

I implore you not to compartmentalize yourself and the implementation of what you are learning in this book. Don't try to eat the right foods and not increase your activity. Don't become a marathon runner and remain a hostage to emotional issues that should be in your past, not your present. Do you want to know how to achieve your health objectives, your zoe life? Recognize, treat, and love yourself as a whole, marvelous creation deserving of abundant health, peace, joy, and happiness.

The ZOE 8 Weight Management Program works because it is a "whole you" program, giving you the physical, emotional, and spiritual tools you need to achieve your health and weight objectives. Now it is time to come up with an individualized strategy just for you. In the next chapter we will show you how to create a customized food plan for *your* specific needs.

Chapter Nine

How to Create a Food Plan That Works for *You*

RELAX, take a deep breath...it is time to create your new food plan, the fourth step in the ZOE 8 Weight Management Program. Remember: it is not a diet; they don't work. It is simply a plan, one that will help *you* choose the foods that will work for *your* specific needs and food preferences.

※

WHILE Ed was away all those weeks at Structure House, he kept me fully informed both about what he was learning there and what Dr. Colbert had told him about candida. He hated the food, and we agreed that the traditional diet-food approach held no hope for him or the other attendees. We didn't believe it likely that anyone there would continue to eat at home the same way they ate at the residential program. We also discussed the dietary dos and don'ts that Dr. Colbert had recommended. I started doing research—something I love, by the way—and read every book I could find on candida. Even though there were common dietary principles in each book, there were also contradictions that left me scratching my head.

I was confused by the conflicting information, so I decided to devise a preliminary food plan that used all the various foods each of the diets had in common and eliminated all the rest. The twist was that Ed had food sensitivities, too, so there could be no corn, no wheat, no yeast, no sugar, no food! At least it seemed that way initially. We had been through this before with our daughter, Taylor, and at that time most of the "allergy-free" foods were also taste-free. Not an option for our family.

Researching was one thing; putting a plan into practice in real life was another. When Ed returned home he threw in another complication. He was meticulously counting calories and recording everything he ate. So every ingredient had to be measured or weighed, counted, and written down. This was the hardest part because I had always been an instinctive cook, preparing meals the way of my Italian ancestors—a little of this and a little of that, recipes that come out of the heart through the hands. We ended up compromising: I cooked, and Ed recorded. This was the meager beginning of the ZOE 8 food plan.

As time went on, we got better at it, and we relentlessly sourced products to substitute for those that had to be eliminated: natural sweeteners instead of sugar, for example, or brown rice pasta instead of the usual wheat version. Our home kitchen became a test kitchen to create recipes using substitute ingredients, many of which we had never used before. To be honest, we threw a lot away. If it did not taste good, no one was going to eat it no matter what the ingredients were. After all, in a year's time, eating three meals a day equates to 1,095 experiences with food, and we had to change every one of them! Creating a customized food plan was going to require planning, research, practice, and patience.

Ed and I are both professionals in the hotel and restaurant business. We are used to developing concepts and putting together business plans and budgets, so we took the same approach to this lifestyle change by first writing a cuisine philosophy. We used the word *cuisine* because we wanted the food to be excellent—we needed it to be. Food and hospitality had been our lives for thirty years, and we were good at it. Besides, the word *diet* was out. A diet is something you go on and then get off of, but this was a complete change, something we had no intention of quitting. This way of eating had to become a lifestyle.

Here's an excerpt of what we wrote while driving through the Texas hill country in the colorful spring of 2002:

> ZOE 8 cuisine is an exciting, responsible, and sustainable cuisine designed for individuals who are losing or maintaining weight, managing and controlling health conditions, or simply maintaining a well-balanced way of eating. It strives to find and use the freshest, finest, whole foods available, without additives or artificial substitutes, to present fare that is appetizing, delicious, innovative, healthful, and appealing to the most discriminating

palates. In doing so, traditional recipes have been deconstructed and then rebuilt, using natural, whole, healthful ingredients, without compromising flavor or appeal, while using classical and contemporary cooking techniques.

From that basic philosophy our food plan began to take shape. We took into consideration not only the food quality but also the purpose for which this journey began. A significant fallacy of the reigning diet philosophy is that food is merely fuel. But in God's design, food is more than mere nourishment and sustenance; food is meant to be a source of enjoyment and pleasure. "Go, eat your food with gladness, and drink your wine with a joyful heart, for it is now that God favors what you do" (Ecclesiastes 9:7). When diet gurus advise us to disassociate ourselves from food, it simply doesn't work—and for good reason: food is a gift from God. Denying ourselves the pleasure of enjoying good, even excellent, food can only result in failure. Maybe that is why only 5 percent succeed in keeping their weight off for three or more years.

PRINCIPLES OF THE ZOE 8 PROGRAM

The ZOE 8 food plan is built upon real food! Very simply put, food as God created it: whole, not fragmented, not reconstituted, altered, or processed. An orange, for instance, as opposed to orange juice; brown rice instead of white rice; nothing artificial; no additives except natural herbs and spices; sea salt as opposed to iodized salt. Foods that are naturally healthy and not associated with the major food allergies or sensitivities. Yeast- or gluten-free whole-grain breads and cereals rather than the traditional American staples. Foods that are naturally lower glycemic: sweet potatoes, not white potatoes. Throughout this chapter we will explain in depth the *why* and *how*, but as you read, keep in mind Dr. Colbert's description of God's food. He describes these foods as living foods, not dead foods—foods that give life, promote health naturally, do not induce or promote obesity, diabetes, cardiovascular disease, or emotional disorders, as opposed to dead foods that rob, kill, steal, and destroy your health.

The ZOE 8 food plan is also built by and for real people! We are not doctors, nutritionists, or even health practitioners, although these professionals are an inseparable part of our team. The food plan is simply the culmination of research, real life, real time, and real results, not only in our family but also now in hundreds of others.

PHASES OF THE ZOE 8 PROGRAM

The program is divided into three phases. *Phase 1,* the first twenty-one days, is meant to begin to bring your body back into balance, to eliminate candida if present, to break food addictions and cravings, and to begin to eliminate food sensitivities and other poachers of your health. *Phase 2* offers a long-term, livable plan to stabilize all your health conditions and achieve body weight goals. The *Sustainable Phase* is the rest of your life, once you have reached your goals and entered a life of health and well-being. Below is a quick overview of the eating guidelines during each phase. We will provide additional guidelines for which foods to eat and which foods to avoid during each phase of the ZOE 8 Weight Management Program in the dos and don'ts section of this chapter.

Phase 1: The First Three Weeks

The first three weeks of your journey are designed to detoxify your body and break unhealthy eating habits. In Phase 1, you will eat no sugar of any kind; no wheat; no corn; no dairy; no fruit; no artificial flavoring, sweeteners, or additives of any kind; no gluten grains; no yeast; no alcohol; no vinegar; no soy sauce; no pickled foods; no smoked, dried, or cured meats; no potatoes, beets, or carrots; no mushrooms; and no deep-fried foods.

Phase 2: Continuing the Benefits

In this phase, which may last as long as you like, your health conditions will stabilize and you will achieve your body weight goals. In Phase 2, you can eat everything that is "legal" in Phase 1, plus fruits, all vegetables except white potatoes, and condiments such as Béarnaise Sauce and Vegenaise.

Sustainable Phase: Making It Last

Once you have reached your health goals—whether they include weight loss, lower blood pressure, lower cholesterol and triglycerides, or a healthy well-being—you can adjust the foods you eat to maintain those goals. Although Phase 2 is sustainable for a long period of time, in this phase you can eat anything except the processed, artificial, high-sugar, fragmented foods that contributed to your health problems in the first place.

DECONSTRUCTION AND RECONSTRUCTION

This principle is the key to personalizing your food plan. Why is this so important? Each of us has a unique and distinct heritage, which includes food preferences formed by our ethnicity, our regional foods, and our family traditions. These are the reasons most diets fail at some point because they are generally all about "low or no," not about your family, your culture, your region. As an example, the cuisine of New Orleans is much different from the cuisine of New York's Little Italy. Both are excellent and reflect the culture and heritage of the people of that region. Far be it from me to take the spice out of life! So a core tenet of the ZOE 8 philosophy is that in order to be sustainable, your food plan must embrace your heritage. You must be free to enjoy your traditional foods without compromising your health or weight.

That is where the deconstruction and reconstruction of recipes comes in. By making a few changes to almost any recipe, you can create a more healthful version of most of your favorite foods. Of course, if your family tradition is the "daily drive-through" or "twenty minutes or it's free delivery," then we encourage you to adopt a cuisine and make a major change!

For example, we go to the Texas coast frequently, and part of that experience is eating shrimp, fish, and other delights from the sea. Cocktail sauce and peel-and-eat shrimp are companions, but the traditional recipe for cocktail sauce includes ketchup, which contains high-fructose corn syrup and other ingredients that were out for us. So was the solution to eliminate the sauce and be tempted to cheat and feel deprived, or create a new recipe using different ingredients to obtain the same taste? We chose the latter. By the example shown below you can see for yourself what a difference it made.

I deconstructed and reconstructed this recipe several times with several products before the new version of our old cocktail sauce was unanimously accepted by the discriminating palates of our taste panel—my family. Now we serve it, say nothing, and it disappears quickly! Almost any recipe can be deconstructed and reconstructed. The trick is knowing the dos and don'ts and finding the alternative food products. Keep reading and you will know what to do.

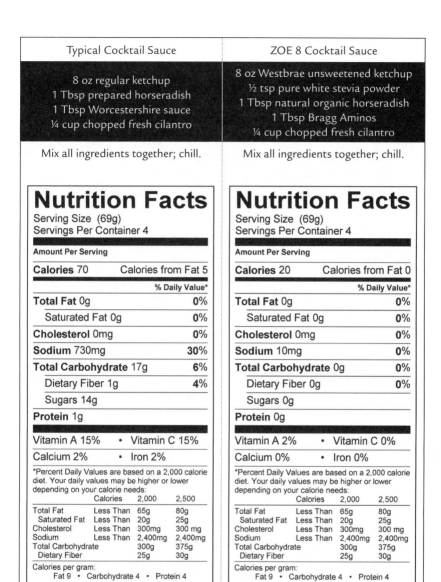

Typical Cocktail Sauce	ZOE 8 Cocktail Sauce
8 oz regular ketchup 1 Tbsp prepared horseradish 1 Tbsp Worcestershire sauce ¼ cup chopped fresh cilantro	8 oz Westbrae unsweetened ketchup ½ tsp pure white stevia powder 1 Tbsp natural organic horseradish 1 Tbsp Bragg Aminos ¼ cup chopped fresh cilantro
Mix all ingredients together; chill.	Mix all ingredients together; chill.

Nutrition Facts

Serving Size (69g)
Servings Per Container 4

Amount Per Serving

Calories 70   Calories from Fat 5

% Daily Value*

Total Fat 0g	0%
Saturated Fat 0g	0%
Cholesterol 0mg	0%
Sodium 730mg	30%
Total Carbohydrate 17g	6%
Dietary Fiber 1g	4%
Sugars 14g	
Protein 1g	

Vitamin A 15% • Vitamin C 15%

Calcium 2% • Iron 2%

*Percent Daily Values are based on a 2,000 calorie diet. Your daily values may be higher or lower depending on your calorie needs:

		Calories	2,000	2,500
Total Fat	Less Than		65g	80g
Saturated Fat	Less Than		20g	25g
Cholesterol	Less Than		300mg	300 mg
Sodium	Less Than		2,400mg	2,400mg
Total Carbohydrate			300g	375g
Dietary Fiber			25g	30g

Calories per gram:
Fat 9 • Carbohydrate 4 • Protein 4

Nutrition Facts

Serving Size (69g)
Servings Per Container 4

Amount Per Serving

Calories 20   Calories from Fat 0

% Daily Value*

Total Fat 0g	0%
Saturated Fat 0g	0%
Cholesterol 0mg	0%
Sodium 10mg	0%
Total Carbohydrate 0g	0%
Dietary Fiber 0g	0%
Sugars 0g	
Protein 0g	

Vitamin A 2% • Vitamin C 0%

Calcium 0% • Iron 0%

*Percent Daily Values are based on a 2,000 calorie diet. Your daily values may be higher or lower depending on your calorie needs:

		Calories	2,000	2,500
Total Fat	Less Than		65g	80g
Saturated Fat	Less Than		20g	25g
Cholesterol	Less Than		300mg	300 mg
Sodium	Less Than		2,400mg	2,400mg
Total Carbohydrate			300g	375g
Dietary Fiber			25g	30g

Calories per gram:
Fat 9 • Carbohydrate 4 • Protein 4

GROCERY STORE DETECTIVES

Another core principle of the ZOE 8 food plan is label reading. Food labels on packaging are divided into two parts: the list of ingredients and the Nutrition Facts panel. Both are important to know how to read and understand.

Interpreting food labels is integral to your success because it helps you make informed food choices for a healthy new you. Ingredients are listed in descending order, so keep in mind that the predominant ingredient is listed first.

As a general guideline, look for labels with fewer ingredients. If there is a paragraph of ingredients full of words you cannot pronounce, then don't buy that product. Put it back on the shelf and look for a better choice. There *are* better choices. Whole, fresh foods do not need ingredient panels: they are what they are. You don't need a list of ingredients for an orange, a blueberry, or a green pepper. When shopping, look for food products that have recognizable, clearly stated ingredients with no additives, preservatives, artificial, or altered ingredients.

Compare these two labels and you will begin to see the difference.

> INGREDIENTS: Organic black beans, water, salt

> INGREDIENTS: Enriched flour (wheat flour), niacin, reduced iron, thiamine mononitrate (Vitamin B1), riboflavin (Vitamin B2), folic acid, partially hydrogenated soybean oil, defatted wheat germ, sugar, cornstarch, high-fructose corn syrup, corn syrup, salt, malt syrup, leavening (calcium phosphate, baking soda), vegetable colors (annatto extract and turmeric oleoresin), malted barley flour

The first label is obviously for canned organic black beans, a wholesome food. Can you tell what food product the second label is for? The second label for a popular low-fat snack cracker is a good example of what is wrong with the standard American diet, which is SAD. It is also a good example of a list of what we call "illegal" ingredients (except for the vitamins used to enrich the devitalized flour), because not one of those ingredients is included in the ZOE 8 food plan.

The Nutrition Facts panel is also important to know how to read. The first item listed in the Nutrition Facts panel is the serving size, usually measured in gram weight. Do you know gram weight vs. ounce weight? Most of us don't. The rule of conversion is that 28 grams equal 1 ounce. If the serving size is 56 g (grams), then divide the serving size by 28, and you will know that the serving size is 2 ounces, or 168 g is 6 ounces, and so on.

Pay close attention to the serving size. Quite often the serving size listed on the label is a smaller portion than what we realistically consume. If the serving size is 2 ounces (56 g) and you actually consume 4 ounces, then that is two servings. So you must multiply the calories, fat, cholesterol, sodium, carbs, and protein listed on the label by two to get the real value of your consumption.

The best choices are always whole, fresh, unaltered, minimally packaged, colorful, naturally healthy foods. They will always be the most nutritious and lowest calorie choices you can make. Learning to read and understand the ingredients list and the Nutrition Facts panel will help you discern what naturally healthy ingredients are. You will become a better shopper and will find it easier to maintain a healthy lifestyle. You will even save money over a period of time and spend less time and money in the doctor's office.

Here's a grocery store hint for you: look high and look low on the shelves, because this is where you will find some good, healthy products. Try this exercise the next time you are in the grocery store: look for the whole oats in the cereal section. Where did you find it? Where did you find the instant, presweetened, flavored, convenience-pack oatmeal? That one was easy to find, wasn't it? The middle shelves contain products from Big Food companies that pay for premium shelf space; you probably even have a coupon for a discount on their products. Just read the labels on a product and determine for yourself if you are going to "buy it" or "shelve it." Your dollars will speak volumes to these companies and help prompt them to get back to more wholesome, naturally healthy products.

Also beware of false health foods. Just because a product is sold in a health food store or in the "health" section of the grocery store does not mean it has naturally healthy ingredients. Read all labels on all products. Knowledge is power. Take a peek in your pantry now and begin to read your labels. Write down the ingredients and see if you would choose anything to eat from that list. What portion of that list is artificial, enriched, or refined? What portion is natural? How many sweeteners did you find?

THE GLYCEMIC INDEX

In spite of the multitude of low-carb fad diets, our bodies crave carbs. We need whole carbohydrates—sugars, starch, and cellulose in their natural forms, not the man-made, low-carb, no-carb varieties that clog the grocery store shelves. Whole carbohydrates provide the raw materials for energy and brain function in the form of glucose and other micro matter.

As we explained in chapter three, the glycemic index helps you identify the most beneficial carbs. It is a ranking of foods, from low to high on a scale of 1–100, based on their overall effect on blood sugar levels. High-glycemic foods are those carbohydrates that break down quickly during digestion, such as refined, nutritionally poor, processed, low-fiber foods. These foods cause a quick spike in blood sugar, then a correspondingly rapid drop. High-glycemic foods tell your body to store fat rather than burn it.

Low-glycemic foods are those that break down slowly, gradually releasing glucose into the blood stream. Low-glycemic foods are high in fiber and nutrients, and they help avoid the drastic and damaging highs and lows of blood sugar fluctuation. Our standard American diet includes too many high-glycemic foods, a situation that is contributing to the diabetes epidemic. When we choose from the lower-glycemic, unrefined, whole foods, our weight, blood sugar, blood pressure, cholesterol, and tryglycerides will become lower, too!

The principle behind the glycemic index helps explain the naturally healthy residents of the Mediterranean countries. Our ZOE 8 food plan actually has a lot in common with the Mediterranean style of eating, though we eat more protein daily. Their diet includes primarily whole, plant-based foods (plentiful vegetables, legumes, whole grains, fruits, and whole nuts) with meat, poultry, and fish eaten only at special meals, not every day. The main source of fat in their diet is olive oil. Most people make their food from scratch, cook in a conventional manner, serve moderate portions, and leisurely eat their meals for maximum enjoyment. This is the way they have eaten for centuries, and it has served them well. We recommend adopting many of the same principles.

THE DOS AND DON'TS OF ZOE 8

To fully understand the details of the dos and don'ts, consult the Body Balance Food Chart located in the back of this book (page 184). This valuable tool came about as we struggled to find the information necessary to accommodate the dos and don'ts on that original pale blue piece of paper Dr. Colbert had given Ed in January 2002. It can still be condensed down to one piece of paper, but it is packed with a lot more information now! This comprehensive chart contains the vital information and principles needed to begin to eat your way to a healthy life. It is the biggest key to personalizing your food plan, maintaining your food culture, and avoiding the foods that may be your personal poisons. Not all whole foods are listed, but you will find enough to get you started on creating your personalized food plan.

Add your own foods as you find them. As mentioned in chapter eight, the foods on the chart already address candida and the major food allergens. If you have a food allergy or intolerance to a food listed, then simply cross it off the list and eliminate that food from your plan. The candida offenders have already been eliminated on the Body Balance Food Chart.

Let's start with a general overview. Each section has a category, i.e., Proteins: calories (cal) per ounce averaged per type (ex. all cuts of beef); energy density rating (ED); fiber gram content; and glycemic index (GI) listed low to high, where applicable. The Fats category lists the predominate type of fat and are all energy dense; the Dairy category lists alternative milks and products, with notes. The Condiments list, Beverage list, Sweetener list, and Notes complete the chart. Following that are some reminders and more specifics on the dos and don'ts.

Proteins

Eat a variety, eat lean, and watch portion size. We all need protein, and based on body weight and activity, some need more than others. What we do not need is excess protein or poor protein choices. Choose protein sources that are unprocessed and of the highest quality and purity—organic, if possible. If you are hooked on deli meats, ask the attendant to print out the nutritional label for your favorite type; you will be surprised at the additives, preservatives, sodium, and nitrites in most of them.

Proteins are allowed during all three phases of the ZOE 8 program; however, when choosing proteins, it is best to look for descriptions like organic, grass-fed, wild-caught, omega-3-enriched, hormone-free, and antibiotic-free. These choices will be better for you and will benefit your health in the long term. For example, grass-fed beef typically has one-third to one-half the fat of a similar cut of grain-fed beef. In fact, the fat content of grass-fed beef is comparable to a skinless chicken breast. Grass-fed beef is also high in the beneficial essential fatty acids called omega-3s (similar to those in fish), as well as vitamin E and CLA (conjugated linoleic acid—a fatty acid that can help people lose weight and also protects against cancer).[1] Vegetarians and vegans, don't lament. You can combine nonanimal-based protein sources such as tofu, legumes, and rice to keep up your protein requirements. We encourage you to read the labels on your protein substitutes to discern the quality of ingredients.

It is all about choices when it comes to both the amount of protein that meets your individual needs and the type of protein you eat. Try protein sources you haven't sampled in a while, and if you don't like fish, then take a good omega-3 supplement. Otherwise, include fish and seafood a few times a week, but consider the source. What you do not want is a weekly dose of mercury. Unfortunately, our fresh and saltwater fish and seafood populations have become dangerous, in many cases, as a result of high concentrations of mercury due to pollution. Ask questions of your fish market, read labels on frozen items, and get educated. Prepackaged meats such as sausages or bacon could be good but are usually laced with nitrites, sweeteners, preservatives, and artificial additives. If you make your own sausage or have your own old-fashioned smokehouse and can cure meat without sugar, then go for it. From a health standpoint protein is important, but it is not the star of your dinner plate.

Veggie carbs

Eat freely, eat a variety, eat colorfully, and don't overcook. These vegetables should be given the starring role on your plate no matter which phase of the ZOE 8 program you are in. They are not listed on the glycemic index, which is good. They contain very little protein and are high in vitamins, minerals, antioxidants, phytochemicals, micronutrients, and more. They are also very filling, producing a feeling of satiety or fullness. As always, look for the highest quality and freshness you can find. What about convenience? Apply the good, better, best rule: canned is good (read label for additives and rinse before using), frozen is better, and fresh is best. Buy organic whenever you can.

Mushrooms are purposely missing from this category and are not included in the food plan because mushrooms are fungi. Are mushrooms a good food? Generally, yes—but not while you are fighting candida or other digestive tract disturbances. If you do not want to live without mushrooms, add them back to your food plan when you have achieved your health objectives.

Starch carbs

Do you suffer from carb confusion? You are not alone. We will explain what we have learned in creating the ZOE 8 food plan. Starch carbs include two types. The first type is what we call *starchy vegetable-based carbs,* which are listed on the glycemic index. The second type is the *grain-based carbs*. This is an important distinction to learn and apply to your food plan. When it comes to starch carbs, eat them with other foods, watch portions and energy density, and eat a variety.

The starchy vegetable-based carbs include legumes (peas, beans, and lentils); soybeans; sweet potatoes, yams, and pumpkins; and sweet root vegetables such as beets and carrots. These tend to be low to mid range on the glycemic index (with sweet root veggies in the high range) and have good amounts of fiber, plentiful nutrients, and incomplete proteins. Because of the starch and sugar content of these carbs, some of them are not included in Phase 1 of the plan. (Again, consult the Body Balance Food Chart on page 184 to see which starch carbs are allowed during Phase 1.) Yes, we do leave white potatoes out of the food plan. White potatoes have been so heavily relied upon as a staple with typical diet regimes that we eliminated them for many reasons. Starchy vegetable-based carbs should play a limited supporting role on your plate. If you must bring them back, do so in the Sustainable Phase. Choose new potatoes and always mix with other vegetables.

The other type of starch carbs is the grain-based ones. This group includes brown and wild rice, and whole grains such as oats, spelt, and quinoa (pronounced *keen-wah*). These foods are very energy dense, contain good fiber, incomplete proteins, and are mid to high on the glycemic index. Grain-based carbs should play a limited supporting role on your plate and should be served with nonstarchy vegetables (see veggie carbs) and protein to lower the energy density of your meals. Some of these foods are the ones that can be ground into flours for breads and baking such as beans, rice, spelt, and oats. In Phase 1 this group is very limited. When your health improves in Phase 2 and the Sustainable Phase, you may choose more from this group.

Limiting both types of these starchy carbohydrates to small portions, especially the grain-based carbs, will contribute to your success in renewing your health and losing weight by improving your metabolism, lowering your blood sugar levels, and much more. This applies to all three phases. Wheat, its derivatives, and other gluten grains have been eliminated from this category. Wheat is one of the major allergens and, because of its gluten content, can be intolerable for those trying to heal their digestive tract. Oats and spelt contain gluten but are more tolerable grains for most people, unless you must avoid gluten entirely because of celiac or Crohn's disease. Corn is eliminated because it is also a major allergen and is a high-glycemic food. If you have uncomfortable symptoms or skin problems after consuming grains of any kind, then avoid them until you reach a higher level of health.

In this category use wheat-free, yeast-free, and sugar-free breads, crackers, and pasta made from non-gluten grains such as brown rice and millet. Read your labels, and you will find suitable products in the frozen food section of your health food store. Breads are by far the biggest challenge, but we have found many excellent products to use. Consult the ZOE 8 Web site (www.zoe8.com) for sources.

Fruit carbs

Eat whole or with other foods, eat a variety, and eat seasonally. Fresh fruits are carbohydrates providing good high-vitamin, high-fiber sources of natural sugars and water. Because they provide natural sugars and are sweet to the palate, fruits are not included in Phase 1 of the food plan. Sugar, natural or otherwise, is a favorite food of candida, and you want to kill it, not feed it. After the first three weeks, when your sugar craving subsides, you can add back in low-glycemic fruits such as berries, green apples, lemons, and limes. Keep the glycemic values of your fruits in the thirties and below while your body balances and your blood sugar stabilizes during Phase 1. If candida is persistent and deeply rooted, then fruit should be eliminated for a longer period of time. However, after achieving your goals you can again enjoy fruits in moderation.

Is fruit juice permissible? It is always best to eat the whole fruit, but yes, in time, fruit juice is permissible. Rules must be applied, though: only freshly squeezed juice from one whole fruit with as much pulp as possible, which should yield about a 2-ounce portion. The problem with fruit juices is that we rarely limit ourselves to a 2-ounce portion. Let's use orange juice as an example. We tend to drink an 8-ounce serving or more, which would be the approximate yield from more than four oranges! Would you sit down and eat four oranges at one time? Probably not. You might get tired of peeling and chewing, and I'm sure you would feel quite full. But you could "drink" four oranges in less than twenty seconds. Unless you need to raise your blood sugar in a hurry, fruit juice should be consumed in its original form—inside the fruit.

Fats

Good fats are essential, so eat and use a variety of them throughout each phase. Watch portions, as fats are all energy dense. In this category I have taken the liberty to include butter, nuts, seeds, oils, coconuts, avocados, and olives. These varied foods are listed under fats even though they contain elements of other categories. These foods are primarily fat and are very energy dense, but they contain the fats essential for you.

Unfortunately, most people have become fat phobic. This is another area of our American food chain that has become "low and no." Entire books have been written about dietary fats, and I will quote from one of the best, *Know Your Fats* by Dr. Mary G. Enig, PhD. She is an internationally renowned nutritionist/biochemist and is known for her detailed research on this subject. Dr. Enig's words are better than mine.

> The important thing to understand is that all fats are basically mixtures of saturated, monounsaturated, and polyunsaturated fatty acids in different proportions....Contrary to prevailing propaganda, fats and oils are very important components of diet. The consumption of naturally occurring, unprocessed or minimally processed fats and oils plays a role in maintaining good health. In addition to the well-recognized need for unprocessed omega-3 and omega-6 fatty acids, there is strong evidence that some of the medium-chain saturated fatty acids such as lauric acid are essential since they are needed for maintaining the natural ability of the individual to fight potentially harmful microorganisms....The bottom line is to consume as many whole foods and whole food mixtures as possible.[2]

So put some good fats back into your food plan, and do it with a good conscience. It will take a while for your mind to adjust to this concept, but your body will immediately love the change.

This does not, however, give you free rein in the fat arena. Always apply the good, better, best rule, and always use unhydrogenated, cold-pressed, natural fats. No margarine! Also avoid deep-fried foods. Learn to pan sauté foods at lower temperatures.

Sweeteners

Sweeteners by any other name are still sweet, and they adversely affect our health. There is hope for retaining sweetness without the harmful effects by eliminating mainstream sweeteners by any name, natural or otherwise, and replacing them with some that are not so well known: stevia, lo han, xylitol, and agave nectar. If you are a honey, maple syrup, or molasses fan, bring them back into your food plan when you have accomplished your health objectives and no longer have weight or blood sugar issues. The bottom line on sweeteners is that your weight issues will begin to melt away if you extract your sweet tooth.

Stevia is the only sweetener used in Phase 1 as it does not affect blood sugar levels and is noncaloric. Stevia is a super-sweet herb native to Paraguay, where it has been used as a sweetener and flavor enhancer for centuries. In America stevia is considered a dietary supplement and not a food product according to the FDA, even though less than ¹⁄₁₆ teaspoon is equivalent to 1 teaspoon of white sugar. I prefer to use the pure powder stevia extract with no other additives.

Lo han is a sweetener derived from the Japanese fruit lo han guo. It also has been used for centuries by the Japanese and Chinese. Lo han is also a noncaloric sweetener and has no glycemic rating. Although not nearly as sweet as stevia, it is still very sweet; so use about ½ teaspoon of lo han to 1 teaspoon of white sugar.

Xylitol is a natural substance found in plants, fruits, and vegetables. It looks and tastes like sugar, but it is not as sweet as stevia or lo han and has 40 percent fewer calories than white sugar. The FDA has approved xylitol as a food additive. Xylitol can be substituted for sugar 1:1 in any recipe, but some people find they cannot tolerate large amounts of this sweetener because of gastrointestinal upset. One of the interesting facts about xylitol is that after much testing, it has been found to reduce tooth decay rates and is endorsed by many dentists.

Agave is a plant-based nectar from the blue agave cactus. Agave has a low glycemic ranking and can be used in any of the ways you use honey or white sugar, but in smaller quantities. Agave is 1.4 times sweeter than white sugar. It is delicious, but beware: 1 tablespoon has 60 calories. It should be used sparingly.

"Dairy"

Real dairy, or typical cow's milk, is one of the major allergens, and for all intents and purposes of ZOE 8, it is considered a processed and altered food. I don't think we will ever get back to what we call "farm milk," the raw, unpasteurized, unhomogenized, cream-rises-to-the-top, unaltered variety that used to be perfectly fine because it was gathered from nonhormonal, grass-fed dairy cows. But this is not the time or place for that controversial subject.

We use alternative "milks" such as the unsweetened varieties of rice milk, soy milk (use in moderation), almond milk, and coconut milk. Label reading and the good, better, best rule apply to these "milks" also. Many are sweetened and have additives in them, so look for the best. If tolerated, goat or sheep's milk may be OK during Phase 1, but not if you need to avoid casein. When your health conditions stabilize and you are ready for Phase 2, then add back in some cheese, but never again what is called "cheese food" or processed cheese. Stick with the high-quality, real stuff. Your body will thank you.

Beverages

There is no substitute for pure water; drink it generously, and drink it first. After that choose noncaffeinated, unsweetened herbal teas served hot or cold during Phase 1. When fruits are added back into your plan at Phase 2, then make lemonade or limeade sweetened with stevia or other sweeteners that are ZOE 8 compliant. But always, always drink plenty of water. Sodas and other diet beverages are permanently off your food plan list.

Consumption of alcohol is a personal choice, but all alcoholic beverages should be excluded until your health objectives are stabilized. As a general rule, avoid beer and distilled liquors because of the yeast and grain content. When it comes to the good, better, best rule for alcohol, white wine is good and red wine is the best; it contains resveratrol, a beneficial antioxidant.

Condiments

There is a wide variety of what we call "legal" condiments available for you. All herbs and spices are wonderful and fill our foods with flavor and interest. Use them generously, but read the labels on all jars. Some contain hidden ingredients such as MSG. Generally, all types of vinegar are out. Most of them are derived from the grains you are trying to avoid, and they upset the body-balancing process. Organic, live apple cider vinegar is one exception and can be added after Phase 1, and the coveted real balsamic vinegar can be added when you are in the Sustainable Phase.

Naturally fermented foods such as sauerkraut and pickles can also be used, but not if the label states vinegar as an ingredient. If you are very adventurous, you can make your own fermented foods, including sourdough starters for bread made the old-fashioned way. Use Bragg Liquid Aminos in place of high-sodium soy and Worcestershire sauces. Use unsweetened ketchup and sweeten it with stevia. Use salsas and hot sauces with good ingredients and without added sweeteners. Look for horseradish and mustard without vinegar (they are available).

A FINAL WORD

You can see now that a wide variety of foods is available to make your own personalized ZOE 8 plan. Just read labels and make the best choices you can wherever you shop. The impact to your health will be remarkable, and you will see measurable evidence as time goes on. You will not only lose weight (if that is your goal), but you will also see improvements in your blood sugar levels, your cholesterol, and your triglycerides.

A final word about the food plan: it will take some time, patience, and practice to create a plan specifically for your needs, but as you can see, the rewards are well worth it. You have to eat for who you are—your body type, your food sensitivities, your preferences, and, of course, your heritage. I hope you have seen that you do not have to give up your traditional favorites; almost all recipes can be made more health-friendly by following the principle of deconstruction and reconstruction. We have spent several years searching out products, and one of our goals for ZOE 8 is to be a resource for you. We are constantly researching and expanding our knowledge of food and nutrition, and it is our absolute delight to share that knowledge with those who are pursuing zoe life.

Now that you are on the way to creating your own food plan, we are going to share with you eight powerful weight-loss strategies that will work for you. So don't change that dial! Oops. We mean, turn the page.

Chapter Ten

Eight Weight-Loss Strategies
That Spell Success

NOW that you have read through the entire food plan, step five of the ZOE 8 Weight Management Program is to use the tools in your ZOE 8 toolbox. "What tools?" you ask. We're about to give you eight strategies that, if followed with discipline, will help you achieve your goals and objectives. You do have goals and objectives, don't you? That is the place to start. Get a notebook, and get ready to write.

STRATEGY #1—KEEP A DAILY JOURNAL

One of the most important things I did in the process of losing 200 pounds was to keep a daily journal. Each day I recorded everything I ate and drank, my weight, and the amount and type of activity or exercise I did. It was eye opening, to say the least. In the past I have kept spiritual journals as well, and I recommend both types.

The primary purpose of keeping a food log is to create awareness of what, when, and how much or how little you eat. And if you will record your emotional state before and after eating, you will also begin to learn more about *why* you eat—reasons besides the primal instinct of true hunger, that is. I can't stress enough how important it is to be completely truthful with yourself as you are taking inventory, setting goals, and keeping your food log. Personal reflection and scrupulous honesty are vital parts of the ZOE 8 Weight Management Program.

Keeping a daily journal is a proven principle of weight-loss success. Participants in the National Weight Control Registry listed journaling as one of the top five components of their success at losing weight and keeping it off. A daily journal not only helps you plan what to eat, but it also provides structure and discipline to other areas of your life as well. If you start feeling overwhelmed at how far you still have to go to reach your destination, just look back at your journal and rejoice at the progress you have made so far. If you feel stuck and don't see the scale moving in the right direction, the answer will be in the pages of your daily journal. Page 129 contains a portion of a sample page from one of my food logs. I began this practice at Structure House where it is mandatory.

In all the weeks and weeks of steady weight loss, I had one week where I actually gained a few pounds. The following week I was in Orlando to see Dr. Colbert, and when I told him about it, he asked to see my journal. He was able to pinpoint the cause just by reading my journal: I had been snacking on too many brown rice cakes by themselves. They are fairly high on the glycemic index, and if I had eaten them with some protein or good fat, they probably would not have contributed to the slight gain I had experienced. The point is that he could diagnose the problem with a quick look at my daily journal.

The format of your journal is not that important. While I was at Structure House, I used the logbooks provided for me. They were very detailed, with hour-by-hour entries and spaces for recording emotional reflections. Lately I have used a very inexpensive record book with blank ruled pages. The important thing is to simply develop the habit of writing everything down.

The benefits of keeping a journal will become even clearer in chapter twelve, "What to Do When Your Engine Stalls." Because it contains a written history of your daily life, the journal is an invaluable tool not only for evaluating progress but also for discerning areas where you need to improve or make adjustments.

I have saved all of my food journals since I began my weight-loss journey in early 2002. In fact, the origin of *The Responsible Cuisine Cookbook* was my daily journal. Elisa and I simply looked back at all the foods I ate during that year, and then we printed out the recipes and edited them into a cookbook. Many of those recipes are included in the back of this book.

STRATEGY #2—LEARN THE PRINCIPLE OF VOLUMETRICS

Now, I like to eat—make no mistake about that! I have learned that you not only are what you eat, but you need to eat for who you are. Let me explain that by helping you understand something called volumetrics.

7-23

Breakfast	Calories
2 slices kamut bread	120
2 tbs. almond butter	210

Lunch	
11 oz. seafood cioppino	220
7oz. sea bass	216
green beans	30

Dinner	
turkey breast, 8oz.	400
gravy	30
broccoli	40
dal (lentils)	120

Snacks	
8 brown rice crackers	60
2 tbs. hummus	90
3 oz. blueberries	45

Total Calories 1595

Total Water (ounces) ₶₶ ₶₶ ₶₶ II
× 8 oz. 136

Activity	Duration
aerobics	30 min.
steps	3134

The weight-management principle of volumetrics centers around the fact that people tend to eat about the same volume (or weight) of food every day. An excellent resource on the topic is the book *Volumetrics* by Dr. Barbara Rolls. Here is the principle in a nutshell, as explained by Dr. Rolls:

> Over the course of a day or two, a person eats about the same weight of food.... Therefore, if you maintain the usual amount of food you eat, yet lower the calories in each portion, you will consume fewer calories and feel just as full.[1]

Restricting the amount you eat, which is what most diet programs recommend, is counterproductive. Your brain is programmed to be satisfied with a certain amount of food, and eating less than that will result in feelings of deprivation that will eventually cause powerful cravings. However, eating the same volume of food but switching to lower-glycemic, less energy-dense foods will help you lose weight while still feeling full.

The energy density of a food has to do with the interplay between fat, carbohydrate, protein, and water. Eating foods with a higher water content, for example, can help you feel full without adding additional calories. Such foods include cooked grains, vegetables, fruits, soups, and stews. "Sometimes," Rolls says, "lowering the energy density of a family recipe is as simple as adding naturally water-rich vegetables. When you do this, you can eat more for the same number of calories, or you can eat your usual portion and take in fewer calories."[2]

Which would make a better snack, a garden-fresh tomato or fat-free pretzel sticks? If you guessed the tomato, you are right. The entire tomato provides only 25 calories, the equivalent of no more than four or five of the tiny pretzel sticks. Now, be honest. Would you be satisfied with only a few bites of the dry, fat-free pretzel sticks? Not likely. You would probably wind up eating far more than the 25-calorie portion size. Obviously, you will feel more satisfied by eating the greater volume of the tomato for the same number of calories.

So the first point to understand about volumetrics is that it is important to eat enough. If you do not eat the volume of food your body is accustomed to, it will backfire on you, stalling your weight loss. Journaling will help you determine your individual volume requirement. We are all different, so you will have to find what works for you. Remember, the goal is to create a food plan specifically for *your* needs and preferences.

There is a qualitative aspect to volumetrics. Not only do you want to choose less energy-dense foods, but you also want to consider what a food is doing for your body nutritionally. What is the sodium content? What about antioxidants and vitamins? How much fat are you getting in an average serving, and what kind of fat is it—saturated fat or one of the more beneficial fats? For example, I could eat 8 ounces of broccoli or 8 ounces of butter. Both are good foods and are part of our ZOE 8 food plan, and I would be eating the same volume whichever one I chose. But there is a huge caloric and nutritional difference between the two.

One of the keys to my success was learning that I needed about 50 to 60 ounces of food each day in order to feel satisfied. By choosing not just lower-calorie foods but lower-glycemic foods, I actually ate my way to a 200-pound weight loss. Again, that is the beauty of the Body Balance Food Chart. We've taken the guesswork out of the equation. Using the chart, you will instantly be able to select lower-glycemic foods that are less energy dense.

There is also a quantitative aspect to volumetrics; you can factor in food cost in addition to volume and calories. After one of our first seminars, I was challenged by one of the participants. She was excited about everything she was learning but also discouraged. "This food plan is fine for people like you," she said, "but there's no way my family can afford to eat this way." She and her husband, an associate pastor, had three children, and I believe the total family income was around $27,500.

Being a "numbers guy," I took this challenge seriously, and I quickly realized that you don't have to spend a significant amount of money to follow the ZOE 8 food plan. Take a look below at A Tale of Two Meals. Both meals contain the same amount of food, 21.5 ounces. But one meal contains more than twice as many calories and costs almost three times as much. Put the principle of volumetrics to work in your food plan, and you can achieve your weight-loss goals without breaking your food budget.

A TALE OF TWO MEALS			
Stir-Fry			
Amount	**Item**	**Cost**	**Calories**
5 oz.	Chicken breast	$1.10	225
1 Tbsp.	Sesame oil	$0.40	100
½ cup	Broccoli	$0.30	15
¾ cup	Brown rice	$0.10	200
½ cup	Cabbage	$0.20	10
½ cup	Carrots	$0.30	20
Total amount: 21.5 oz. Total cost per person: $2.40 Total calories per person: 570		Total cost per oz.: $0.11 Total calories per oz.: 26.5	

Prime Rib			
Amount	**Item**	**Cost**	**Calories**
9 oz.	Prime rib	$5.04	630
6 oz.	Baked potato	$0.30	190
1 oz.	Butter	$0.16	200
3 oz.	Spinach	$0.10	20
½ oz.	Cream	$0.40	50
1 oz.	Sour cream	$0.20	50
1 oz.	Cheese	$0.20	115
Total amount: 21.5 oz. Total cost per person: $6.40 Total calories per person: 1,255		Total cost per oz.: $0.30 Total calories per oz.: 58.5	

The grocery list on the next page further explains the quantitative aspect of volumetrics. Compare the price and calorie counts of these food items purchased at our local grocery store. This kind of information is valuable for helping you plan meals and prepare your grocery list. For foods that are too calorie-dense or too expensive, look for replacements.

GROCERY LIST					
	Per pound		Per ounce		Per cup	
Item	$	Calories	$	Calories	$	Calories
Green beans	$1.69	72	$0.11	4.5	$0.85	36
Asparagus	$2.49	72	$0.16	4.5	$1.25	36
Yellow squash	$1.49	60	$0.09	3.75	$0.75	30
Zucchini	$0.79	60	$0.05	3.75	$0.40	30
Yams	$0.69	400	$0.04	25	$0.35	200
Brown rice	$0.74	1,200	$0.05	75	$0.37	600
Sirloin beef (all natural)	$5.89	960	$0.37	60	$2.95	480
Prime ribeye	$10.99	1,360	$0.69	85	$5.50	680
Salmon (fresh Atlantic)	$5.99	640	$0.37	40	$3.00	320
Lobster (tail)	$20.00	400	$1.25	25	$10.00	200
Butter	$2.48	3,200	$0.16	200	$1.24	1,600
Olive oil	$3.18	3,840	$0.20	240	$1.59	1,920

The chart on page 134 shows one of my favorite recipes: cioppino, a traditional Italian seafood stew. It is so filling, nutritious, and volumetric! Now, this dish is made with seafood, but for purposes of illustration I have shown the effect if the dish were to be made with chicken, pork, or beef, for example. Notice how the calories and cost vary with the protein used. Made with seafood, it is high cost but lower in calories and fat. Chicken would be the least expensive but comes with a modest increase in calories, and while beef or pork would be moderate in cost, it would be the highest in calories and fat. It is all about choices, you see.

STRATEGY #3—DRINK PLENTY OF WATER

In addition to adding water-rich foods to your diet, you need to make sure you are staying adequately hydrated. We cannot overstate the need for you to drink enough water each day—not beverages that contain a lot of water, such as tea or coffee, but actual water. It should become your beverage of choice.

CIOPPINO RECIPE	
Serves 4–6.	
Ingredients	**Protein**
1 cup diced onion 2 oz. olive oil 2 oz. minced garlic 1 ½ tsp. oregano 2 cups fresh tomato, diced ½ bay leaf ½ tsp. thyme 1 tsp. black pepper	**3 lbs. red snapper, shellfish, or fish** Total calories: 1,560 Calories per oz.: 32.5 Total cost: $24.00 Cost per oz.: $0.50
2 oz. fresh basil, chopped 1 Tbsp. parsley 1 small pinch saffron ½ tsp. dry basil 2 oz. tomato paste ½ tsp. crushed red pepper 1½ cups chicken stock (2 ¾ cups chicken or meat recipe) 52 oz. canned diced tomatoes	**3 lbs. chicken** Total calories: 2,160 Calories per oz.: 45 Total cost: $3.00 Cost per oz.: $0.06
3 lbs. protein (see Protein column) *Include in seafood recipe only:* 8 oz. clam juice 2 tsp. fish base (substitute liquid in can of oysters) 8 12-oz. can whole baby clams	**3 lbs. beef or pork ribs** Total calories: 4,320 Calories per oz.: 90 Total cost: $6.00 Cost per oz.: $0.13
Sauté onions and garlic in olive oil. Add 1⅓ cups of chicken stock; reduce for 10 minutes. Add the rest of the ingredients (chicken/beef) and simmer until onions are tender. For seafood: Add seafood just prior to serving.	

Water facilitates intracellular activity, which regulates all of our bodily functions. Water helps move food through the digestive tract, carries nutrients to our cells, lubricates our joints, and maintains body temperature. In addition, water flushes excess weight and toxins out of the body. Water is vitally important, yet about half of us are mildly dehydrated on a given day.[3] Some estimates run even higher, stating that three out of four people don't drink enough water.[4]

The majority of your body weight—some 60 to 70 percent—is made up of water. As you lose water through normal processes each day, that water needs to be replaced. Don't wait until you are thirsty to start drinking water; by that time you may already be slightly dehydrated. Symptoms of dehydration include headache, fatigue, dry mouth or throat, and even a dry cough. You need extra water when spending time outdoors, during activity, or on very hot days.

How much water should you drink? At a minimum you should be drinking the recommended eight glasses a day, or 64 ounces. (If that sounds like a lot, consider this: it is the equivalent of drinking two Big Gulps of soda over an entire day.) For weight loss, however, a better formula is to take your weight and divide it by two, then use the resulting number as a guideline for how many ounces of water to drink each day. For example, if you weigh 180 pounds, you should be drinking 90 ounces of water. There is an upper limit to this formula, depending on how overweight you are, but it gives a good estimate for most people and helps you individualize your water needs.

Dr. Colbert advised me to drink room-temperature water rather than chilled water. The stomach is a furnace, he said, and you will not want to put ice water in your furnace! I use a 16-ounce glass to keep track of my water consumption, and I record each one in my journal. I start the day by drinking one of those 16-ounce glasses as soon as I get up, then I drink a second one with breakfast. I drink another glass during the morning; one before lunch and one with lunch; another during the afternoon; one before dinner and one with dinner. That totals 128 ounces—a full gallon—per day, an excellent goal for my weight. Drinking water before a meal helps me moderate my food intake.

When you first start increasing your water intake, you may experience more frequent "pit stops"; however, the number of trips to the bathroom will become less frequent after a few days.

What benefits can you expect from increasing your water intake? First of all, your metabolism will function more efficiently. "A strong metabolism requires a lot of water to be stored within your body. Water drives all the chemical reactions that are needed to burn calories both at rest and during exercise."[5]

In addition, your digestion will improve and you will probably find yourself eating less. People are often unable to distinguish between true hunger and thirst. And your exercise will be much more effective. Increasing your activity level will require additional water to support your muscles. Drinking a glass of water before exercising will help you work harder and burn more calories, and drinking a glass of water afterward will help flush toxins released by the muscles from your body.

According to fitness expert Bob Greene, "Active muscles not only store more water, they store more glycogen. Glycogen is a form of carbohydrate that is stored in your muscles. Along with fat, it is used as an energy source when you exercise. The more fit you become, the more glycogen is stored within your muscles. This allows you to work at higher levels of exercise, which will help you become even fitter. Remember that every gram of glycogen within your body holds about 2.5 to 3 grams of water."[6]

STRATEGY #4—ADD ORGANIZATION TO YOUR LIFE

To be successful at anything, you must start with a vision, then take it to a plan. Get a new vision for yourself, and then make that vision into a plan for your life. One of the purposes of the ZOE 8 program is to help you organize or add structure to your life in order to help you achieve your health or weight-loss goals.

According to the dictionary, *structure* is something arranged in a definite pattern of organization, the way in which parts are arranged or put together to form a whole. (No wonder the founders of Structure House chose this name.)

Arrange your life, build a structure for the whole you—body, mind, and spirit. Is your life structured for success? What is your plan for different areas of your life? Establish a thought-out, comprehensive, and organized daily routine.

I once heard a man on television, I believe his name is Mike Murdoch, say that the secret of your future success is hidden in your daily routine. Now that is a powerful truth. Think about that. What is your daily routine? What do you eat, think, say, and do every day?

I have dramatically changed the structure of my life over the past three years. My daily routine now includes the following:

1. I pray or meditate before I get out of bed. I keep a Bible at hand and relevant spiritual books—in addition to my tattered yellow

legal pad with all the scriptures and notes that have carried me through.

2. I eat a couple of brown rice crackers (15 calories) to break my fast and get my fat-burning machine started. (You are storing fat until you give yourself something to burn. Flip the switch every morning.)

3. When trying to lose weight or inches, I exercise five or six mornings a week—three full-resistance workouts and two short (fifteen- to twenty-minute) aerobic sessions. If I am in a maintenance mode, I only do two free-weight workouts. In the evening I do forty-five to sixty minutes of aerobics (elliptical machine only for me these days) on two of my non-weight-training days. On weight-training days I do fifteen minutes of aerobics in the evening. I always take one or two days of rest per God. When in maintenance mode, I don't do either the morning or evening aerobics. When maintaining, I work out once, not twice a day. The two-a-days are too much for more than a six- or eight-week period.

4. I always eat lunch and dinner.

5. I consume 100 to 150 ounces of water every day.

6. I take one day of rest almost every week, no work.

7. If in a losing mode, I journal water, exercise, steps, and food and calorie intake.

8. I try to sleep six or seven hours, which is very adequate for me. I try to completely relax for a couple of hours before bed by light reading or watching mindless movies, detective shows, or comedies.

9. I pray and/or read from my bedside spiritual library just before I go to sleep every night. I open and close my day with my mind and heart on God.

STRATEGY #5—RELY ON THE POWER OF PRAYER

If you could have seen me the way I was three years ago compared to the way I am now... well, who'd a thunk it? As I have said before, what you see now is an outward manifestation of an inward transformation, and this next strategy had a great deal to do with it.

Now, I'm going to ask you to trust me on this one. We are all at different places in our faith life, or you might not even have one. But I'm asking you to have enough faith in me, and in the truth of my story, to try this strategy, regardless of your views on God, faith, or prayer. You see, I believe I would never have made the successful journey to health without prayer, and lots of it. As I mentioned earlier, I began and ended each day in prayer during the four weeks I spent at Structure House. I continued the practice when I returned home, and I still keep a yellow legal pad by my bedside, using it to record Bible verses that speak to me at a particular time and any insights or thoughts I have about the scriptures I am studying. I don't have words to tell you what a valuable tool this has become. Like my food journal, that yellow legal pad is a history of my progress and a source of great inspiration and motivation for me and now, through our seminars, Web site, and this book, for many others.

In this section I want to share with you some of the things I have learned about the power of prayer. Let me say first that the Bible gives a clear answer for the reason you don't have whatever it is you need: "You do not have, because you do not ask God" (James 4:2). That is a great incentive to pray: if you don't ask, you will not receive! Jesus said much the same thing when he instructed his disciples to pray and expect an answer: "Ask and it will be given to you; seek and you will find; knock and the door will be opened to you. For everyone who asks receives; he who seeks finds; and to him who knocks, the door will be opened" (Matthew 7:7–8).

The power of prayer is so great, Jesus said, that even faith as small as the tiniest seed could move mountains: "I tell you the truth, if you have faith as small as a mustard seed, you can say to this mountain, 'Move from here to there' and it will move. Nothing will be impossible for you" (Matthew 17:20).

How can you be sure God will answer *your* prayer? Pray according to his will. "This is the confidence we have in approaching God: that if we ask anything according to his will, he hears us. And if we know that he hears us—whatever we ask—we know that we have what we asked of him" (1 John 5:14–15).

Now do you see how important it is to know God's will for your health and your weight?

Here's how I made the commitment to change:

- I asked God to make me the man he planned for me to be.
- I prayed that he would make dead to me anything that would harm me.
- I relied on God's Word: "The one who is in you is greater than the one who is in the world" (1 John 4:4)…"I can do all things through Christ who strengthens me" (Philippians 4:13, NKJV).

It was amazing how God answered those prayers, especially the fact that I completely lost my taste for fine wine; it no longer appealed to me the way it once had. Remember, food and wine were my business, and our restaurant holds monthly events where we feature different vineyards and labels. I was able to host the wine dinners, enjoying the food without being tempted by the wine.

One of the prayers I still pray every day comes from the following passage of Scripture, in which we are instructed to put on the armor of God:

Be strong in the Lord and in his mighty power. Put on the full armor of God so that you can take your stand against the devil's schemes. For our struggle is not against flesh and blood, but against the rulers, against the authorities, against the powers of this dark world and against the spiritual forces of evil in the heavenly realms. Therefore put on the full armor of God, so that when the day of evil comes, you may be able to stand your ground.

—EPHESIANS 6:10–13

Start praying this scripture daily. Speak it over yourself, your loved ones, and others. Put on the armor of God and stand—your battle is not with chocolate and ice cream but with spiritual forces set on destroying your health!

STRATEGY #6—THE POWER OF POSITIVE WORDS

Positive thinking plus positive words can revolutionize your life. When I was overcoming the emotional roadblocks in my life (remember, my big issue was rejection), Dr. Mark Jones instructed me to say to myself continually: "I am an approved and acceptable person." That was very difficult for me at first. I did not feel approved or acceptable in the least. But *feelings lie.* I had to reprogram myself, and you will, too.

Remember what you learned in chapter six: thoughts produce corresponding feelings and emotions. It is not the other way around. What you think about will determine your feelings, so it is absolutely crucial to change old, negative thought patterns to new, positive thought patterns, which will produce positive feelings and emotions.

One of the best ways to change your thoughts is to hear yourself say aloud the positive principles you want to establish in your mind. You not only are what you eat, but you are also what you think and speak. That is why Mark encouraged me to keep saying over and over, "I am an approved and acceptable person." You know what happened? I said that to myself long enough that I began to *feel* approved and accepted—and that motivated me to change my behavior. I also learned to look *through* my feelings to the facts. When I coupled behavior modification techniques like this one with the ZOE 8 food plan and the proven weight-loss strategies in this chapter—poof! I started melting, just as Don Colbert had predicted.

Use the list of affirmations included in this section to help you start changing the way you think about yourself and your life. It is a great idea to record your own voice speaking these affirmations onto a CD or cassette tape. Listen to it while you are driving in the car, while you are getting dressed in the morning, or before you go to bed at night. You may feel silly at first, but I guarantee that if you will consistently use these affirmations, the payoff will be enormous—but you will not! You will be shrinking because you firmly believe you are worth taking care of and that you deserve to be healthy and happy.

ZOE 8 AFFIRMATIONS

The following affirmations will help reprogram your "internal software" with life-changing attitudes based on God's Word. Repeat these statements aloud daily.

I am beautiful, capable, and lovable. I am valuable. I love myself unconditionally and nurture myself in every way. I am unique, the apple of God's eye.

I am a child of God. I love people and show love, warmth, and friendship to all. I am healed of all my childhood wounds, and I hold no account of wrong done to me. I can be intimate with myself and others. All of my relationships are based on integrity and respect.

I am intelligent and have great creativity. I can concentrate easily. I can analyze and solve problems. I learn quickly and have an excellent memory. I have the mind of Christ. I make decisions with confidence.

I am diligent, faithful, and have a spirit of excellence. Whatever I put my hand to will prosper. God always causes me to triumph in Christ.

I let go of things I cannot control. I have the courage to change the things I should change, the serenity to accept the things I cannot change, and the wisdom to know the difference. I have no need to control people or situations. I am controlled by the Holy Spirit.

I am a success. I can do anything I put my mind to. I can do all things through Christ, who strengthens me. I see each day as a new and positive adventure. I give thanks in all things.

I express my potential more and more each day. I see problems as exciting challenges that cause me to grow stronger and stronger in my faith. I visualize myself as the person God wants me to be. I see myself achieving my goals and fulfilling God's purpose for my life.

I live every day with passion and power. I feel strong, excited, passionate, and powerful. I feel tremendous confidence. I have all the abilities I need to succeed.

Every cell in my body vibrates with health, healing, vitality, and love. I am healthy and strong and filled with vitality. Jesus took every sickness and every disease away from me.

I awaken each day feeling healthy and alive with energy. Any tension I feel is simply a signal to relax, release, and let go. I always have more than enough energy to do all I want to do.

All that I am, I derive from Jesus. He is always in my thoughts, and I pray without ceasing. Jesus is my strength, my joy, my peace. He is with me wherever I go, and he promised never to leave me or forsake me.

I surrender my life to Jesus Christ. I have a wonderful, fulfilling relationship with Jesus. I trust my conscience, which is led by the Holy Spirit. I feel God's presence at all times.

I walk in the fruit of the Spirit of love, joy, peace, patience, goodness, gentleness, faith, meekness, and self-control. I am sustained by the love of Christ. The peace of God rests upon me.

I do not worry about anything. In everything, I give thanks to God and give my cares to him. The peace that passes understanding guards my heart and mind, and I remain calm no matter what happens around me.[7]

STRATEGY #7—THE POWER OF POSITIVE RELATIONSHIPS

Another book I discovered after I had already achieved my weight-loss goals—*God Will Make a Way* by Henry Cloud and John Townsend—has some very good information. The authors point out the power of positive relationships: "People who have sustaining, supporting relationships tend to lose more weight, and keep it off for longer periods, than those who don't. We were not built or designed to be alone."[8]

King Solomon stated the same principle over two millennia ago: "Two are better than one, because they have a good return for their work: if one falls down, his friend can help him up. But pity the man who falls and has no one to help him up" (Ecclesiastes 4:9–10).

A good support network of family and friends can make the difference between success and failure in a weight-loss program. It is important to establish relationships with those who can help you along the way. Be selective in whom you confide, however. A close friend or family member may or may not be the best person. Yet it is vitally important to form "safe" relationships with one or more people with whom you can be open and vulnerable. Perhaps you can confide in a pastor or counselor at your church or community center. The concept of community is powerful—witness the success of twelve-step groups, many of which are held in churches now. If you have no one close to encourage you, then consider joining a support group.

Also, enlisting someone to follow the ZOE 8 program with you can be a tremendous boost to your success. Couples, families, and close friends do well following the program together. If you are a part of our Internet family, you will find support from others who are on the same journey, and you can communicate with them regularly. We now offer our own support program through the www.zoe8.com Web site.

STRATEGY #8—TAKE APPROPRIATE NUTRITIONAL SUPPLEMENTS

Unless you eat a perfectly balanced diet, pure, natural supplements are essential components in balancing your body to achieve your health and weight-loss goals. Always remember, however, that *supplements are not substitutes*. In other words, they are supplements to healthy eating, not a substitution for good nutrition. The best way to get the nutrients you need is to get them through whole, organic foods, but sometimes our bodies need the extra boost that a high-quality supplement can offer.

Dr. Don Colbert often says that supplements are bridges, not highways. Like prescription drugs, they are temporary solutions. His Bible Cure series is an excellent resource. He recommends specific supplements for each different health condition you may be facing. There are thirty titles in the series now, each on a different disease or condition, and we recommend them highly.

While losing 200 pounds I used supplements for adrenal and gallbladder support, CoQ_{10}, and Nystatin (a prescription medication for severe candida). Over time I added glucosamine and omega-3 oils. I still see Dr. Colbert several times a year, and he fine-tunes my supplement intake at each visit.

There are so many supplements on the market and a glut of information—some helpful, some confusing, and some downright absurd—about supplements on the Internet and in popular books. While many good products are available, there is also a lot of junk out there. And because supplements are unregulated by the FDA, there is no standard for quality. Therefore, we believe you need an expert (licensed practitioner, MD, chiropractor, pharmacist, etc.) to analyze your body and tell you what supplements you should be taking. If you need help locating a health-care practitioner with expertise in supplements, we recommend you call Nutri-West at (800) 443-3333. We have also found several outstanding compounding pharmacies and can provide you with information on our Web site (www.zoe8.com).

Always let your regular physician know what supplements you use because they can react differently if you are taking prescription medications or cause complications if you require surgery.

The following are supplements that we either take ourselves or frequently recommend to ZOE 8 participants. Remember that not all supplements are equal. It is extremely important to read the label, paying thorough attention to the directions for use, source of ingredients, potency, percent of daily value, and recommended dosage. Most supplements will have a date stamped on the bottle indicating when the efficacy may begin to diminish. Very important, particularly if you have food sensitivities, is the notation on the bottle: "Contains no starch, salt, sugar, wheat, corn, yeast, milk or dairy products, or preservatives." Almost all supplements from a health store will have such a disclaimer.

- *Multivitamin:* Everyone should take a good multivitamin daily as a general supplement to your diet. Many companies produce vitamins directed toward women, men, or children. Some of the quality high-support multivitamins require a dosage of three times a day to maintain consistent levels.

- *CoQ$_{10}$ (coenzyme Q$_{10}$):* An antioxidant, CoQ$_{10}$ prevents damage from free radicals. It is used to slow aging, increase energy, lose weight, strengthen the heart, improve the immune system, lower blood pressure, and enhance endurance and aerobic performance.

- *Probiotics:* A general term for products containing beneficial or good bacteria, probiotics are used to maintain a healthy digestive tract, reduce cholesterol, support the immune system, and prevent cancer. They also displace bad bacteria and yeast.

- *CLA (conjugated linoleic acid):* A natural omega-6 fatty acid found in grass-fed beef and dairy products, CLA builds muscle, burns fat, increases thermogenesis (burns calories), and is a cancer-fighting antioxidant.

- *Coleus forskolin:* This is used to increase fat burning, stimulate lean body mass, prevent fat storage, improve thyroid function, lower blood pressure, and enhance insulin secretion.

- *CortiSlim:* This brand-name product mitigates the effect of cortisol, the body's stress hormone, decreases appetite, prevents fat storage, and increases fat burning.

- *DSF Formula:* This proprietary product from nutriceutical company Nutri-West is available only through affiliated health practitioners. It mitigates the effects of stress, supports function of the adrenal glands, prevents "burnout," improves digestive system, and helps stabilize blood sugar.

- *Fiber Wisdom:* This zero-calorie, taste-free soluble inulin fiber dissolves easily in beverages. It helps metabolize fats and carbohydrates and flush waste. It is considered a probiotic because it feeds the good bacteria in the colon.

- *Fish oil:* A good source of the essential fatty acid omega-3, fish oil promotes muscle growth, reduces blood clotting, suppresses inflammation, protects the heart and blood vessels, and helps lower blood pressure. Note: Fish oil should not be used without a doctor's supervision by anyone taking blood-thinning drugs.

- *Flaxseed oil:* Containing the essential fatty acids omega-3 and omega-6, flaxseed oil is used to reduce inflammation associated with inflammatory diseases such as arthritis and psoriasis. It reduces cholesterol, lowers risk of heart attack and stroke, and protects against cancer. Note: Flaxseed oil should not be used without a doctor's supervision by anyone taking blood-thinning drugs.

- *Glucosamine:* This amino acid combination found in joint cartilage has been shown to decrease inflammation and protect joints and tendons from injury by rebuilding and repairing cartilage.

- *Green tea:* Unlike black tea, green tea contains active compounds of polyphenols and flavonols, which have cancer-fighting antioxidant properties. Green tea enhances immune function, reduces cholesterol and triglycerides, and may help with weight loss.

- *5-HTP:* A derivative of the amino acid tryptophan, which helps the body make serotonin, 5-HTP is an important neurotransmitter that plays a critical role in sleep, mood regulation, pain control, and inflammation. It should not be used by people taking certain drugs used to treat depression, especially SSRI (selective serotonin reuptake inhibitors) or MAO (monoamine oxidase inhibitors) antidepressants.

- *Moducare:* This brand-name product formulated from a patented blend of plant sterols helps regulate the immune system.

- *MSM:* A metabolite of DMSO, a well-known solvent used topically for pain relief in anti-inflammatory conditions, MSM promotes relief of arthritis pain and stiffness, stimulates immune function, and supports connective tissue. It should not be taken by anyone with a known sensitivity to sulfur.

- *Relora:* Relora is another brand-name product that helps control cortisol levels. It promotes relaxation, restful sleep, and weight control. It also helps control nervous eating through stress relief.

- *Rhodiola rosea:* This supplement contains golden root, which has been used for hundreds of years to treat colds and flu-like symptoms. It promotes weight loss, relieves stress, enhances immune system, improves cognitive function, and enhances athletic performance.

- *Tanalbit:* This brand-name product containing plant tannins provides gastrointestinal support. It helps relieve bloating, gas, diarrhea, yeast and bacterial overgrowth, and inflammation resulting from food sensitivities and intolerances.

For more information on supplements, effective dosages, and possible drug interactions, check the following Web sites: www.drcolbert.com (Dr. Don Colbert) and www.supplementwatch.com (Supplement Watch).

Now that you have learned what foods to eat and what foods to avoid, as well as these eight important strategies for success, it is time to "Get Up and Get Moving." In the next chapter you will learn the dramatic benefits of even a modest increase in your activity level, and you will learn how it can be fun, not drudgery.

Chapter Eleven

Get Up and Get Moving

YOU knew this moment was coming, didn't you? At some level we all know that physical activity is an essential part of our existence. We were designed and engineered for movement, and lots of it. Yet our technologically advanced society has obsessively engineered our environment for comfort, convenience, and efficiency. We enjoy magnificent benefits from such enhancements; however, there is a growing, glaring problem with our so-called evolution.

As we have pointed out, America—and other "advanced" societies—are experiencing a rampant growth in life-destroying obesity, diabetes, cardiovascular disease, and other chronic conditions. We have become less fit and much sicker. Our quest for quality of life has resulted in the loss of the very thing we desire. We may be advanced technologically, but in many aspects—especially when it comes to health—we are not experiencing quality of life. And one of the main reasons is a completely sedentary lifestyle facilitated by the technologies we crave as consumers.

Good news: no matter "what condition your condition is in" at the moment, you can quickly and dramatically improve. *Better news:* no matter what your socioeconomic status, physical condition, or life's experience, you can achieve zoe abundant life—a life you can enjoy to the fullest.

How do I know this for a fact? Because I have done it, and so can you.

In January 2002 I weighed somewhere in the 470s or 480s. There is no way to know for sure because I hadn't been near a scale for ten years—not since I had eclipsed the 350 mark back in 1992. Most doctors' offices do not even have scales for weighing people larger than 350 pounds, let alone home scales.

"How does it feel?" Bob Dylan asked in the sixties. Not "like a rolling stone" at 470-plus pounds, that is for sure. I hurt. Every minute of every day I hurt. My joints and bones ached from the weight they admirably supported. My muscles had atrophied from disuse and the strain of short, crushing bursts of movement as I walked from one resting stop to another. My knees were shot; they throbbed all the time. Never in my life will I forget the excruciating pain I experienced in my hamstrings and lower back when I had to walk more than twenty or thirty yards without being able to stop and sit and allow my muscles—such as they were—to rest.

A trip to the grocery store, for instance, required at least two stops in the restroom—not for the usual purpose but to give my legs a break. As my back muscles locked up, I would break out in a sweat, and it was all I could do not to scream. I was a full-body charley horse. After another twenty or thirty yards, it would start all over again. I would be gasping for breath so hard that my chest ached.

Every few months I experienced either a dislocated rib (pushed out of place by my girth), or a pinched nerve, or a few cracked ribs from tumbles brought on by my lack of balance and ability to control my momentum once I tripped or stumbled.

In short, my life was all about pain. I realize that very few readers can possibly relate to all my troubles, and I'm grateful for that. I sincerely hope you or your loved ones never know what I'm talking about. I share my reality with you to emphasize two things. First, if I was able to achieve my zoe life, enjoying everything I want to do with no physical impairment, anyone can do the same. Second, the ZOE 8 program is for everyone. The people with the most to gain from our program are not people in poor condition, but those whose health is good or even great—and who never want to experience any, not to mention all, of the physical problems I did.

HOW I STARTED MOVING

I got moving during my twenty-eight-day stay at Structure House. During my intake and evaluation I received the lowest rating for fitness. That, coupled with my bad knees, limited my activities to very short walks, workouts in a chair with resistance bands, and workouts in the swimming pool. I partially fit in one of their mechanical apparatuses called the Nu-Step. I could work the arms or legs separately, but not at the same time, as designed.

I was extremely blessed by two women I mentioned earlier. Cassie, the assistant director of the physical training program, became a friend and supporter, encouraging me from day one. Debbie was a "for hire" trainer who specialized in helping severely impaired or injured individuals and what I have come to lovingly call "supertankers" like me. Debbie was an athlete who had suffered a serious injury and was "rehabbed" in water. She had become an expert in water training and was also a very strong masseuse, a perfect combination for me. Over a four-week period I learned to work out in the pool and with the resistance bands. My last week there I walked, rather than drove, the quarter mile from my room to the dining hall. Of course it hurt, and there were two strategically placed benches for breaks, but I did it.

When I returned home I was down to about 440 pounds and ready to move, one day at a time, one step at a time. For the next four months, in addition to all the strategies previously presented—complete adherence to what we now call the ZOE 8 food plan, and intense prayer and emotional healing—I purposed every day to increase my activity. I also began receiving regular deep tissue and trigger point massage therapy. I am eternally grateful I could afford the support I needed. I often worry how individuals who are not as blessed financially can climb out of a hole as deep as mine was. I believe God will provide the means that we will one day be able to help people of every background and socioeconomic circumstance.

I walked a few more steps each day, or swam one more lap, or pulled on a stronger band, and afterward my massage therapist would release the lactic acid in my muscles and work until I—get this—felt good. Yes, *good*. Day by day the pain subsided, and I could do a little bit more. I had a doctor friend with a rehab clinic who let me go in after hours to use the exercise equipment. I was reclaiming my life—one day, one pound, one inch at a time.

After five months, I met a personal trainer at the rehab clinic and began genuine workouts. I am sure people were smirking behind my back and making fun of me, but I didn't care. I was on a mission from God, and I knew it. As Cloud and Townsend titled their book, *God Will Make a Way*—and he did. My trainer, Harold, was a godsend. He patiently worked me, massaged me, and helped me heal. He is a beautiful human being—one of many God sent my way—to whom I am most grateful.

Now, fast-forward a year, and I'm 200 pounds lighter and a well-oiled workout machine. I went from feebly lifting a 40-pound bar a few times to weight training three days a week with a workout weight of 135 pounds for twenty-four reps, and another three to five days a week of aerobics for thirty to sixty minutes at 3.8 miles per hour walking or 5.5 to 6 miles per hour on the elliptic.

Oh, yeah. Remember those knees? The ones the orthopedist had told me I would need to have replaced? Well, I still have them, and they don't hurt. I do lunges and squats, cover as much as seven to ten miles a day between my daily activity and workouts, and I feel good—head to knees to toes.

Enough about me, already. Let's get you moving.

START WHERE YOU ARE

If you are in a depleted physical condition when you begin, you may need physical or massage therapy to help release taut muscles and get rid of toxins that have built up in your system. The massages were the key to unlocking my muscles, and it made a huge difference in regaining my mobility. Don't worry if you are unable to do any aerobic exercise at all, or if you cannot go for long walks. In fact, we don't even talk about exercise when someone first starts the ZOE 8 Weight Management Program; we save it for step number five. And when we do reach the point where physical movement is needed, we emphasize the word *activity* rather than *exercise*, because the important thing is to just get up and get moving!

Let's read what Rusty recently told us about his improvements in this area:

ZOE 8 TESTIMONY

I used to snack on junk food and drink six to eight sodas a day while riding around the oil fields in my pickup. My work required long hours in the truck, and I relied on convenience stores for lunch and snacks. My weight was out of control and I knew I needed to make some serious changes, so I started by getting rid of the sodas. Then I attended a ZOE 8 seminar, and it turned my life around.

Just by preparing lunch at home and packing ZOE-friendly snacks for the road, I lost 35 pounds in my first three months on the program. I also started increasing my activity, and now I have so much more energy—plus a bright new outlook.

I can now walk the golf course with my son, something I was never able to do before the ZOE 8 program. This has been such a postive step in my life, and I am so glad I made the time and commitment to the program. The ZOE 8 team has been a great support.

—Rusty G.

The key is to start wherever you are and increase your activity gradually. You want to avoid injury, and you also don't want to overtrain—it can actually prevent you from losing weight if you keep your calorie level too low to compensate for the increased energy expenditure.

For most people exercise is an intimidating word, painting a picture of pain, sweat, tight clothing, torturous equipment, and the feeling that "this is really for someone else, not me." The result is that you put off exercise, relegating it to something you will do someday—along with eating right and cleaning out the garage.

In the ZOE 8 Weight Management Program, exercise is simply activity— the kind you do every day even if it is walking from the couch to the refrigerator. Of course, we want to help you go a little further than that to achieve your physical goals. The following eight steps will get you started, and you will not need a gym in order to begin being active. Resolve to be consistent and more active every day. The results will astound you!

THE 8 STEPS OF ZOE ACTIVITY

1. **Consult your doctor or health practitioner** to determine your level of physical health.

2. **Believe in yourself.** Movement is a necessary part of life. No matter what your physical condition is now, believe that it can improve, step by step, day by day, by simply increasing your daily activity. Find your motivation to get moving in the direction of physical health, the zoe kind. You can "just do it!"

3. **Set your goals.** Only you know what activity level is realistic for you. If you have been sedentary, begin by just walking. If you are more active, walk briskly, ride a bike, or try a new activity such as yoga, Pilates, swimming, dancing, or gardening. *You* decide the activity that fits *you*. But you must do something and keep doing it. Set short-term and long-term goals, and involve others in your plan.

4. **Invest in time and planning** to achieve your goals. You are important. All of us have twenty-four hours in a day; no one has more or less. Plan at least thirty minutes of your chosen activity in addition to your daily tasks, and over time work your way up to sixty minutes or more. Soon it will become routine. Plan to rest, too. Getting adequate sleep is essential to your overall health. What can you change in your twenty-four hours to make time for activity? Watch less TV? Get up a little earlier?

5. **Invest in a pedometer** to count the steps you walk in a day. The ultimate goal is 10,000 steps a day or more, but if you are at 1,000 steps today, go for 1,500 steps tomorrow. Taking more steps every day can easily fit into your daily routine by simply parking your car farther away, taking the stairs, not taking the shortcut, walking the dog, walking with a friend, or grocery shopping. Adding steps to your day is an easy way to increase your activity while doing everyday tasks. What can you do to increase your steps?

6. **Invest in a set of resistance bands** and follow the simple illustrations enclosed in the box. Resistance bands are readily available, inexpensive, and easy to use. They can be used sitting or standing, by young or old, by the active or inactive, at home and away. Consistently adding this activity in addition to tracking your steps with a pedometer will gradually result in weight loss and a more toned body.

7. **Increase your activity.** As you get moving and become more fit, increase your level of activity. Being more active will become a way of life. Add more movement and have some fun. Play a sport, learn ballroom dancing, just keep walking, enjoy water aerobics, swimming, exercise videos, hiking, mountain biking, tai chi, join a gym—you choose. Increasing your level of activity and maintaining it consistently is a key to long-term physical health. Keep moving!

8. **Celebrate your accomplishments.** Incentives keep us motivated. Find ways, other than a pint of ice cream, to reward yourself. You may want to buy new clothes, take a long-awaited trip, go to a movie, spend time with friends, or have a party. It is your choice, but plan for rewards.

I got moving by simply focusing on adding activity to my daily routine. I started parking my car farther from the entrance, gradually increasing the distance until I was parking at the end of the lot. I started walking the dog, going a little farther each time. I started walking up a flight of stairs rather than taking the elevator. In my hotels now I walk two flights up or three flights down.

There are many pounds to be lost or gained in our daily routine. Everyone, regardless of fitness level, should begin increasing the activity in their daily routine, then move on to more targeted and intense activities.

THREE TYPES OF FITNESS

There are three basic types of fitness with corresponding types of activity.[1] I will explain all of them in this section, give you some specific ideas for increasing your fitness level, and share with you a couple of easy, fun, and effective workouts. In addition to the information contained here, ZOE 8 publishes a monthly activity on our ZOE 8 Web site.

Structural fitness

The first type is structural fitness, which refers to your overall ability to function in daily life and your ability to exercise, specifically your degree of mobility, flexibility, and stability. Stretching exercises are the primary activity for increasing structural fitness. Most people do not pay enough attention to this type of exercise because, by itself, it does not burn fat. However, improving your balance and stability will help you perform all kinds of activities more effectively.

Check your local library or bookstore, where you will find a multitude of resources that include stretching exercises with detailed instructions and photos. An excellent online resource is www.exercise.about.com, where you will find articles and instructions for beginners to advanced exercisers. If you are interested in a structured form of flexibility training, you may want to take a class in tai chi, yoga, or Pilates. These exercise programs require no or minimal equipment, and you can often find inexpensive classes through community colleges, church and civic groups, or your local YMCA. Instructional videos are also available if you prefer exercising at home. The most extensive source for exercise videos I have found is Collage Video, www.collagevideo.com. They have hundreds of videos, all of which are staff reviewed and rated for difficulty, and they even have videos for seated workouts for those with limited mobility.

Cardiovascular fitness

The second type of fitness is cardiovascular fitness, which is achieved by increasing aerobic activity, also called cardio for short. *Aerobic* refers specifically to oxygen, so aerobic exercise is any form of activity that increases the amount of oxygen your heart and lungs deliver to your muscles.

If you have been basically inactive, one of the best ways to begin an aerobic exercise program is simply to start walking. Swing your arms while you walk, and you will strengthen your heart while really working the long muscles of your legs—also important for stability and strength. One of my favorite aerobic exercises is the one I started when I was still a "supertanker"—water aerobics.

Stair climbing is one of the most aerobic exercises you can perform—and another one you do not need equipment for. I have an elliptical machine at home (that is all I use for aerobics today besides swimming and walking), and they are available at every gym or fitness center. Of course, there is always aerobic dancing, cycling, rowing, skiing, and skating.

Rather than using a formula for achieving a target heart rate during aerobic exercise, most trainers today prefer to use what is known as perceived exertion level. For one thing, it is awkward to stop exercising to measure your heart rate (unless you are using sophisticated equipment that measures it for you), and further, the formulas for target heart rate cannot possibly measure your actual oxygen consumption. Your heart rate can also be influenced by your emotional state, medications you have taken, the weather (if you are outdoors), and even caffeine consumption. What is important to know is that for fat-burning purposes, you want to work at a moderate intensity, for a longer period, than for cardio purposes, which requires a higher intensity level in shorter workouts.

There are several different perceived exertion scales, most of them numbered from one to ten, but all of them are based on how deeply you are breathing, how hard you are working, and whether you are still able to carry on a conversation. If you can sing, you are not working hard enough; if you can carry on a conversation, even though you are breathing hard and breaking a sweat, you are working at a moderate, fat-burning speed (around levels five to six); and if you are working too hard to utter more than a few words, you are working at an intense cardio level (seven to eight on the scale).

PERCEIVED EXERTION SCALE

Paige Waehner has a humorous spin on the perceived exertion scale:[2]

Level 1: *I'm watching TV and eating bon bons.*

Level 2: *I'm comfortable and could maintain this pace all day long.*

Level 3: *I'm still comfortable, but am breathing a bit harder.*

Level 4: *I'm sweating a little, but feel good and can carry on a conversation effortlessly.*

Level 5: *I'm just above comfortable, am sweating more, but can still talk easily.*

Level 6: *I can still talk, but am slightly breathless.*

Level 7: *I can still talk, but I don't really want to. I'm sweating like a pig.*

Level 8: *I can grunt in response to your questions and can only keep this pace for a short time period.*

Level 9: *I am probably going to die.*

Level 10: *I am dead.*

Take the plunge into fitness

When I started out to reclaim my health, I began in a swimming pool. Land activities, including walking, were out of the question because of my weight and broken-down knees. I was blessed to spend four weeks in a very upscale institution that had experts in water therapy and, of course, a heated indoor pool (it was winter at the time). So let me save you time and money by sharing what I learned.

As you would with any workout program, ask your health practitioner to check you out first. Once you are cleared, you want to start in the water as you would any other activity: slowly, in order to determine your fitness level and to prevent injury. Water workouts should be structured just like a typical workout, with a three- to seven-minute gentle warm-up, followed by a fifteen- to forty-minute session that brings you to your targeted level of exertion, and finishing with a gentle five-minute cool down. That is the really fun part, just floating around with gentle arm or leg movements.

Just like walking or jogging, water is ideal for aerobic or fat-burning exercise, which requires longer, less aggressive activity. Believe it or not, water is also great for anaerobic or muscle-building activity, just like weight lifting. Instead of barbells or hand weights, muscle training in the water requires special gloves or "noodles," which you can purchase at any grocery store or pool supply. Or you can even use a couple of plastic jugs filled with water—anything that will increase resistance. Trust me, you can get an incredible power workout in the water, one that will work your entire body.

One of the great benefits of water is buoyancy. In waist-high water, 50 percent of your body weight is supported by the water itself; in chest-high water, 85 to 90 percent of your body weight is supported. Therefore, all water activity is *no impact,* so no matter your weight or the condition of your knees, ankles, or so forth, you can dramatically improve your health. For me, it was water only for about three months, followed by a season of water and land exercise. To this day I involve water exercise during the summer because it is cool, fun, relaxing, and effective.

Now, a very important note. The water temperature must be 82 degrees or higher. Why? Just like whales, when submerged in cooler water, our bodies go into fat storage mode—not good! The University of Florida released a study recently that indicated our appetites increase after exercise in cooler water—also not good.[3] The warmer the water, up to 94–96 degrees, the better.

Muscular fitness

Muscular fitness, the third type of fitness, is improved by strength training, weight training, or resistance training. Don't think this is only for bodybuilders or fitness fanatics! Everyone should want to increase lean muscle mass because it revs up your metabolism, causing you to burn more calories even at rest. So both cardio and strength training are important parts of a balanced activity regimen; one burns fat outright, and the other builds muscles that help you burn fat more efficiently.

I have a complete home gym now and work out extensively, but my first gymnasium was a chair; I worked out with elasticized bands of different lengths and colors. So absolutely anybody can begin a strength-training program. Since my purpose is not to write an exercise book (maybe I will do that some day), I will limit myself here to explaining how you can get a full body workout for just $9.95.

That is right, you do not have to spend a lot of money on a gym membership or expensive equipment. All you need is a chair and a set of resistance bands, which can be bought for around ten dollars at stores like Wal-Mart and Target. You will find a wider selection at www.bodytrends.com, and they also have a helpful chart and FAQ section to help you determine which bands are right for your needs.

Resistance bands are sometimes viewed as the underdog of the workout world, but I assure you that even iron-pumping gym rats will break a sweat with them. (A gym rat myself now, I can say this with some authority.) Resistance bands have the unique ability to provide resistance throughout the entire movement. When you use free weights, you don't necessarily get that continuous resistance. With bands you can concentrate on both the lifting and lowering phase of each exercise. The result is that your muscles are challenged in a completely different way, which can help you avoid boredom. Not only will you be able to challenge your muscles, but you will also be able to perform numerous exercises with one little piece of equipment. The most important aspect of lifting with bands is control: take your time and focus on what you are doing.

Many different types of bands are available. The thicker the band, the more difficult your workout will be. It is a good idea to get several different levels of thickness as some exercises may require less resistance than others. Different resistance levels are generally color-coded. A great feature of the pre-packaged sets is that they usually come with three levels, providing you the ability to advance as you get stronger. Many kits also come with illustrated workout guides. The bands can be used for upper body exercises such as chest presses and bicep curls, and the band can be wrapped around a chair to get some great lower body work as well.

The best part of all? Resistance bands are portable, affordable, and provide you with the ability to exercise anytime and anywhere. You can exercise in groups for support or in the privacy of your home or hotel room when traveling. A compact and considerably less expensive alternative to gym equipment, exercise bands are an ideal way to change up your current workout routine or a wonderful way to get one started.

As your fitness level progresses, weight training is an excellent way to get results. All public gyms today feature weight machines, which are safe. These machines isolate and work individual muscles or muscle groups. Even better than weight machines are free weights, which yield a greater benefit because the "free" aspect forces you to utilize stabilizing muscles at the same time you are targeting a specific muscle group. For example, a bicep curl on a weight machine works only the bicep muscle. Doing bicep curls with free weights, however, not only works your bicep muscle but also strengthens your chest, back, and abdominal muscles as well.

Free weights do not initially require the use of big bars. As you are building up your muscles and overall strength, dumbbells are great. And free weights are not just for the guys! Elisa regularly works with 10- to 20-pound hand weights with excellent results. After four months on the resistance bands, I started using the weight machines and dumbbells. Today I use heavy bar weights and dumbbells for specific muscle exercises.

WARM UP, WORK OUT, COOL DOWN

Whatever kind of exercise you are doing, you need to be sure to start with a warm-up period—five to ten minutes of light cardio work. Follow that with a series of stretching exercises. It is important to warm up *before* stretching; "cold" muscles are prone to tears or overstretching injuries. End your workout with a similar cool-down period. Gradually slow the intensity of your workout and wind up with some plain old-fashioned walking. Add a few final stretches; now that your muscles have been thoroughly worked they will be able to stretch further and you will get the maximum benefit from increasing your flexibility, cardio, and muscular fitness.

WHEN CALORIES COUNT

OK, you have started yourself moving. Now, what?

Up until now we have not discussed how many calories you should be eating in order to lose weight. The ZOE 8 food plan does not focus on calories, because if you are not eating the right foods, the number of calories you consume may be irrelevant. Once you are eating the best foods for your specific needs, however, calories do count. So, after you have conquered your roadblocks (candida, food sensitivities, hormones, etc.), and you have your personalized weight-loss strategy in place and have started moving more, then it becomes important to watch your calories.

I will give you some formulas for calculating your calorie requirements in a moment, but first I want you to remember this very important point: nothing ever stays the same. Whatever your physical condition, wherever you are in your health continuum, each day you will go forward or backward based on your choices of food, emotions, and activity. Albert Einstein said, "No problem can be solved from the same level of consciousness that created it." Likewise you cannot maintain the same level of activity if you desire to change your physical reality—and this is true whether you are just starting out or have been exercising regularly.

I have personally learned this principle. For a one-year period I lost an average of 4.2 pounds a week, eating an average of 1,752 very volumetric calories per day. I made my calories count, and I was never hungry. I also worked out three times a week, once I was able, with weights and aerobics. My daily routine activity—parking the car at the end of the lot, taking the stairs rather than the elevator—remained consistent. For an eight-month period my weight stayed the same. I was content. I was fit. I stopped increasing my activity, and all was well.

That is, until I stopped exercising for the next eight months, yet continued to eat the same. The result: weight gain. Now, I had stopped exercising in order to deal with a medical circumstance; I had no choice. It was frustrating but very valuable as a case study in Einstein's thinking about not staying at the same level that created the problem. I subsequently have resumed and even increased my activity—time, type, and intensity—for the past six months. The result: a higher fitness level than ever and, of course, weight loss. Today my personal aerobic sessions have gone from fifteen to twenty minutes, to forty-five to sixty minutes. That is all the time I have, so from here it is an increase in intensity by increasing the resistance on my elliptical.

CALORIES IN VS. CALORIES OUT

If you have invested in a pedometer, you will be able to calculate the number of calories you burn while walking. The following chart will give you an idea of the number of calories you can burn while doing other activities.

Why is knowing the number of calories burned important? The basic mathematical principle of weight loss is that you have to burn more calories than you consume.

Keep in mind that this chart is based on calculations for a person weighing 150 pounds. The calories burned during a particular activity will always vary in proportion to body weight. For example, a person weighing only 100 pounds will burn approximately ⅓ fewer calories than the numbers presented here, so you would multiply the number of calories burned by 0.7 to get a more accurate calculation. For a 200-pound person, multiply by 1.3. The heavier you are, the more calories you will burn during an activity.

Working harder or faster will only slightly increase the calories burned during exercise. A better way to burn up more calories is to increase the time spent on your activity.

CALORIES BURNED PER HOUR

Sedentary Activities	Vigorous Activities (over 350 cal/hr)
Lying down or sleeping, 90	Aerobic dancing, 546
Sitting quietly, 84	Basketball (recreational), 450
Sitting and writing, card playing, etc., 114	Bicycling (12 mph), 410
	Circuit weight training, 756
Moderate Activities (150–350 cal/hr)	Cross-country skiing (5 mph), 690
Bicycling (5 mph), 174	Football (touch, vigorous), 498
Canoeing (2.5 mph), 174	Jogging (5 1/2 mph), 740
Dancing (ballroom), 210	Jumping rope, 750
Gardening, 323	Racquetball, 588
Golf (twosome, carrying clubs), 324	Running (10 mph), 1280
Horseback riding (sitting to trot), 246	Skating (9 mph), 384
Light housework, cleaning, etc., 246	Scrubbing floors, 440
Swimming (25 yds/min), 275	Swimming (50 yds/min), 500
Tennis (recreational doubles), 312	Tennis (recreational singles), 450
Volleyball (recreational), 264	
Walking (2 mph), 220	
Walking (3 mph), 320	

Thus, you cannot maintain a constant level of activity—let's say aerobics at 75 percent of your maximum heart rate three times a week for a twenty-minute period—and expect continual results in terms of weight loss. Eventually you reach a balance between your body weight, calorie consumption, and fitness. That means, for example, that you can start out on a campaign to lose twenty pounds by going from a sedentary lifestyle to sixty minutes of aerobics, as mentioned above. You maintain a caloric intake of 1,800 calories a day. And let's say that for a period of eight weeks you consistently lose two pounds a week. Suddenly, your weight loss stops. You have hit a plateau...or have you?

What has actually happened is that you have achieved a balance between calories in and calories out. You will need to increase your activity in duration or intensity; otherwise, you will stay where you are for a while. As we age, we need to carefully balance our energy intake and outtake because our metabolism, left on its own, will slow down. Increasing activity and balancing activity with calorie consumption is a lifelong process necessary to achieve and maintain an abundant life.

Now, there are several formulas for calculating the number of calories required to maintain your current body weight. Individual requirements may vary due to differences in metabolism, but the following guidelines will give you a starting point.

The Harris-Benedict formula is a widely used tool. We present it here because this particular formula allows for differences between gender and factors in age, weight, height, and activity level. Basal metabolic rate (BMR) is the amount of energy, expressed in calories, needed to maintain your body at rest. Keep in mind that this formula is for *maintaining* weight. In order to *lose* weight, you will need to eat fewer calories per day, or, of course, burn more through increased activity. A good rule of thumb is to reduce your intake by 500 calories per day, which will result in a slow, steady loss of approximately one pound per week. (There are 3,500 calories in one pound; eliminating 500 calories per day for seven days equals 3,500 calories.)

HARRIS-BENEDICT FORMULA FOR WOMEN

STEP 1

BMR = 655 + (9.6 x weight in kilos) + (1.8 x height in cm) - (4.7 x age)

Notes: 1 inch = 2.54 cm • 1 kilogram = 2.2 lbs.

Example of BMR

You are thirty-two years old.

You are 5 feet 4 inches tall (64 inches x 2.54 = 162.5 cm).

Your weight is 185 pounds (185 divided by 2.2 lbs. = 84 kilos).

Your BMR is 655 + (80 6) + (291) - (150) = 1602 calories.

HARRIS-BENEDICT FORMULA FOR WOMEN

STEP 2

To determine your total daily calorie needs, now multiply your BMR by the appropriate activity factor, as follows:

If you are sedentary (little or no exercise)
Calorie calculation = BMR x 1.2

If you are lightly active (light exercise/sports 1–3 days/week)
Calorie calculation = BMR x 1.375

If you are moderately active (moderate exercise/sports 3–5 days/week)
Calorie calculation = BMR x 1.55

If you are very active (hard exercise/sports 6–7 days/week)
Calorie calculation = BMR x 1.725

HARRIS-BENEDICT FORMULA FOR MEN

STEP 1

BMR = 66 + (13.7 x weight in kilos) + (5 x height in cm) - (6.8 x age)
Notes: 1 inch = 2.54 cm • 1 kilogram = 2.2 lbs.

Example of BMR

You are twenty-five years old.
You are 6 feet tall (72 in. x 2.54 = 182.9 cm).
Your weight is 220 pounds (220 divided by 2.2 = 100 kilos).
Your BMR is 66 + (1370) + (914) - (170) = 2180 calories.

STEP 2

To determine your total daily calorie needs, now multiply your BMR by the appropriate activity factor, as follows:

If you are sedentary (little or no exercise)
Calorie calculation = BMR x 1.2

If you are lightly active (light exercise/sports 1–3 days/week)
Calorie calculation = BMR x 1.375

If you are moderately active (moderate exercise/sports 3–5 days/week)
Calorie calculation = BMR x 1.55

If you are very active (hard exercise/sports 6–7 days/week)
Calorie calculation = BMR x 1.725

Depending on your activity level and your individual metabolism, you may lose faster or slower. Men tend to lose faster than women, for example. It is important that you lose fat, not muscle, so cutting your calories lower than the above recommendation may actually be counterproductive. As with everything in the ZOE 8 program, you will need to find the calorie level that works for *your* particular body type and lifestyle. Over a period of time, your daily food journal will provide the answer.

If you find the Harris-Benedict mathematical formula too challenging, use the Mayo Clinic guidelines shown below. The Mayo Clinic chart is not as precise, but it will give you a ballpark number you can tweak to your individual requirements.

MAYO CLINIC CALORIE GUIDELINES FOR WEIGHT LOSS		
Your weight in pounds	**Daily calorie goal**	
	Women	**Men**
250 or less	1,200	1,400
251 to 300	1,400	1,600
301 or more	1,600	1,800

You should never drop below the minimum recommended calorie guidelines, i.e., 1,200 calories for women or 1,400 calories for men. Doing so will put you at risk of not getting the nutrients you need. It will also slow down your metabolism and keep you from losing any weight at all.

Remember, if you are eating whole foods and following the ZOE 8 principles, including activity, *you will lose weight.*

And, if you get to the point where your weight loss slows dramatically or stalls, then the next chapter contains the secret to getting you revved up again.

Chapter Twelve

What to Do When Your Engine Stalls

IT would be wonderful if you followed the ZOE 8 Weight Management Program to a "T" and lost a pound or three a week, without fail, until you reached your goal. But it is not likely to happen that way. Why? Our bodies are remarkably adaptive, and after a period of steady weight loss your body will begin to feel comfortable at its new weight and will want to settle in and stay there. Your metabolism reaches what is called a set point, a place on your internal fat-burning thermostat that your body seeks to defend. In order to change the setting on your thermostat, you must either increase your fat-burning activities or retool your food plan—or both.

But first of all, you must determine whether you have truly reached a plateau or whether your body is simply adjusting to biological, emotional, or seasonal changes. Most people tend to weigh more in the winter months, whether through a decrease in activity or biological programming that tells the body to increase fat storage in cold weather. Also, if you start to lose body fat too quickly, your metabolism will slow down and conserve fat as a form of self-preservation. In addition, if you are not eating enough calories, your metabolism will stall and hold on to fat reserves.

Also remember that you may experience an initial weight gain (or slower loss) due to an increase in water consumption. Over a period of several weeks, your body will begin to absorb and utilize the extra water efficiently, and you will lose any water weight you have accumulated. Remember that what shows up as a loss on the scale can be water, fat, or muscle. The goal is to lose fat, not muscle, so it is important not to lose weight too fast.

In order to reach a true plateau, you must first have been losing weight consistently. If that is the case, and you go at least three weeks without further loss, then you have probably reached a plateau—and that is the point at which your engine truly stalls and you need to make some adjustments.

A ZOE 8 SELF-DIAGNOSTIC TOOL

To help you determine why your weight loss has stopped or slowed down, give your weight-loss program a checkup. This is a chance to fine-tune your weight management program, and that is why we made it step number seven of the ZOE 8 Weight Management Program. The following sections contain a series of questions to use as a self-diagnostic tool for fine-tuning your program.

Check your commitment and expectations

- Are you operating from spiritual conviction or the strength of your will?
- Reread your commitment to change. Are you committed?
- What expectations did you have when you started the program?
- How have those expectations changed?
- How realistic are your expectations?

Review your goals

- How realistic are your goals?
- What progress have you made toward your goals?
- How long have you been on the program?
- How much weight have you lost?
- How many inches have you lost?
- Are you wearing a smaller size of clothing?

Remember that the scale is only one tool for measuring your progress; don't get so caught up in that number that you lose sight of your overall progress.

Review your daily journal

- Check your "cheating" level.
- Have you been honest in recording what and how much you eat?
- How consistent have you been in following the food plan?
- What changes do you need to make to become more consistent?

Are you encountering food sensitivities?

- Have you been tested for food sensitivities?
- What were the results of the testing?
- Have you successfully eliminated problem foods from your diet?

If you have not been tested for food sensitivities, we strongly recommend it and will try to help you find a health practitioner near you.

Are you having hormone problems?

- Have you had your hormone levels checked?
- What were the results of the testing?
- Were supplements recommended?
- How long have you been taking these supplements, and how well are they working?

Are you getting enough sleep?

- How well are you sleeping?
- Are you getting adequate rest, or do you still feel fatigued?
- What do you need to do in order to increase the amount of sleep you get or improve the quality of your sleep?

Do you need a physical exam?

- When was the last time you had a physical exam?
- When was the last time you had your body chemistry checked through blood work?
- What problems were identified?
- Have you made any improvements in those problems?
- Are you taking prescription medications? Remember that these medications can interfere with weight loss.
- Are you taking a daily multivitamin and appropriate supplements?

Check your food-plan compliance

- Are you eating enough?
- What is your average caloric intake?

- Is it above or below the recommended level you set after reading chapter eleven?
- Are you eating three meals a day?
- What is your average water intake?
- Are you meeting your daily requirement? If not, why?
- Do you read food labels when you shop? Are you watching for sugar, corn, and yeast disguised as other ingredients?
- How balanced is your diet? How many low-glycemic foods as opposed to high-glycemic foods do you eat?
- Check your consumption of salt and sugar.

Too much salt in your diet will cause water retention, making you appear puffy and hindering weight loss. Too much sugar will add calories and cause hunger cravings. How are you doing when it comes to reducing salt and sugar?

Check your activity level

- How much aerobic exercise have you been doing?
- Can you increase the time you exercise or the number of times you exercise per week?
- Have you increased the number of steps you take each day? Walking is great exercise, it requires no special equipment, and you can take a friend with you.
- What are you doing to increase activity in your everyday routine?
- Are you taking the stairs instead of the elevator?
- Are you parking farther from the entrance?
- What can you do to burn more calories throughout the day?

Are you eating for emotional reasons?

- How often do you eat in response to stress?
- What steps are you taking to control stress?
- What emotions or situations are causing you to eat inappropriately?
- How have you worked on changing that?

We highly recommend the book *God Will Make a Way* by Dr. Henry Cloud and Dr. John Townsend. The following quotes are from the chapter on weight loss and health.[1] Do any of these emotional reasons for eating apply to you?

Emptiness inside. "Food represents love and can compensate for a lack of relationships. It doesn't reject, it has a satisfying quality, and it is always available." The association of food and love begins the first time a mother feeds her newborn baby.

Control deficits and boundary problems. "God designed us to develop ownership and responsibility over our lives, so that we could be free to live and choose him and his way....However, many people struggle" with this freedom. "Food becomes the only arena in life in which the person can make free choices, the only arena that does not involve pleasing others" or facing rejection.

Unhappiness. Eating to medicate emotional pain can result in self-condemnation, self-hatred, and unrelenting guilt. "Since you can't run from yourself, people who struggle with self-condemnation can't escape the doubt and self-criticism, and some use food as an anesthetic from the pain. Yet...all anesthetics wear off."

Entitlement. Some people feel "they should be able to eat whatever they want, whenever they want"—they deserve it. This is actually a denial of reality.

Intimacy. Some people, uncomfortable with their sexuality, allow their weight to "hide their attractiveness, ensuring that they will avoid any sexual or romantic scenarios. Of course their sexuality is not gone; it is simply buried."

While God intends for us to enjoy food, we should never use it as a way to replace love.

IMPROVEMENTS OTHER THAN WEIGHT LOSS

Weight loss is not the only measure of success. Are your clothes fitting better? Are you feeling better? Do you have more energy? How has your overall health improved?

IT IS NOT A DIET; IT IS A LIFESTYLE

Above all, keep in mind that this is not a diet. This program is about making lifestyle changes. You do not have to do it all at once. Take small steps at first, and implement additional changes over time. Slow, gradual progress is actually the best kind for your body. Losing too much weight too fast puts additional stress on your body and can cause you to lose skin and muscle tone.

So be patient with the program, and be patient with yourself. We all want quick fixes, but that is what has gotten us where we are. Make your weight-loss program a matter of prayer, commitment, and faithfulness. As you stick with it, everything will seem to come together all at once, and your good habits will become part of your character. One of the ladies in a ZOE Plus support group we have started where we live in Boerne, Texas, has coined a new word: *clickage.* That is what occurs when everything finally clicks into place—spiritually, emotionally, and physically—and the ZOE 8 principles become your way of life. Don't give up, and you will reach clickage, too!

Finally, be realistic. We all have days when we slip up and stray from the program. We make poor choices and regret them later, or we give in to the taste temptations that constantly bombard us. When that happens, and it will, be kind to yourself and don't let it derail you. As they say in New Jersey, just "fuggedaboutit" and go on with your life and your new zoe lifestyle. That is the healthy, abundant life you were meant to enjoy.

Chapter Thirteen

Zoe: The Life You Were Meant to Live

Ed I have talked a lot about my desire for you to discover the zoe life that I have experienced and live it to the fullest as God designed it. It hasn't been easy sharing some very personal stories in these pages, but I wanted you to see where I came from so you can appreciate where I am now. And Elisa and I want the same thing for you—the very best in life.

So *how* can you achieve zoe life? And *why* should you make the effort? Please read on.

HOW: ALL YOU NEED IS LOVE (DUM DUM, DAH DAH DUM)

"All you need is love," sang the Beatles, and while they may have had something different in mind than I do, I can't sum it up any better than that. Love is the four-letter word above all words.

I believe God *is* love. In fact, it says so in Scripture: "God is love. Whoever lives in love lives in God, and God in him" (1 John 4:16).

An amazing quality of love is that it never fails. One of the most beautiful descriptions of love—not passion, as we sometimes think of love today, but the essence of transcendent love—is found in the Bible, in the thirteenth chapter of First Corinthians. The following is my paraphrase of how the apostle Paul described love:

> A man may have all knowledge, faith that can move mountains, may give all his possessions to the poor and may even be willing to give up his life—but if he does not have love, his knowledge and good deeds have gained him nothing. Nothing at all. Love is patient, love is kind, it does not envy, it does not boast, and love is not proud. Neither is love rude or self-seeking. Love does not anger easily, and one who loves does not keep score—he "keeps no record of wrong." Love does not delight in the evil around us, but rejoices

in truth wherever it is found. Love bears all things, believes all things, hopes all things, and endures all things. Love never fails.

Let me say that again: *love never fails.* What a hard concept for any human living on this planet in these times to grasp, let alone live out! That was certainly me at one time. However, I am confident today that if I "faint not" ("And let us not be weary in well doing: for in due season we shall reap, if we faint not" Galatians 6:9, KJV), and if I stand resolute in truth and faith, then I cannot fail.

I need to love myself—my spirit, my mind, and my body. I need to love my God. I need to love those whom God has personally ordained to be in my life and I in theirs—my wife, my children, my friends and family, fat people, thin people, healthy and unhealthy people who somehow, some way come into my life and the ZOE 8 program. And now you, a reader of this book.

Sound a little crazy? Well, I have already been there and done that, as they say. I have already *not* loved myself, my body, my life. That is not only crazy, it is deadly—and painfully so. Now I choose, with conviction, to passionately, unyieldingly operate in the spirit of love. The stakes are high. I want everything my heavenly Father desires for me. Every single thing. "All I need is love," and I will have all those things.

We have made this the final step of the ZOE 8 program because at the end of every ZOE 8 seminar I emphatically implore people to be in relationship and to live in love. We all have parents, family, a pastor, a friend, a dog—someone or something that allows us to love and be loved. If that isn't the case for you, then Elisa and I offer to love you. There is always room for more love.

SEE THE NEW YOU

As you work on becoming the "new you," remember that there will be challenges and setbacks. Nothing of true value comes without effort and persistence. Having become a consistent lifter of weights, I fully appreciate the essentialness of "resisting" and "pressing through." Each of us must "lift the weight" and do the work necessary to get the rewards that are ours for the taking—you know, things like peace, joy, happiness, health, fun. How does that sound? As those challenges or setbacks or even bad choices occur (yes, I still mistakes every day), remember to love yourself and your life.

Remember that love is kind and does not anger easily. Be kind to yourself. And when all else fails, praise God we have the "F" word: forgive yourself and anyone else connected to your circumstance.

During June 2002 I had an experience I will never forget. I was a few months into my battle with candida and had been to a follow-up after my first meeting with Dr. Don Colbert. I would occasionally fax him questions regarding new food ideas or physical issues that popped up. At that point I had lost about fifty to sixty pounds. In response to a fax I had sent, Don scribbled some answers to my questions and included a personal note. He asked me to daily close my eyes and see myself as I was going to be—thinner, healthy, happy. He went on to encourage me to believe in that vision and said that he believed in that with and for me.

When I read Don's note, I went to my bedroom and wept. Despite the wonderful people in my life, people who truly cared for me, I had always felt alone in the confines of my mind and the depths of my soul. I was alone not because of the actions or behaviors of others, but because of my own inner view of myself. Reading those words on a faxed page from Don, not only did I not feel alone at long last, but also I felt the strength and power of his confidence and faith. I began to believe. I began to "see" the "new" Ed.

You need to see yourself every day as the person you desire to be. The new you may be the same physically as you are today or dramatically different. That you may be filled to overflowing with peace and joy, as opposed to anxious or depressed. That you may be married as opposed to single. Whatever, you need to be sure you have a vision of yourself that includes or exceeds life beyond all your goals and dreams. You should wake up in the morning and not get out of bed without taking a moment to close your eyes and admire yourself as you are going to be.

Most of all you must *believe* that vision. That takes faith. Faith is the evidence of things hoped for but not yet seen, the Bible says. (See Hebrews 11:1.)

Now, here is an offer you can't beat. Faith, for some, requires development, just like building muscles. For a season of my life, I needed to rely on Don's faith. I also relied on the faith of my pastor, Dub Jones. I was too weak on my own, but the faith of these godly men supported me. This is as God intended. We need others. We need those "safe" relationships I talked about earlier. Elisa and I not only offer to love you, but we have faith available for you, too!

One other very important point about how you see yourself. I have learned that the people who truly know us and love us usually have a more accurate view of us than we have of ourselves. My children frequently see themselves as failed, or incapable, or even unattractive in certain ways. I see my children as they are: marvelously complex, beautiful, capable. Sure, from time to time any of us may need to lose some weight, perhaps even a lot. But none of us are a number on a scale. We are not Madison Avenue models or airbrushed photos. None of us are simply a "condition," such as diabetic; we are not our disease. We are all magnificent creations, capable of love, and needing love. Do not view yourself through the eyes of the world. View yourself, the whole you—spirit, mind, and body—through the eyes of someone who loves you.

WHY: WHERE DO YOU GET YOUR MOTIVATION?

Why did I do what I did when I did it? That was the question I frequently received: what finally motivated me? Truthfully, the answer has changed over the past three years.

Initially, I thought it was some kind of miracle, or something beyond my comprehension. For whatever reason, I finally came into touch with the right doctor, the right body of knowledge, and literally dozens of specific support people—all at exactly the right moment. I was somehow led to be in the right place at the right moment to hear life-changing messages from amazing men of God: John Hagee at a Fourth of July camp meeting we decided to attend at the last minute; an impromptu visit to hear Dr. Creflo Dollar, who pastors World Changers Church International, as we were driving through Atlanta; hearing guest speaker John Bevere one evening at Cornerstone Church; finding books that affirmed everything God was saying to me as I peeled off all my outer layers: John Eldredge's *Wild at Heart*; John Hagee's *The Seven Secrets*; R. T. Kendall's *Total Forgiveness*; Cloud's and Townsend's *God Will Make a Way* (all great reads, by the way).

Did all of this happen by chance? Did I turn fifty, and suddenly everything clicked? Not by a long shot. I knew there had to be a bigger answer out there. As we began giving ZOE 8 seminars, I began to focus on the "why now" question. While we were talking about it one day, Elisa said to me, "God's time is all the time. He is always ready; we aren't."

It took a while for me to process what she was saying, but Elisa's comment evolved to a belief that crystallized one day listening to Dr. Creflo Dollar. "We must initiate our blessings," he said. As Creflo spoke, I realized that Elisa was right: God's time is all the time. He sits painstakingly on the sidelines, heart breaking, as he waits upon his children to seek the blessings that are ours for the asking. Just as we cannot live our children's lives, our heavenly Father allows his children to find their own way.

So how did I "initiate my blessings"? It is clear and simple in hindsight. First, in total desperation I decided to address my weight one last time. But this time, as I told my wife and pastor before I set out, I knew the answer was not with any weight-loss clinic, any doctor, or any so-called formula. I was going away to primarily isolate myself from everything in order to seek God. So, first I turned it over to him—not just in prayer, but in action.

Second, when God opened a door through Chris Hagee, and Diana Hagee made a call to Mary Colbert, who made an opening for Don to see me, I said yes. I walked through that door without fear or hesitation. My "miracle" happened when I walked off the porch of the Kendall Inn in Boerne, Texas, said good-bye to my wife and kids, got in my car, and headed out on I-10 toward my future. I initiated my blessing by taking that action.

INITIATE YOUR BLESSING

Similarly, *you* must initiate *your* blessing by doing something. You have begun your future by reading this book, and I believe that is no accident. For whatever reason, you chose to pick up this book and have thus initiated something for yourself or a loved one. Congratulations!

So back to motivation. Where do you get it? It is simple; refer back to the *how* at the beginning of this chapter. "All you need is love." If you don't love yourself enough to enter into your zoe life, then do it for those I call the innocents—you know, the ones who are guilty of loving you, who suffer emotionally by watching you engage in behaviors, actions, or attitudes that rob you—and them—of the full potential of your life.

This isn't about weight or pounds or people with "weight" problems. This applies to smokers and compulsive over-trainers and workaholics and people who just aren't happy. It applies to people who aren't in love with themselves or God or anyone else enough to initiate their own blessings. This message—this zoe life—is for everyone.

While conducting interviews for this book, we stumbled upon a truly remarkable insight into the "why now" question. Connie Reece, our writer, noted during hours of interviews that I had indicated my distress over the fact that due to a complex business situation—the only venture we had ever participated in that was a potential disaster of major proportions—coupled with my inability to get adequate life insurance, I was haunted by the thought that if I died, my legacy to Elisa and the children would be financial ruin. They would not be able to deal with the potential economic catastrophe I had gotten us into. I believed deep inside that I had robbed this incredibly wonderful woman of the marriage and the life she deserved. I had humiliated my kids in front of their friends by my size, and I had frequently allowed myself to put work and business ahead of them. I really, really wanted to leave the world of pain in which I was living, but not if it meant further depriving my family.

So if I had a compelling motivation, it was the love of my family and perhaps some remnant of pride or self-dignity, yet it was pretty much at a subconscious level. The simple truth is that I finally got to the point where God was the only way, and I had just enough faith in God to let him take me where I am today.

We have covered a tremendous amount of information in this book. There is a lot of truth for you to chew on and digest. So take your time; remember that love is patient and that getting healthy is a labor of love. And yes, others—including us at ZOE 8—can help, but the truth of the matter is that only you can do it. In fact, as God did for me, when you seek him and his abundant life on your own behalf, he will bring into your life every person, strategy, and resource you need.

BREAK ON THROUGH TO THE OTHER SIDE

What is your "it"? You know, the thing you absolutely fear and dread, the thing you feel most uncomfortable about? When you not only face your "it," but also plow right through it, you open the door into the realm of your greatest promise, your greatest joy, your greatest peace. You will initiate a season of blessing and favor that will usher in abundant life—a life that exceeds your desires, even your imagination.

For Christ that "it" was the cross, which was just three days from heaven and his eternal rule at the right hand of God. For the ancient Hebrews "it" was disobedience and lack of faith that kept them wandering forty years in the wilderness, just one day from the Promised Land. For me "it" was rejection—the fear of losing my wife and the destruction of a family—and a replay of my past and all that came with it.

Again, what is your "it"? Come on over to the other side. Your "it" is a lie, a device of our eternal enemy to keep you from a heaven on earth of blessings and abundant life. Come on over to the other side. Live a life not of promise, but of prosperity. Not of potential, but of power. Live your life, not a lie. Come on over to the other side!

We all need to "break on through to the other side," in the words of Jim Morrison of the Doors (not exactly an exemplary figure, but the music and culture of the 1960s is obviously part of my heritage).

How do you break through? When most churches preach the message of the cross of Christ, they focus on the why and how of the cross. Are they wrong? Absolutely not. But we shouldn't focus on the cross to the point that we forget about the resurrection. Jesus did not stay on the cross, and the grave could not hold him. He was resurrected to new life—the same new life that can be ours now and forevermore!

That is what ZOE 8 is all about—breaking through your "it" and getting beyond the past and into your future. It is about living again, living fully, living abundantly. Remember what I said about the number eight back at the very beginning? Eight is the number that represents new beginnings, new growth, new life. It is the number of resurrection. Now, you have to go through the cross (your "it") in order to get to the resurrection (your zoe life).

How can you know you are ready to break on through to the other side? Love and peace. As I said earlier, God is love. And perfect love, according to the Bible, drives out fear (1 John 4:18) and results in perfect peace (Isaiah 26:3).

So, take your "peace and love" temperature (told you I was a child of the sixties). See if you are too hot or cold. When you are "observing to do all things," when you are in healthy, safe relationships, you will register 98.6 on the peace and love thermometer. And if you get a little too hot or cold from time to time, it is no big deal. Go back to step one, or follow my wife's scientific approach to curing what ailed her when learning to eat the right things: ask God. Offer a sincere prayer to our heavenly Father asking him to show you any areas you can fine-tune. And listen—because you will get an answer.

Why don't we try it now? Say this with me:

Father God, I thank you for the cross and the victory of the resurrection. I want to break on through to the other side and abide with you in peace, joy, and prosperity. I want to be passionately in love with myself and my life. I want to have fun. Please show me— gently, lovingly, and clearly—any thought, behavior, or circumstance of mine that blocks my way to the other side. I want to experience abundant life here and now—not someday, but today. Thank you, heavenly Father.

OK now, let's have some fun and enjoy life. There's a little—no, even a lot of "heaven on earth" available for us, and it is available here and now. It is zoe life—the life God desires for you—the life you deserve and desire for yourself and your loved ones.

See you on the other side!

The Eight Steps of the ZOE 8 Weight Management Program

HOW do you put the wealth of information presented in this book into an action plan? Here are the eight steps of the ZOE 8 Weight Management Program as we present them in our seminars. Reading through the steps below will help refresh your memory of the principles you have learned.

STEP 1: WHERE ARE YOU NOW?

If you don't know where you are, how can you know where you are going?

You must determine your starting point not just from a physical standpoint, but from a spiritual and emotional standpoint as well. We recommend taking a complete inventory of the following:

Spiritual inventory

- What is your belief regarding the existence and nature of God?
- What have you discovered about your purpose in life?
- What are your beliefs concerning God's design for your health?
- Have you ever considered your health or weight a spiritual issue?
- What social interactions have you had of a spiritual nature (church, synagogue, mosque, twelve-step or other support group, fellowship, etc.)?

Emotional inventory

- Why have you not found a solution to your weight or health problems before now?
- What has been your greatest obstacle: lack of information or lack of motivation?
- What unresolved issues from your past still trouble you today?
- How are these issues related to your weight or health problems?
- What is your level of contentment?
- How would you describe your outlook on life?
- How often do you feel overwhelmed? What do you do about these feelings?
- What is missing in your life?

Physical inventory

- Describe any conditions you have that require medical treatment.
- Locate any records you have relating to your blood pressure and any lab work such as cholesterol and triglycerides, glucose or blood sugar, etc.
- List any minor health problems, including aches and pains you just put up with.
- List any prescription medications and nutritional supplements you take.
- What is your family history of disease?
- What surgeries have you had? When? What impact did the surgery have on your health or weight management?

STEP 2: WHERE ARE YOU GOING?

If you don't know where you are going, how will you be able to get there?

Spiritual goals

- What are your specific goals regarding your spiritual life?

- Have you discovered your purpose in life?
- What are you doing to fulfill that purpose?
- What inspirational books have you read lately? Make a list of books you plan to read.

Emotional goals

- What are your goals for achieving contentment in life?
- What issues from your past do you want to resolve, and what would that resolution entail?
- What negative behaviors would you like to replace with positive ones?
- What attitudes do you need to change?
- What are your goals for personal relationships?
- Describe how you would feel in your vision of zoe, life to the fullest.

Physical goals

- Define at least ten specific goals that address your weight and health issues.
- What can you not do now, because of your health or weight, that you would like to do in the future?

STEP 3: IDENTIFY YOUR ROADBLOCKS

Roadblocks are a source of frustration, but once identified they are a source of hope.

The eight most common roadblocks are the following:

- Prescription medications
- Stress
- Hormones
- Lack of sleep
- Food sensitivities and intolerances
- Candida
- Sabotage
- Compartmentalization

STEP 4: SET OUT ON YOUR JOURNEY

The ZOE 8 philosophy: Eat your food in the form God made it.

Review the Body Balance Food Chart and the dos and don'ts. Remember the "good, better, best" rule. Always choose the highest-quality, naturally healthy, whole foods available; use organic when possible. Always read food labels—become a grocery store detective.

- Phase 1—three weeks
- Phase 2—until weight and/or health conditions are stabilized
- Sustainable Phase—the rest of your life

STEP 5: CHECK YOUR TOOLBOX

Your ZOE 8 toolbox—don't leave home without it.

- Daily journal
- Volumetrics
- Hydration
- The power of prayer
- The power of positive words and positive relationships
- Nutritional supplements

STEP 6: GET UP AND GET MOVING

Start where you are, and increase activity gradually.

- Get moving spiritually through forgiveness.
- Get moving emotionally by moving beyond the past: "Let your past be your past at last."
- Get moving physically with ZOE Activity: 8 Steps to Get You Moving!

Work on all three types of fitness.

- *Structural fitness*: flexibility, mobility, and stability—do simple stretching exercises, or for more advanced structural fitness, do tai chi, yoga, or Pilates.
- *Cardiovascular fitness*: aerobic exercise; for fat-burning, lower intensity for longer intervals; for cardio, higher intensity for shorter intervals.

- *Muscular fitness*: weight training or resistance training with free weights, machines, or resistance bands; free weights provide the best full-body workout.

STEP 7: FINE-TUNE YOUR PROGRAM

For maximum performance, don't neglect regular tune-ups.

- Check your commitment level.
- Check your expectation level.
- Review your goals: are they realistic?
- Check your food journal for clues.
- Are you sleeping enough?
- Are you managing stress?
- Have you been tested for food sensitivities?
- Have you had a comprehensive physical exam?
- Are you eating enough?
- What is your average caloric intake?
- Are you drinking enough water?
- Are you getting too much salt or sugar?
- Have you increased your activity level?
- Have you increased the number of steps you take each day?
- Are you reading food labels and watching for hidden ingredients?
- How balanced is your diet?
- Are you eating enough low-glycemic foods?
- Are you taking a daily multivitamin and appropriate supplements?
- Are you on prescription medications that interfere with weight loss?
- Are your clothes fitting better?
- Are you feeling better?
- Do you have more energy?
- How has your overall health improved?

STEP 8: DISCOVER *ZOE*—GOD'S LIFE

Zoe is the life you were meant to live. Zoe is the life
you deserve to live.

Nourish your spirit the same way you nourish your body each day.

- How do you feed your spirit each day?
- Have you developed an attitude of gratitude for God's blessings in your life? List some of them.
- The essential nature of God is love. How loving are you by nature?

See yourself as you really are.

- How have you changed the way you see yourself since starting ZOE 8?
- Rely on loved ones for a true view of yourself.
- Don't measure your worth by a number on the scale.
- Remember that you are a whole person—spirit, mind, and body—with unique gifts and talents as well as a unique purpose.

Take your "peace and love" temperature.

- Move past your "it" and cross over to the other side.
- Ask your heavenly Father for assistance.
- Enjoy your zoe life, and don't forget to have fun!

BODY BALANCE FOODS

Phase 1 foods are shaded in gray

EAT A VARIETY, EAT LEAN, AND WATCH PORTIONS AND ENERGY DENSITY			EAT FREELY, EAT A VARIETY, EAT COLORFULLY, DON'T OVERCOOK, ALL LOW ENERGY DENSITY			EAT WITH OTHER FOODS, WATCH PORTIONS & ENERGY DENSITY, EAT A VARIETY					EAT WHOLE OR WITH OTHER FOODS, EAT A VARIETY, EAT SEASONALLY		
PROTEINS 1 oz or noted	**Cal per** oz	**ED per** oz	**VEGGIE CARBS** 1 oz or noted	**Cal** per oz	**Fiber** grams per oz	**GI low-high**	**STARCH CARBS** 1 oz or noted	**Cal per** oz	**Fiber** grams per oz	**ED per** oz	**GI low-high**	**FRUIT CARBS** 1 each or 1C=cup or noted	**Cal**	**Fiber** 1 avg size
Anchovy	9	0.32	Acorn Squash	10	0.32	24	Black Beans	37	0.57	1.32	5	Blackberries 1C	74	5.90
Beef	69	2.46	Artichokes	12	0.25	25	Garbanzos	46	0.70	1.64	5	Blueberries 1C	82	1.90
Bluefish	35	1.25	Asparagus	7	0.23	26	Soy Beans	49	0.57	1.75	5	Boysenberries 1C	66	3.60
Chicken	65	2.32	Bamboo Shoots	5	0.19	27	Great Northerns	28	0.94	1.00	5	Cranberries 1C	46	1.10
Clams	42	1.50	Bean Sprouts	8.6	0.22	28	Kidney Beans	23	0.27	0.82	5	Lemon	17	0.00
Cod	30	1.07	Bell Peppers (all)	7	0.33	30	Lentils	32	1.00	1.14	5	Limes	20	0.00
Crab	24	0.85	Bok Choy	3	0.41	32	Lima Beans	35	1.00	1.25	5	Mulberries 1C	61	1.30
Crayfish	30	1.07	Broccoli	8	0.28	38	Navy Beans	32	0.52	1.14	5	Raspberries 1C	61	3.70
Eggs 1 lg	79	2.82	Brussels Sprouts	10	0.39	39	Pinto Beans	22	0.35	0.78	18	Apricot dried 10	83	1.03
Flounder	58	2.07	Butternut Squash	11	0.35	45	Buckwheat	96	0.28	3.42	22	Cherries 1C	104	0.58
Grouper	33	1.17	Cabbages (all)	6	0.22	46	Split Peas	32	0.54	1.14	24	Plums	36	0.40
Haddock	32	1.14	Cauliflower	7	0.45	46	Tapioca (dry)	98	0.02	3.50	25	Grapefruit 1/2	38	0.24
Halibut	40	1.42	Celery	4	0.19	47	Carrots	12	0.29	0.42	29	Prunes each	20	0.17
Lamb	73	2.60	Chili Peppers (all avg)	11	0.50	48	Green Peas	23	0.66	0.82	31	Pomegranate	104	0.31
Lobster	28	1.00	Chives	2	0.01	50	Tortillas, Spelt (G)	10	0.84	0.35	38	Apple	81	1.06
Mussels	50	1.78	Cucumber	3	0.17	54	Black eyed Peas	27	1.40	0.96	38	Persimmon	118	2.50
Oysters	10	0.35	Eggplant	6	0.28	55	Brown Rices	31	0.08	1.10	40	Strawberries	45	0.79
Pork	65	2.32	Garlic	1	0.01	57	Wild Rice	29	0.09	1.03	41	Pears	98	2.30
Salmon	61	2.17	Sweet Beans	10	0.95	59	Sweet Potato	29	0.22	1.03	42	Nectarines	67	0.54
Sardines	25	0.89	Greens (all avg)	8	0.27	63	Spelt flour (G)	100	3.20	3.57	42	Oranges	62	0.56
Scallops	25	0.89	Kale	9	0.22	64	Beets	9	0.23	0.32	42	Peaches	37	0.56
Sea Bass	30	1.07	Kohlrabi	8	0.30	66	Oatmeal dry (G)	107	1.90	3.82	42	Tangerines	37	0.28
Shrimp	28	1.00	Leeks	17	0.32	68	Rice Crackers	120	2.00	4.28	46	Grapes 1C	102	0.70
Smelts	24	0.85	Lettuces (all avg)	4	0.20	68	Rice Pasta	33	0.44	1.17	50	Dates (3)	69	0.35
Snapper	36	1.28	Okra	9	0.25	71	Millet	91	0.89	3.25	51	Mangos	135	1.70
Sole	20	0.71	Onions (all avg)	8	0.11	75	Breads 1 slice avg	80	0.56	2.85	52	Banana	105	0.57
Swordfish	44	1.57	Radishes	4	0.15	75	Pumpkin	9	1.25	0.32	53	Kiwi	46	0.84
Tofu	33	1.17	Scallions	7	0.23	97	Parsnips	22	0.61	0.78	56	Currents 1/2 C	204	1.10
Trout	43	1.53	Sea Veggies (all avg)	10	0.00	n/a	Amaranth flour	102	0.28	3.64	56	Raisins 1/2 C	244	1.05
Tuna	52	1.85	Snow Peas	4	0.90	n/a	Bean flours	107	2.44	3.82	58	Apricot fresh 3	51	0.64
Turkey	54	1.92	Spaghetti Squash	9	0.40	n/a	Chickpea flour	103	1.35	3.67	59	Papaya	117	2.04
			Spinach	11	1.32	n/a	Quinoa	104	1.65	3.71	59	Pineapple	77	0.84
			Swiss Chard	6	0.25	n/a	Rice flour	104	1.60	3.71	61	Figs (3)	141	2.31
			Tomatoes	24	0.57	n/a	Soy Flour	121	4.87	4.32	65	Melons 4 oz	57	0.50
			Water Chestnuts	14	0.14	n/a	Turnips	28	0.19	1.00	73	Watermelon 1C	50	0.48
			Yellow Beans	8	0.95	n/a	Arrowroot flour	100	0.95	3.57				
			Yellow Squash	5.6	0.31									
			Zucchini	4	0.12									

BODY BALANCE FOODS (continued)

Phase 1 foods are shaded in gray

GOOD FATS ARE ESSENTIAL, EAT & USE A VARIETY, WATCH PORTIONS				CHOOSE UNSWEETENED, USE WITH OTHER FOODS			READ LABELS FOR INGREDIENTS AND CALORIES	

FATS 1 Oz / Tbls (oils)	Type Fat	Cal per oz	Fiber grams per oz	"DAIRY"	GI	Cal per oz	CONDIMENTS 1 Tbls	Cal per Tbls
Almond Butter	M	176	0.42	Almond Milk		10	Apple Cider Vinegar	0
Almonds	M	167	1.40	Feta Cheese		39	Braggs Aminos	0
Avocado	M	29	1.90	Goats Milk		30	Herbs, all	0
Avocado Oil Tbls	M	120	0	Kefir, unsweet		45	Horseradish	0
Brazil Nuts	P/M	186	0.65	Live Yogurt	36	30	Hot Sauces	10
Butter	S	108	0	Parmesan		79	Miso	0
Coconut	S	99	7.00	Rice Milk		20	Salsa	10
Coconut Milk	S	65	0	Ricotta		28	Spices, all	0
Coconut Oil Tbls	S	120	0	Romano		30	Unsweet Ketchup	5
Flax Oil Tbls	P	120	0	Soy Milk	44	12	Whole Grain Mustard	0
Flaxseeds Tbls	P	48	2.70					
Grapeseed Oil Tbls	P	120	0	Real dairy is not what it used				
Hazelnuts	M	179	1.10	to be, if tolerated choose				
Hickory Nuts	M	190	1.79	organic, no hormone, raw			Beverages	
Macademia Nut Oil Tbls	M	120	0	if possible			Herb Teas	0
Macademia Nuts	M	199	1.50				Natural Lemonade	0
Extra Virgin Olive Oil Tbls	M	120	0				Natural Limeade	0
Olives	M	25	0.70				WATER	0
Pecans	M	190	0.45				There is no substitute	
Pine Nuts	P/M	146	0.31				for water, drink generously	
Pumpkin Seed Oil Tbls	P	120	0				Choose water first	
Pumpkin Seeds	P	154	0.63					
Safflower Oil Tbls	P	120	0					
Sesame Oil Tbls	P/M	120	0	Sweetners			NOTES:	
Sesame Seeds	P/M	161	1.40	Agave tbls	11	60	Phase 1 Foods	
Soy Nuts	S	129	0	Stevia	0	0	GI= Glycemic Index	
Spanish Peanuts	M	162	0	Xylitol tbls	8	58	Low less than 56	
Sunflower Seeds	P	162	1.20				Medium 56- 69	
Valencia Peanuts	M	160	0.90	Stevia is your best choice			High more than 69	
Vegenaise	M	180	0	Use others sparingly			G= Contains Gluten	
Walnut Oil Tbls	P	120	0				Fiber RDA = 25 g or more	
Walnuts	P	182	1.30				28 Grams = 1 oz.	

P = polyunsaturated
S = saturated
M = monounsaturated
Read label on nut butters, no sugar
no additives, no hydrogenated

ED= Energy Density
The lower the density the better
ED= Calories divided by gram weight
Low .05-1.59
Medium 1.60-4.09
High 4.10 - 10

Seven-Day Meal Plan With Recipes

THE following recipes and menu suggestions are from our *Responsible Cuisine Cookbook.* The menus are merely suggestions to give you ideas for creating healthy, appetizing, and delicious recipes and menus for you and your family. The menu items presented here are a mixture of selections from Phase 1, Phase 2, and the Sustainable Phase. (Be careful during Phase 1; give your body the time it needs to balance itself.) We have omitted desserts in these recipes, although we eat many delicious desserts during Phase 2 and the Sustainable Phase. Some of these recipes, which feature berries, green apples, nuts, spices, ice cream made with coconut milk, and even chocolate, are available through our Web site, www.zoe8.com.

SEVEN-DAY MEAL PLAN	
Day 1	
Breakfast	Poached Eggs, Pico de Gallo, Quick Guacamole
Lunch	Hamburgers, Quinoa Tabouli
Dinner	Incredible Summer Slaw, Shrimp and Chicken Jambalaya
Day 2	
Breakfast	Hot and Creamy Quinoa Cereal, Cinnamon Butter, Spelt or Millet Toast
Lunch	Grilled Chicken Fajitas, Sautéed Onions and Peppers, Avocado Salad
Dinner	Garbanzo Bean Salad, Seafood Cioppino, Garlic Bread

SEVEN-DAY MEAL PLAN	
Day 3	
Breakfast	Machacado Breakfast Tacos
Lunch	Summer Garden Salad, Sun-Dried Tomato and Tuna Pasta
Dinner	Roasted Herb Chicken, Bombay Basmati Rice, Sautéed Baby Spinach
Day 4	
Breakfast	Frittata Primavera
Lunch	Cajun Chicken Breast, Whipped Butternut Squash, Cajun Rice
Dinner	Field Greens Salad, Lemon Grape Seed Oil Dressing, Mediterranean Pasta, Broccoli Italian Style
Day 5	
Breakfast	Scrambled Eggs Fiesta, Hacienda Pinto Beans
Lunch	Grilled Shrimp Salad, Sesame Ginger Dressing
Dinner	Minestrone, Broiled Sirloin with Tomato and Breadcrumb Crust, Braised Cabbage and Peas
Day 6	
Breakfast	Sunrise Chicken Breast Chimichurri
Lunch	Salad Niçoise, Garlic Herb Dressing
Dinner	Shepherd's Pie, Green Beans Palermo
Day 7	
Breakfast	French Toast, Mixed Berry Compote
Lunch	Broiled Salmon Steak, Pecan Quinoa, Tomato Cucumber Relish
Dinner	Zucchini Carpacio, Braised Beef, Brown Rice Risotto
Bonus Recipes	
Soups	Gazpacho, Vegetarian Chili, Roasted Eggplant and Tomato Soup, Lentil Soup and Meatballs
Salads	Crispy Calamari Salad
Snacks	Cajun Nut Mix, Hummus

Day 1

Poached Eggs
Phase 1, 2, and Sustainable
Serves 4

2 cups water (approx. amount needed to
  make 2 inches of water in skillet)
1 tsp. apple cider vinegar*
¼ tsp. salt
4 large eggs

Pour 2 inches of water in a medium nonstick skillet and bring to a boil. Reduce heat and simmer. Add vinegar and salt to the simmering water. Crack eggs one at a time into a shallow dish and slide each whole egg into the simmering water. Do not overcrowd the pan or allow the eggs to touch. Simmer eggs for 4–5 minutes until yolks are cooked and whites are firm. Remove eggs with a slotted spoon, drain, and place on serving plates.

Tip: Serve with 2 slices of buttered spelt or millet toast.

*See our list of recommended resources for purchasing ZOE 8–compliant foods (page 219).

7-oz. serving (including toast): 390 calories, 19 g total fat (6 g sat. fat), 565 mg cholesterol, 300 mg sodium, 32 g carbohydrate (4 g fiber, 2 g sugar), 20 g protein

Pico de Gallo
Phase 1, 2, and Sustainable
Makes 3½ cups

2½ cups fresh tomatoes, diced
1 cup onion, diced
½ cup cilantro, chopped
½ cup Serrano peppers, minced
Pinch of sea salt
Squeeze of lemon juice (eliminate for Phase 1)

Mix all ingredients in a bowl. Chill and serve as a condiment with eggs.

Tip: You can also serve pico de gallo with beans or fajitas. (See Day 2 lunch.)

3-oz. serving: 20 calories, 0 total fat (0 sat. fat), 0 cholesterol, 5 mg sodium, 5 g carbohydrate (1 g fiber, 3 g sugar), 1 g protein

Quick Guacamole
Phase 1, 2, and Sustainable
Serves 8

16 oz. Hass avocado halves (about 4 avocados)
8 oz. red salsa*
Sea salt

Crush avocados to desired consistency. Add salsa and mix. (Can pulse in food processor if desired.) Add sea salt to taste. (Add lemon juice in Phase 2 if desired.)

*See our list of recommended resources for purchasing ZOE 8–compliant foods (page 219).

4½-oz. serving: 170 calories, 15 g total fat (3 g sat fat), 0 cholesterol, 120 mg sodium, 9 g carbohydrate (5 g fiber, 2 g sugar), 2 g protein

LUNCH

Hamburgers
Phase 1, 2, and Sustainable
Serves 4

1¼ lbs. lean ground sirloin
1 tsp. cracked black pepper
1 tsp. dry mustard
1 tsp. unsweetened ketchup*
Millet hamburger buns (buttered and grilled, broiled, or toasted)

Optional Toppings

Sliced tomato
Sliced onion
Lettuce
Pico de gallo
Guacamole
Pepper rings
Green grilled onions
Salsa
Vegenaise* (eliminate for Phase 1)

Mix hamburger ingredients together and divide into four 5-oz. patties. Heat broiler and place burgers 4 inches from broiler. Broil burgers until desired doneness. Approximate cooking times: 6 minutes for rare, 8 minutes for medium rare, 10 minutes for well done. Turn burgers halfway through the cooking process. (The same process can be followed if you choose to grill or panfry your burgers.) Place on sliced buns and add your choice of toppings.

See our list of recommended resources for purchasing ZOE 8–compliant foods (page 219).

5-oz. serving (without toppings): 370 calories, 7 g total fat (5 g sat fat), 75 mg cholesterol, 270 mg sodium, 40 g carbohydrate (5 g fiber, 0 sugar), protein 34 g

Quinoa Tabouli
Phase 1, 2, and Sustainable
Serves 4

1½ cups quinoa
2 medium-sized cucumbers, peeled, seeded, and diced
½ cup fresh parsley, chopped
2 Tbsp. fresh lemon juice (eliminate for Phase 1)
1 tsp. fresh garlic, minced
1 Tbsp. olive oil
Sea salt and pepper to taste

Cook quinoa according to package directions. Let cool, and place in large bowl. Add remaining ingredients, mix thoroughly, and chill.

4½-oz. serving: 280 calories, 7 g total fat (1 g sat fat), 0 cholesterol, 20 mg sodium, 47 g carbohydrate (4 g fiber, 0 sugar), 9 g protein

DINNER

Incredible Summer Slaw
Phase 2 and Sustainable
Serves 8

2 cups radicchio, shredded
1½ cups endive, sliced
2 cups fresh tomato, chopped
1 lb. fresh peas
1 small yellow banana chili pepper
¼ cup fresh cilantro, chopped
1 small cucumber, chopped
½ cup black olives, sliced
⅛ tsp. sea salt
½ tsp. cracked black pepper
2 cloves garlic, minced
¼ tsp. oregano
3 Tbsp. grape seed oil
3 Tbsp. olive oil
2 Tbsp. fresh lemon juice

1 Tbsp. apple cider vinegar*

Toss all ingredients in a large bowl and serve.

*See our list of recommended resources for purchasing ZOE 8–compliant foods (page 219).

6-oz. serving: 180 calories, 13 g total fat (2 g sat fat), 0 cholesterol, 190 mg sodium, 13 g carbohydrate (4 g fiber, 5 g sugar), 4 g protein

Shrimp and Chicken Jambalaya
Phase 1, 2, and Sustainable
Serves 6

1¼ lb. chicken breast, cubed
1¼ lb. shrimp, peeled and deveined*
3 Tbsp. butter
Sea salt and pepper to taste
2 Tbsp. olive oil
4 cloves garlic, chopped
⅓ cup green onion, chopped
⅓ cup red onion, diced
⅓ cup each of yellow, red, and green bell pepper, diced
¼ cup celery, diced
¼ cup fresh parsley, chopped
¼ tsp. thyme
2 cups short-grain brown rice
4¾ cups chicken stock
1¾ Tbsp. Cajun spice mix (read label)

Sauté chicken and shrimp in butter over medium heat, adding salt and pepper to taste. Remove chicken and shrimp from heat; set aside in bowl. In same pan, heat olive oil, garlic, and vegetables. Sauté until vegetables are translucent. Add rice and continue to sauté for 5 minutes. Add chicken stock and Cajun spice and cook until rice is tender. Add chicken and shrimp and toss, adding water if mixture is too dry. Serve in large bowls.

* If you have food sensitivities to seafood, use 2½ lbs. of chicken and eliminate the shrimp.

12-oz. serving: 480 calories, 19 g total fat (8 g sat fat), 170 mg cholesterol, 450 mg sodium, 40 g carbohydrate (5 g fiber, 1 g sugar), 35 g protein

Day 2

Hot and Creamy Quinoa Cereal
Phase 1, 2, and Sustainable
Serves 1

⅔ cup quinoa*
½ tsp. butter
Unsweetened soy milk*
1 tsp. pecans, chopped
¹⁄₁₆ tsp. stevia (if extra sweetness is desired)

Cook quinoa according to package directions. Add remaining ingredients and serve.

See our list of recommended resources for purchasing ZOE 8–compliant foods (page 219).

5½-oz. serving: 120 calories, 8 g total fat (3 g sat fat), 10 mg cholesterol, 20 mg sodium, 10 g carbohydrate (1 g fiber, 1 g sugar), 3 g protein

Cinnamon Butter
Phase 1, 2, and Sustainable
Makes 1/2 cup

1 stick unsalted butter, softened
½ tsp. cinnamon
¾ Tbsp. agave nectar* (eliminate for Phase 1)

Bring butter to room temperature and mix in cinnamon and agave. Place in glass container and refrigerate.

Tip: Cinnamon butter is a great addition to your breakfast choices and can be stored as you would regular butter.

See our list of recommended resources for purchasing ZOE 8–compliant foods (page 219).

1-oz. serving: 180 calories, 19 g total fat (12 g sat fat), 50 mg cholesterol, 0 sodium, 0 carbohydrate (0 fiber, 3g sugar), 0 protein

Spelt or Millet Toast
Phase 1, 2, and Sustainable
Serves 1

2 slices spelt or millet bread,* toasted
2 Tbsp. cinnamon butter (recipe above)

Toast bread and spread with cinnamon butter.

Tip: Almond butter* also tastes delicious with these breakfast menu items.

See our list of recommended resources for purchasing ZOE 8–compliant foods (page 219).

2 slices: 250 calories, 2 g total fat (0 sat fat), 0 cholesterol, 250 mg sodium, 38 g carbohydrate (4 g fiber, 0 sugar), 6 g protein

LUNCH

Grilled Chicken Fajitas
Phase 1, 2, and Sustainable
Serves 4

2 lbs. boneless skinless chicken breasts and thighs
2 Tbsp. olive oil
1 tsp. granulated garlic
½ tsp. sea salt
1 tsp. cracked black pepper
1 tsp. cumin powder
Spelt tortillas

Cut chicken into strips; place in bowl and add olive oil, garlic, sea salt, black pepper, and cumin powder. Marinate for 30 minutes. Heat broiler and place chicken 4 inches from broiler and cook for 15 minutes, turning as necessary. Serve on warmed spelt tortillas. Top with pico de gallo, guacamole (recipes under Day 1 breakfast), and sautéed onions and peppers (recipe below).

8-oz. serving (with 1 tortilla but no toppings): 440 calories, 15 g total fat (3 g sat fat), 160 mg cholesterol, 560 mg sodium, 22 g carbohydrate (1g fiber, 1g sugar), 53 g protein

Sautéed Onions and Peppers
Phase 1, 2, and Sustainable
Serves 6

1 Tbsp. olive oil
4 cloves garlic, chopped
2 large onions, sliced
1 tsp. cracked black pepper
2 large red, yellow, orange, or green bell peppers, sliced

In medium skillet, heat olive oil. Add chopped garlic and sauté lightly to release flavor. Add sliced onions, cracked black pepper, and bell peppers; sauté over medium heat until cooked.

4-oz. serving: 60 calories, 3 g total fat (0 sat fat), 0 cholesterol, 0 mg sodium, 9 g carbohydrate (2 g fiber, 4 g sugar), 1 g protein

Avocado Salad
Phase 1, 2, and Sustainable
Serves 4

2 large heads Bibb lettuce
3 large avocados, crushed
3 cups Tomato-Cucumber Relish (recipe under Day 7 lunch)
Garlic Herb Dressing (recipe under Day 6 lunch)
½ cup pepitas (pumpkinseeds), toasted

Wash and arrange lettuce leaves; top with avocados and relish. Drizzle with dressing and sprinkle with toasted pepitas.

8-oz. serving: 270 calories, 23 g total fat (4 g sat fat), 0 cholesterol, 125 mg sodium, 13 g carbohydrate (7 g fiber, 3 g sugar), 8 g protein

DINNER

Garbanzo Bean Salad
Phase 1, 2, and Sustainable
Serves 6

15-oz. can garbanzo beans, drained and rinsed (read label)
1 cup cucumber, chopped
¼ cup onion, chopped
¼ cup tomato, chopped
¼ cup red bell pepper, chopped
1 Tbsp. parsley, chopped
½ cup olive oil
¼ tsp. cracked black pepper
¼ tsp. oregano
Sea salt to taste

Mix all ingredients; toss, chill, and serve.

4½-oz. serving: 250 calories, 19 g total fat (3 g sat fat), 0 cholesterol, 210 mg sodium, 18 g carbohydrate (4 g fiber, 4 g sugar), 4 g protein

Seafood Cioppino
Phase 1, 2, and Sustainable
Serves 6

4 Tbsp. olive oil
4 cups onions, diced
⅓ cup fresh garlic, chopped
1½ cups chicken stock
1½ tsp. oregano

2 cups fresh tomatoes, chopped
1 bay leaf
½ tsp. thyme
1 tsp. cracked black pepper
4 Tbsp. fresh basil, chopped
1 Tbsp. fresh parsley, chopped
Pinch of saffron
½ tsp. dried basil
4 Tbsp. tomato paste
½ tsp. crushed red pepper
1 cup clam juice*
56 oz. canned whole tomatoes (read label), chopped
2 tsp. oyster liquid*
8-oz. can whole baby clams*
¾ lb. mixed fish and shellfish, including oysters*

Heat olive oil in stockpot, adding onions and garlic and sautéing lightly. Add chicken stock and simmer for 10 minutes. Add all other ingredients except seafood and simmer for 20 minutes. Add seafood just before serving; heat through.

Tip: This recipe freezes well. It also can be made in a Crock-Pot; just add the clams and fish about 20 minutes before serving as fish doesn't take long to cook.

*If you have food sensitivities to seafood, substitute chicken, beef, or pork.

8-oz. serving: 80 calories, 3 g total fat (0 sat fat), 15 g cholesterol, 300 mg sodium, 9 g carbohydrate (1 g fiber, 4 g sugar), 4 g protein

Garlic Bread
Phase 2 and Sustainable
Serves 8

¼ tsp. granulated garlic
¼ tsp. cracked black pepper
¼ tsp. oregano
¼ tsp. crushed red pepper
16 slices spelt sourdough bread,* thinly sliced (¼-inch thick)
½ tsp. extra-virgin olive oil

Mix garlic, cracked black pepper, oregano, and crushed red pepper. Place bread slices on a baking sheet, spray with olive oil, and sprinkle with spice mixture. Place about 4 inches from broiler and broil for about 3–4 minutes until browned.

See our list of recommended resources for purchasing ZOE 8–compliant foods (page 219).

1½-oz. serving: 120 calories, 2 g total fat (0 sat fat), 0 cholesterol, 300 mg sodium, 22 g carbohydrate (1 g fiber, 1 g sugar), 4 g protein

Day 3

BREAKFAST

Machacado Breakfast Tacos
Phase 1, 2, and Sustainable
Serves 4

1 tsp. butter
½ onion, chopped
2 chili peppers, seeded and minced
1 large tomato, seeded and drained
8 large eggs, beaten
2 cups black beans
½ lb. lean shredded beef
4 spelt tortillas*
3 Tbsp. salsa

Sauté butter, onion, and peppers in skillet over medium heat until vegetables are softened. Add tomatoes and eggs; scramble until cooked. Remove from heat. In separate pan or microwave, heat black beans, and mash. Heat shredded beef, and warm tortillas according to package directions. Assemble all ingredients on the tortillas and top with salsa.

*See our list of recommended resources for purchasing ZOE 8–compliant foods (page 219).

14-oz. serving: 480 calories, 19 g total fat (6 g sat fat), 585 mg cholesterol, 380 mg sodium, 46 g carbohydrate (11 g fiber, 6 g sugar), 39 g protein

LUNCH

Summer Garden Salad
Phase 1, 2, and Sustainable
Serves 4

2 medium tomatoes
4 oz. fresh green beans
1 head endive
¾ cup radicchio, shredded
1 Tbsp. sunflower seeds

1 Tbsp. fresh garlic, minced
1 Tbsp. olive oil
Sea salt and cracked black pepper to taste
1 Tbsp. fresh herbs (parsley, chive, mint), finely minced

Steam green beans and cut into 1-inch pieces; place in large salad bowl. Chop tomatoes, quarter and slice endive, and shred radicchio; add to green beans. Add sunflower seeds, garlic, olive oil, salt and pepper. Finely mince parsley, chive, mint, or any mixture of your favorite fresh herbs and add to salad. Toss and serve.

5-oz. serving: 60 calories, 4 g total fat (0 sat fat), 0 cholesterol, 105 mg sodium, 6 g carbohydrate (4 g fiber, 2 g sugar), 2 g protein

Sun-Dried Tomato and Tuna Pasta
Phase 1, 2, and Sustainable
Serves 4

16-oz. package brown rice penne pasta*
1 Tbsp. olive oil
2 Tbsp. garlic, chopped
28-oz. can crushed tomatoes (read label; no salt added)
½ cup sun-dried tomatoes, chopped
1 Tbsp. capers (packed in oil)
1 can tuna packed in olive oil (not drained)
½ can anchovy fillets, whole
12 black olives, sliced
½ tsp. crushed red pepper
2 tsp. oregano
1 tsp. cracked black pepper
12 jumbo black olives, sliced
2 Tbsp. fresh parsley, chopped

Cook pasta according to package directions; set aside. Heat olive oil in saucepan and sauté garlic until golden brown. Add tomatoes and simmer for 5 minutes. Add capers, tuna, anchovy fillets, and spices; simmer for 20 minutes. Add black olives and chopped fresh parsley. Toss with pasta and serve.

*See our list of recommended resources for purchasing ZOE 8–compliant foods (page 219).

14-oz. serving: 540 calories, 20 g total fat (3 g sat fat), 30 mg cholesterol, 800 mg sodium,* 74 g carbohydrate (8 g fiber, 8 g sugar), 19 g protein (*To reduce sodium, look for items without added salt and items packed in water or oil, not in brine.)

Roasted Herb Chicken
Phase 1, 2, and Sustainable
Serves 6

Whole roasting chicken (3 lbs. or more)
1 Tbsp. olive oil (olive oil spray, no additives)
1 tsp. sea salt
1 Tbsp. cracked black pepper
1 Tbsp. granulated garlic
1 tsp. oregano
1 tsp. basil
1 tsp. sage
1 tsp. paprika

Preheat oven to 400 degrees.

Remove the neck and giblets, rinse chicken in cold water, and pat dry. Place the chicken on a rack in a shallow roasting pan, breast side up, and coat entire chicken with olive oil. Pat chicken with assorted spices and spray with olive oil. Roast in oven for approximately 1 hour, until the juices run clear or the internal temperature reaches 170 degrees in the thickest part of the breast. Remove chicken from oven and let sit for 10 minutes before carving.

8-oz. serving: 510 calories, 37 g total fat (10 g sat fat), 165 mg cholesterol, 470 mg sodium, 2 g carbohydrate (1 g fiber, 0 sugar), 39 g protein

Bombay Basmati Rice
Phase 1, 2, and Sustainable
Serves 12

1½ Tbsp. ghee (clarified butter)
1½ cups onion, chopped
⅛ tsp. saffron
1 tsp. garam masala (Indian spice mix)
½ tsp. cinnamon
½ tsp. ginger
1 lb. brown basmati rice
4 cups chicken broth

In a medium saucepan heat ghee and onion. When onion is clear, add spices and sauté for about 2 minutes. Add rice and coat with mixture. Add chicken broth; cover and cook for about 45 minutes, until rice is cooked.

5-oz. serving: 170 calories, 4 g total fat (2 g sat fat), 10 mg cholesterol, 190 mg sodium, 31 g carbohydrate (3 g fiber, 2 g sugar), 4 g protein

Sautéed Baby Spinach
Phase 1, 2, and Sustainable
Serves 6

1 Tbsp. fresh garlic, chopped
1 Tbsp. olive oil
32 oz. fresh baby spinach
¼ tsp. sea salt
½ tsp. cracked black pepper

Sauté garlic in olive oil in medium saucepan until golden. Reduce heat and add spinach. As spinach starts to wilt, cover pan. When wilted, stir, cover, and remove from heat. Sprinkle with salt and pepper. Serve hot, cold, or at room temperature.

5½-oz. serving: 60 calories, 3 g total fat (0 sat fat), 0 cholesterol, 280 mg sodium, 6 g carbohydrate (4 g fiber, 2 g sugar), 4 protein

Day 4

BREAKFAST

Frittata Primavera
Phase 1, 2, and Sustainable
Serves 3

¾ Tbsp. olive oil (or butter)
½ cup red bell peppers, chopped
½ cup onions, thinly sliced
½ cup zucchini, thinly sliced
½ cup tomato, chopped and drained
½ tsp. cracked black pepper
6 large eggs, beaten
1 Tbsp. fresh basil, chopped
1 Tbsp. fresh parsley, minced
Sea salt to taste

In a large nonstick skillet, heat ½ Tbsp. olive oil on medium heat; add chopped red bell peppers and sauté for two minutes. Add sliced onions and sauté for 5 minutes or until soft. Add zucchini and tomatoes and sauté 2 minutes. Add pepper, beaten eggs, basil, and parsley. Let eggs set; do not scramble. As eggs begin to set, loosen sides with a heat-resistant spatula and continue to cook on medium heat (adjust heat as necessary); cover to finish cooking the top. When top is cooked, loosen frittata, slide onto serving platter, and cut into wedged portions. Sprinkle with sea salt if desired.

4-oz. serving: 130 calories, 8 g total fat (3 g sat fat), 275 mg cholesterol, 85 mg sodium, 4 g carbohydrate (1g fiber, 2 g sugar), 9 g protein

LUNCH

Cajun Chicken Breast
Phase 1, 2, and Sustainable
Serves 6
6 boneless skinless chicken breasts (4 oz. each)
1 Tbsp. olive oil
2 Tbsp. Cajun spice mix (read label)

Coat chicken breasts with olive oil and spice mix. Place in oven and broil (about 4 inches from broiler) for 20 minutes, turning after 10 minutes. Serve with your choice of vegetables and Cajun Rice (recipe below).

Tip: You can also grill Cajun chicken according to your favorite method.

4-oz. serving: 150 calories, 4 g total fat (1 g sat fat), 70 mg cholesterol, 75 mg sodium, 0 carbohydrate (0 fiber, 0 sugar), 27 g protein

Whipped Butternut Squash
Phase 1, 2, and Sustainable
Serves 4
3 butternut squash (about 4 ½ cups)
Butter and cinnamon to taste

Cut squash in half and steam until tender. Scoop out pulp and mash. Serve with butter and a touch of cinnamon.

6-oz. serving: 100 calories, 3 g total fat (2 g sat fat), 0 cholesterol, 5 mg sodium, 18 g carbohydrate (5 g fiber, 4 g sugar), 2 g protein

Cajun Rice
Phase 1, 2, and Sustainable
Serves 10
2 Tbsp. olive oil
2 Tbsp. garlic, chopped
¼ cup celery, chopped
1 cup red, yellow, and green bell peppers, chopped

2 cups short-grain brown rice
¼ tsp. fresh thyme
½ tsp. crushed red pepper
1¾ Tbsp. Cajun seasoning mix
5 cups chicken broth*
¼ cup fresh parsley, chopped

Heat olive oil in a medium saucepan and add garlic, celery, and peppers. Sauté over medium heat until slightly cooked and soft. Add rice and thyme; continue to sauté until rice is shiny, about 4 minutes. Add red pepper, seasoning mix, and chicken broth and bring to a boil. Reduce heat, cover, and simmer for 45 minutes or until rice is cooked. Remove from heat and stir in parsley.

Tip: In addition to being served as a side dish, Cajun Rice can be added to soup or stew.

*See our list of recommended resources for purchasing ZOE 8–compliant foods (page 219).

6-oz. serving: 160 calories, 4 g total fat (0 sat fat), 0 cholesterol, 260 mg sodium, 29 g carbohydrate (2 g fiber, 1 g sugar), 4 g protein

DINNER

Field Greens Salad
Phase 1, 2, and Sustainable
Serves 4

4 oz. mixed field greens
1 avocado
1 carrot, shredded
1 fresh tomato, chopped
1 Tbsp. sunflower seeds
½ cup sunflower sprouts

Mix all ingredients in a salad bowl and toss with your choice of Lemon Grape Seed Oil Dressing (recipe below) or Garlic Herb Dressing (recipe under Day 6 lunch).

4-oz. serving (without dressing): 120 calories, 9 g total fat (2 g sat fat), 0 cholesterol, 20 mg cholesterol, 11 g carbohydrate (4 g fiber, 2 g sugar), 4 g protein

Lemon Grape Seed Oil Dressing
Phase 1, 2, and Sustainable
Makes 2 ½ cups

½ cup grape seed oil

1 cup canola oil
½ cup fresh lemon juice (eliminate in Phase 1)
1 tsp. fresh lemon peel
2 tsp. garlic, chopped
2 Tbsp. shallot, chopped
¼ tsp. white pepper
½ tsp. sea salt

Mix all ingredients in salad dressing cruet or glass measuring cup. If you prefer a creamier texture, mix ingredients in a blender or small food processor. Pour onto your favorite salad.

Tip: Store leftover dressing in refrigerator for up to 2 weeks.

1-oz. serving: 180 calories, 20 g total fat (2 g sat fat), 0 cholesterol, 30 mg sodium, 1 g carbohydrate (0 fiber, 0 sugar), 0 protein

Mediterranean Pasta
Phase 1, 2, and Sustainable
Serves 6

2 Tbsp. extra-virgin olive oil
6 garlic cloves, chopped
28-oz. can whole peeled tomatoes, chopped in food processor (or crushed tomatoes)
½ cup sun-dried tomatoes, chopped with tomatoes in food processor
½ tsp. cracked black pepper
½ cup fresh basil chopped slightly, loosely packed
¼ tsp. red pepper flakes (optional)
15-oz. can artichoke hearts, drained, quartered
15-oz. can black olives, drained, halved
¼ lb. fresh baby spinach
1 Tbsp. pine nuts
1 16-oz package brown rice penne pasta*
Grated Parmesan cheese (Sustainable Phase)

In a medium saucepan heat 1 Tbsp. olive oil; add chopped garlic and sauté lightly but do not brown. Add tomatoes and pepper, simmering for 10 minutes. Add basil, pepper flakes, artichoke hearts, olives, and spinach; simmer for 10 minutes. Add nuts and reduce heat to low. Cook pasta according to package directions and transfer to large bowls. Pour sauce over pasta and top with grated Parmesan cheese if desired.

*See our list of recommended resources for purchasing ZOE 8—compliant foods (page 219).

8-oz. serving: 230 calories, 7 g total fat (1 g sat fat), 0 cholesterol, 530 mg sodium, 41 g carbohydrate (6 g fiber, 4 g sugar), 5 g protein

Broccoli Italian Style
Phase 1, 2, and Sustainable
Serves 4

1 head broccoli
2 Tbsp. olive oil
¼ tsp. granulated garlic
¼ tsp. sea salt
¼ tsp. cracked black pepper
¼ tsp. sesame seeds

Separate broccoli florets and cut stems to about 1½ inches. Steam until cooked to desired tenderness. Remove from steamer and arrange on serving platter. While still hot, drizzle olive oil and sprinkle garlic, salt, black pepper, and sesame seeds over florets. Serve at room temperature.

6-oz. serving: 110 calories, 8 g total fat (1 g sat fat), 0 cholesterol, 100 mg sodium, 8 g carbohydrate (5 g fiber, 3 g sugar), 5 g protein

Day 5

BREAKFAST

Scrambled Eggs Fiesta
Phase 1, 2, and Sustainable
Serves 4

1 Tbsp. unsalted butter
½ cup red bell peppers, chopped
½ cup green peppers, chopped
1 Tbsp. jalapeno pepper, minced (about 1 pepper)
½ cup onion, chopped
6 large eggs
1 fresh avocado, sliced
4 Tbsp. fresh salsa
15-oz. can vegetarian refried black beans*
4 spelt tortillas*

Heat butter in a sauté pan and add peppers and onion; sauté until slightly soft. Beat eggs in a separate bowl and add to pan. Reduce heat and cook until eggs are scrambled. Serve with avocado slices, salsa, refried black beans, spelt tortilla, and pico de gallo (recipe under Day 1 breakfast).

*See our list of recommended resources for purchasing ZOE 8–compliant foods (page 219).

Per serving (including tortilla and toppings): 400 calories, 21 g total fat (6 g sat fat), 420 mg cholesterol, 590 mg sodium, 39 g carbohydrate (8 g fiber, 6 sugar), 20 g protein

Hacienda Pinto Beans
Phase 1, 2, and Sustainable
Serves 10

1 Tbsp. olive oil
2 cups onion, chopped
4 cloves garlic, chopped
6 cups water (reduce water to 3 cups if using canned beans)
2 cups dry beans* (or two 15-oz. cans)
2 cups fresh tomatoes, chopped
½ cup fresh cilantro, chopped
2 jalapenos, chopped
½ tsp. crushed red pepper
1 Tbsp. cumin
1 Tbsp. oregano

*Soak beans according to package directions.

In a stockpot heat olive oil. Add onion and garlic and sauté lightly. Add water, beans, and remaining ingredients; simmer for 2 hours. If using canned beans, simmer for about 1 hour.

8-oz. serving: 200 calories, 2 g total fat (0 sat fat), 0 cholesterol, 10 mg sodium, 34 g carbohydrate (10 g fiber, 3 g sugar), 12 g protein

LUNCH

Grilled Shrimp Salad
Phase 1, 2, and Sustainable
Serves 4

1½ lbs. medium to large shrimp,* shell and tail off
2 Tbsp. olive oil
1 tsp. granulated garlic
¼ tsp. sea salt
1 tsp. cracked black pepper
1 Tbsp. fresh parsley, chopped
1-lb. bag of mixed lettuces
1 cup fresh tomatoes, diced

Wash shrimp and place in bowl. Add olive oil, garlic, salt, pepper, and parsley. Coat shrimp thoroughly and marinate for 10–20 minutes. Heat broiler; place shrimp on baking sheet 4 inches from broiler and cook for 7 minutes, or until shrimp have turned pink. Do not overcook. Remove from oven and let cool slightly. Place lettuce and tomatoes in bowl and toss with Sesame Ginger Dressing (recipe below). Add shrimp, lightly toss, and serve on a platter.

Tip: You can also grill shrimp for this recipe according to your favorite method.

* If you have food sensitivities to seafood, you can substitute cubed boneless, skinless chicken breast for shrimp.

8-oz. serving (without dressing): 260 calories, 10 g total fat (2 g sat fat), 260 mg cholesterol, 380 mg sodium, 5 g carbohydrate (1 g fiber, 1 g sugar), 36 g protein

Sesame Ginger Dressing
Phase 1, 2, and Sustainable
Makes 2½ cups

¼ cup sesame oil
¼ cup toasted sesame seeds
1½ cups olive oil
⅓ cup Bragg's Liquid Aminos*
⅛ cup fresh ginger
⅛ cup fresh garlic, minced
½ Tbsp. crushed red pepper

Mix all ingredients together and place in salad dressing cruet or glass measuring cup. Pour over salad and serve.

Tip: Store leftover dressing in the refrigerator for up to two weeks.

See our list of recommended resources for purchasing ZOE 8–compliant foods (page 219).

1-oz. serving: 210 calories, 22 g total fat (3 g sat fat), 0 cholesterol, 0 mg sodium, 1 g carbohydrate (0 fiber, 0 sugar), 0 g protein

DINNER

Minestrone
Phase 1, 2, and Sustainable
Serves 12

2 Tbsp. olive oil
4 cloves garlic, chopped
1 medium onion, chopped
2 celery stalks, chopped (with leaves)
2 cups green cabbage, chopped
28-oz. can whole tomatoes, chopped in food processor

4 cups water (more or less for desired heartiness of soup)
¼ cup fresh basil, chopped
¼ cup fresh parsley, chopped
1 tsp. rosemary
¼ tsp. oregano
Sea salt and cracked black pepper to taste
2 cups fresh baby spinach
15-oz. can white beans, rinsed

Heat olive oil in stockpot, adding garlic, onion, celery, and cabbage. Sauté until vegetables are tender. Add tomatoes, water, and spices, and simmer for 30–45 minutes. Add spinach and beans. Stir and simmer for 5 minutes until spinach is wilted and soup is thoroughly heated.

9-oz. serving: 100 calories, 3 total fat (0 sat fat), 0 cholesterol, 150 mg sodium, 16 g carbohydrate (5 g fiber, 4 g sugar), 5 g protein

Broiled Sirloin with Tomato and Breadcrumb Crust
Phase 1, 2, and Sustainable
Serves 4

1¾ lbs. top sirloin
2 Tbsp. olive oil
1 tsp. cracked black pepper
1 tsp. granulated garlic
1 large fresh tomato, sliced
¾ cup coarse seasoned millet breadcrumbs

Set oven on broil, and place sirloin on oiled broiler pan or sheet pan. Rub sirloin with 1 Tbsp. olive oil and season with cracked black pepper and garlic on both sides. Cover surface of meat with sliced tomato. Generously coat tomatoes with breadcrumbs and drizzle with 1 Tbsp. olive oil. Broil for approximately 10 minutes (rare), 15 minutes (medium), or 20 minutes (well done).

Tip: Instead of purchasing breadcrumbs loaded with preservatives, make your own by grating the ends of loaves of millet bread.

6-oz. serving: 380 calories, 22 g total fat (7 g sat fat), 130 mg cholesterol, 95 mg sodium, 2 g carbohydrate (0 fiber, 1 g sugar), 43 g protein

Braised Cabbage and Peas
Phase 1, 2, and Sustainable
Serves 6

1 Tbsp. olive oil
2 Tbsp. garlic, chopped

1 head green cabbage, sliced (about 6 cups)
1 cup chicken broth*
½ cup parsley, chopped
1 cup frozen green peas
½ tsp. black pepper

Heat olive oil in sauté pan over medium heat; add chopped garlic. Sauté garlic slightly, and add cabbage. Cover and steam for 5 minutes. To braise cabbage, add chicken broth; reduce heat and simmer for about 10 minutes. Stir in parsley and peas. Cover and cook for an additional 5 minutes or until the cabbage is tender. Season with pepper.

*See our list of recommended resources for purchasing ZOE 8–compliant foods (page 219).

5½-oz. serving: 70 calories, 3 g total fat (0 sat fat), 0 cholesterol, 140 mg sodium, 9 g carbohydrate (3 g fiber, 4 g sugar), 3 g protein

Day 6

BREAKFAST

Sunrise Chicken Chimichurri
Phase 1, 2, and Sustainable
Serves 1

1 spelt bagel, split and toasted
1 tsp. butter
2-oz. grilled chicken breast
2 eggs, poached (recipe under Day 1 breakfast)
3 asparagus spears, steamed
1½ Tbsp. Chimichurri Sauce (recipe below)

To assemble on serving plates, spread bagel with butter and layer with chicken breast, poached eggs, asparagus spears, and sauce.

Per serving: 630 calories, 34 g total fat (15 g sat fat), 670 mg cholesterol, 445 mg sodium, 29 g carbohydrate (5 g fiber, 4 g sugar), 47 g protein

Chimichurri Sauce
Phase 1, 2, and Sustainable
Makes 3 cups

1 cup olive oil
3 Tbsp. garlic, chopped
2 Tbsp. shallots, chopped

2 cups flat leaf parsley
1 cup fresh cilantro
1 red bell pepper, chopped
3 Tbsp. pepperoncini, chopped
1 Tbsp. apple cider vinegar*

Place all ingredients in a food processor and process until the contents become a rough paste. Use as a sauce or marinade.

*See our list of recommended resources for purchasing ZOE 8–compliant foods (page 219).

1-oz. serving: 130 calories, 13 g total fat (2 g sat fat), 0 cholesterol, 45 mg sodium, 1 g carbohydrate (1 g fiber, 0 sugar), 0 protein

LUNCH

Salad Niçoise
Phase 1, 2, and Sustainable
Serves 4

½ head butter lettuce, broken apart
1 cup black olives, sliced
12 oz. white albacore tuna
1 cup fresh tomato, chopped
1 ½ cups celery, chopped
½ cup green onions, chopped
2 Tbsp. sunflower seeds
1 15-oz. can great northern beans, rinsed
2 Tbsp. Italian parsley, chopped
2 Tbsp. pine nuts
1 tsp. Herbes de Provence
Sea salt and cracked black pepper to taste

Combine all ingredients and arrange on serving platter. Dress with Garlic Herb Dressing (recipe below) and serve.

8-oz. serving (without dressing): 290 calories, 16 g total fat (2 g sat fat), 15 mg cholesterol, 660 mg sodium, 17 g carbohydrate (6 g fiber, 2 g sugar), 21 g protein

Garlic Herb Dressing
Phase 1, 2, and Sustainable
Makes 1 3/4 cup

1 cup extra-virgin olive oil
¼ cup apple cider vinegar* (eliminate in Phase 1)
4 Tbsp. garlic, minced

1 Tbsp. shallots, minced
3 fresh basil leaves, minced
2 tsp. fresh oregano, minced
½ tsp. fresh thyme, minced
½ tsp. fresh parsley, minced
½ tsp. fresh tarragon, minced
½ tsp. fresh mint leaves, minced
Sea salt and cracked black pepper to taste

Mix all ingredients together in glass measuring cup, and use as a salad dressing or marinade for poultry or fish. If you prefer a creamier texture, then mix ingredients in a blender or small food processor.

Tip: This is a versatile dressing; you may substitute dried herbs for fresh; you may also use your choice of herbs or use lemon instead of the vinegar. Add more herbs for a more intense flavor.

*See our list of recommended resources for purchasing ZOE 8–compliant foods (page 219).

1-oz. serving: 170 calories, 19 g total fat (3 g sat fat), 0 cholesterol, 20 mg sodium, 1 g carbohydrate (0 fiber, 0 sugar), 0 protein

DINNER

Shepherd's Pie
Phase 1, 2, and Sustainable
Serves 8

2½ lbs. lean ground beef
1 Tbsp. olive oil
4 garlic cloves, chopped
1 cup onions, chopped
1 cup red bell pepper, chopped
1 tsp. cracked black pepper
½ tsp. garlic powder
¼ tsp. rosemary
¼ tsp. sage
¼ tsp. tarragon
1 large head cauliflower, trimmed into florets
Sea salt and white pepper to taste
2 cups frozen petite green peas (cooked according to package directions)

Preheat oven to 350 degrees.

In a sauté pan, brown ground beef; drain and set aside. In the same pan, add olive oil, garlic, onions, and peppers; sauté until soft. Add spices and ground beef; let simmer on low heat for about 10 minutes. Remove from heat. Steam cauliflower until tender; drain well and pat dry. Puree cauliflower in a food processor until it reaches the consistency of mashed potatoes. Season with salt and pepper. Spread ground beef mixture on bottom of casserole dish, spread peas over beef, and top with a layer of cauliflower puree. Bake for 20 minutes.

13-oz. serving: 420 calories, 19 g total fat (7 g sat fat), 120 mg cholesterol, 220 mg sodium, 19 g carbohydrate (7 g fiber, 8 g sugar), 43 g protein

Green Beans Palermo
Phase 1, 2, and Sustainable
Serves 8

1 lb. fresh green beans
1½ tsp. extra-virgin olive oil
2 garlic cloves, chopped
Sea salt and cracked black pepper to taste
Almonds, slivered (optional)

Cut ends off green beans and wash thoroughly. Steam beans for about 10 minutes or until desired tenderness is reached. Heat olive oil in sauté pan; add garlic and cook, but do not let it brown. Add green beans and toss in pan until coated. Remove from heat to serving dish; season with salt and pepper, and top with slivered almonds if desired.

Tip: This dish can be served hot, cold, or at room temperature.

2-oz. serving: 80 calories, 7 g total fat (1 g sat fat), 0 cholesterol, 5 mg sodium, 4 g carbohydrate (1 g fiber, 1 g sugar), 1 g protein

Day 7

BREAKFAST

French Toast
Phase 1, 2, and Sustainable
Serves 4

3 large eggs
¼ cup unsweetened soy milk*
½ tsp. ground nutmeg
½ tsp. ground cinnamon
1 Tbsp. unsalted butter
8 slices millet bread

In a pie plate, whip eggs until smooth, adding soy milk, nutmeg, and cinnamon. Heat butter in a sauté pan over medium heat. Briefly soak slices of bread in egg mixture and cook on both sides until golden brown, adding more butter to pan as necessary. Hold on heated platter until ready to serve.

Tip: After Phase 1, serve with Cinnamon Butter (recipe under Day 2 breakfast) or Mixed Berry Compote (recipe below).

See our list of recommended resources for purchasing ZOE 8–compliant foods (page 219).

4 ½-oz. serving (without butter or compote): 270 calories, 10 g total fat (4 g sat fat), 215 mg cholesterol, 210 mg sodium, 32 g carbohydrate (4 g fiber, 1 g sugar), 11 g protein

Mixed Berry Compote
Phase 2 and Sustainable
Makes 3 cups
1 cup frozen unsweetened blueberries
1 cup frozen unsweetened strawberries
1 cup frozen unsweetened blackberries
1 cup water
$\frac{1}{16}$ tsp. pure stevia powder*
2 tsp. arrowroot powder

Place berries and 3/4 cup water in a small saucepan and cook about 15 minutes. Sweeten with stevia to taste. Mix ¼ cup water with arrowroot powder and add to mixture; simmer until thickened. Remove from heat. Serve with pancakes or waffles.

Tip: When adding stevia to increase sweetness, do not add more than ¹⁄₁₆ tsp. at a time.

See our list of recommended resources for purchasing ZOE 8–compliant foods (page 219).

4-oz. serving: 40 calories, 0 total fat (0 sat fat), 0 cholesterol, 0 sodium, 10 g carbohydrate (3 g fiber, 7 g sugar), 1 g protein

LUNCH

Broiled Salmon Steak
Phase 1, 2, and Sustainable
Serves 4
4 salmon steaks or salmon fillets (7 oz. each)
1 Tbsp. olive oil
1 Tbsp. dried dill
½ tsp. cracked black pepper
1 Tbsp. granulated garlic

Coat salmon with olive oil and sprinkle with dill, pepper, and garlic. Place salmon 4 inches under broiler and broil for approximately 5–8 minutes.

7-oz. serving: 390 calories, 24 g total fat (5 g sat fat), 115 mg cholesterol, 115 mg sodium, 1 g carbohydrate (0 fiber, 0 sugar), 40 g protein

Pecan Quinoa
Phase 1, 2, and Sustainable
Serves 8

1 cup uncooked quinoa
1 Tbsp. olive oil
½ tsp. garlic, chopped
2 cups chicken broth or vegetable broth*
1 oz. pecans, chopped
2 tsp. fresh parsley, chopped
⅛ tsp. sea salt
¼ tsp. white pepper

Rinse and drain quinoa thoroughly. In a 1½ quart saucepan, heat olive oil and lightly sauté garlic. Add quinoa, broth, pecans, parsley, salt, and pepper; bring to a boil. Reduce heat and simmer until all water is absorbed (10–15 min.). Mix and serve.

*See our list of recommended resources for purchasing ZOE 8–compliant foods (page 219).

3-oz. serving: 120 calories, 5 g total fat (1 g sat fat), 0 cholesterol, 180 mg sodium, 16 g carbohydrates (2 g fiber, 0 sugar), 4 g protein

Tomato-Cucumber Relish
Phase 1, 2, and Sustainable
Makes 3 cups

1½ cups fresh tomatoes, diced and seeded
1½ cups cucumber, diced
2 tsp. apple cider vinegar*
1 Tbsp. olive oil
1 tsp. cracked black pepper
½ tsp. sea salt
½ tsp. granulated garlic
1½ tsp. fresh cilantro, chopped
1½ Tbsp. red onion, finely diced

Mix all ingredients and place in a small bowl. Store leftover relish in a small glass jar for up to 5 days in the refrigerator.

*See our list of recommended resources for purchasing ZOE 8–compliant foods (page 219).

1½-oz. serving: 20 calories, 2 g total fat (0 sat fat), 0 cholesterol, 80 mg sodium, 2 g carbohydrate (0 fiber, 1 g sugar), 0 protein

DINNER

Zucchini Carpacio
Phase 1, 2, and Sustainable
Serves 4

2 oz. arugula
1 zucchini, peeled and thinly sliced
3 Tbsp. extra-virgin olive oil
1 Tbsp. cracked black pepper
Pinch of sea salt

Note: Create each serving individually on a small plate.

Place ½ oz. arugula in the center of each plate; arrange zucchini slices around arugula, each slice slightly overlapping the other. Drizzle olive oil over arugula and zucchini; sprinkle with pepper and sea salt to taste. Can also be served with Lemon Grape Seed Oil Dressing (recipe under Day 4 dinner) or Garlic Herb Dressing (recipe under Day 6 lunch).

2½-oz. serving: 110 calories, 11 g total fat (2 g sat fat), 0 cholesterol, 5 mg sodium, 3 g carbohydrate (1 g fiber, 1 g sugar), 1 g protein

Braised Beef
Phase 1, 2, and Sustainable
Serves 6

2 Tbsp. olive oil
2½ lbs. boneless chuck roast
3 medium onions, diced
2 large celery stalks, diced
2 medium red bell peppers, chopped
28-oz. can whole tomatoes, chopped in food processor
2 cups beef broth (read label)
1½ Tbsp. minced garlic (about 6 cloves)
2 bay leaves
1 tsp. oregano
1 tsp. fresh rosemary, finely chopped, stems removed
1½ tsp. cracked black pepper
¼ tsp. sea salt
2 Tbsp. arrowroot

Preheat oven to 425 degrees.

Heat olive oil in roasting pan and brown roast. Add vegetables and sauté lightly about 10 minutes. Add other ingredients except arrowroot; cover, and cook in oven until meat is fork tender. Remove meat and skim fat. Reduce sauce by ¼ by boiling on stovetop. Stir in arrowroot to thicken sauce. When sauce reaches desired thickness, return meat to sauce.

Tip: For variety, try lamb, veal, or pork shanks with the same preparation. (This is a great Crock-Pot recipe!)

12½-oz. serving: 320 calories, 16 g total fat (5 g sat fat), 75 mg cholesterol, 420 mg sodium, 19 g carbohydrate (4 g fiber, 10 g sugar), 25 g protein

Brown Rice Risotto
Phase 1, 2, and Sustainable
Serves 8

2 Tbsp. olive oil
2 Tbsp. garlic, chopped
2 cups short-grain brown rice
½ cup green onions, chopped
4 cups chicken stock*
¾ cup frozen peas

In a saucepan, heat olive oil; add chopped garlic and sauté lightly. Add rice and onions; cook until rice is translucent and coated. Heat chicken stock in a separate pan and add it one cup at a time to the rice until all stock is absorbed; stir frequently. Add peas with the last cup of stock. When all stock is absorbed, remove mixture from heat and cover for 5 minutes. Do not overcook or rice will become mushy. Stir and serve.

*See our list of recommended resources for purchasing ZOE 8–compliant foods (page 219).

6-oz. serving: 230 calories, 5 g total fat (0 sat fat), 5 mg cholesterol, 300 mg sodium, 40 g carbohydrate (3 g fiber, 1 g sugar), 5 g protein

Bonus Recipes

SOUPS

Gazpacho
Phase 1, 2, and Sustainable
Serves 12

3 cups tomato juice (read labels)
6 cups V-8 juice (low sodium, read label)

1 Tbsp. cracked black pepper
1 tsp. sea salt
¼ tsp. cayenne pepper
¼ cup olive oil
2 cups beef stock
1 Tbsp. ground cumin
1 tsp. Bragg's Amino Acid*
2 tsp. chili powder
2 tsp. garlic, minced
2 Tbsp. fresh cilantro, chopped (for garnish)
1 cucumber, chopped (for garnish)

Combine all ingredients in food processor and pulse until thoroughly mixed. Place in large bowl and chill for 2 hours. Serve in chilled bowls. Garnish with chopped cilantro and cucumber. Add jalapenos if you like it hot.

Tip: You can substitute vegetable or chicken stock for beef stock, if you prefer. You can also garnish with avocado or other chopped vegetables of your choosing.

*See our list of recommended resources for purchasing ZOE 8–compliant foods (page 219).

8-oz. serving: 90 calories, 5 g total fat (1 g sat fat), 0 cholesterol, 400 mg sodium, 9 g carbohydrate (1 g fiber, 6 g sugar), 2 g protein

Vegetarian Chili
Phase 1, 2, and Sustainable
Serves 10

1 large eggplant, peeled and diced
1 tsp. sea salt
⅔ cup olive oil
1 medium yellow onion, diced
2 medium bell peppers, diced
1 medium red pepper, diced
2½ tsp. garlic, chopped
3¼ cup canned crushed tomatoes with juice
1½ Tbsp. chili powder
2½ tsp. oregano
1¼ tsp. black pepper
1¼ tsp. fennel seed
¾ cup pinto beans, dry (cooked) or canned and rinsed
3 Tbsp. dill
2½ tsp. ground cumin
2½ tsp. basil
6 Tbsp. fresh parsley, chopped

1½ cup garbanzo beans, canned and rinsed

Peel and dice eggplant; place in colander and sprinkle with sea salt. Let stand 1 hour, then pat dry. Heat oil in stockpot. Add eggplant, onion, peppers, and garlic; sauté until tender. Add rest of ingredients and simmer for 45 minutes. Serve hot.

11-oz. serving: 290 calories, 16 g total fat (2 g sat fat), 0 cholesterol, 440 mg sodium, 30 g carbohydrate (8 g fiber, 7 g sugar), 8 g protein

Roasted Eggplant and Tomato Soup
Phase 1, 2, and Sustainable
Serves 12

2 Japanese eggplants
3 whole tomatoes
1 onion, quartered
2 red bell peppers
4 cloves garlic
2 sprigs basil
2 sprigs thyme
2 sprigs oregano
1 tsp. sea salt
1 tsp. cayenne pepper
1 Tbsp. olive oil
3 quarts chicken stock*

Preheat oven to 450 degrees.

Coat eggplant, tomatoes, onion, and peppers with olive oil. Roast in oven until color starts to change and the skins split open. Put roasted vegetables and all other ingredients in a stockpot and simmer for 45 minutes. Let cool slightly, then puree in food processor. Strain through strainer, heat if necessary, and serve.

*See our list of recommended resources for purchasing ZOE 8–compliant foods (page 219).

9-oz. serving: 50 calories, 2 g total fat (0 sat fat), 0 mg cholesterol, 60 mg sodium, 8 g carbohydrate (2 g fiber, 4 g sugar), 1 g protein

Lentil Soup and Meatballs
Phase 1, 2, and Sustainable
Serves 10

3 Tbsp. olive oil
3 celery stalks, chopped
1 large onion, chopped
3 cloves garlic, chopped

8 cups water
2 cups lentils (washed and rinsed thoroughly)
1 tsp. thyme
1 tsp. sea salt
1 tsp. cracked black pepper
1 cup baby spinach

Heat olive oil in stockpot. Add celery, onion, and garlic; sauté until tender. Add water, lentils, and spices; simmer until the lentils are tender, approximately 1 hour. Add spinach and drop in meatballs (recipe below); simmer for 15 minutes.

Meatballs

½ lb. ground sirloin, pork, or veal
1 tsp. cracked black pepper
½ tsp. sea salt
¼ tsp. crushed red pepper

Mix all ingredients thoroughly in a bowl. Form into small ½-inch meatballs and drop into simmering soup.

9-oz. serving: 160 calories, 2 g total fat (0 sat fat), 10 mg cholesterol, 330 mg sodium, 23 g carbohydrate (13 g fiber, 2 g sugar), 16 g fiber

SALADS

Crispy Calamari Salad
Phase 2 and Sustainable
Serves 4

8 oz. mixed calamari pieces
½ Tbsp. olive oil
2 tsp. granulated garlic
2 tsp. black pepper
4 oz. arugula
½ cup carrots, shredded
½ cup black olives, sliced

Cut calamari into pieces; coat in olive oil and spices. Place on broiler pan and broil until crispy. In a salad bowl combine arugula, carrots, and olives. Top with crispy calamari and toss with Lemon Grape Seed Oil Dressing (recipe under Day 4 dinner).

4-oz. serving: 90 calories, 3 g total fat (0 sat fat), 130 mg cholesterol, 180 mg sodium, 7 g carbohydrate (2 g fiber, 1 g sugar), 10 g protein

SNACKS

Cajun Nut Mix
Phase 1, 2, and Sustainable
Use unsalted and no-oil-added roasted nuts and seeds.

Olive oil cooking spray
1 cup raw hulled sunflower seeds
1 cup soy nuts
1 cup pecan halves
1 cup pumpkinseeds
1 cup almonds
1 Tbsp. Cajun spice mix*
Sea salt

Preheat oven to 350 degrees.

Lightly spray olive oil on a baking sheet. Place nuts and seeds on baking sheet; spray lightly with olive oil. Sprinkle Cajun spices and salt to lightly coat mixture. Roast mixture until lightly browned, approximately 15 minutes; turn halfway through cooking process. Remove from oven; toss and season once more. Let cool completely. Store in airtight container and refrigerate.

*See our list of recommended resources for purchasing ZOE 8–compliant foods (page 219).

2-oz. serving: 310 calories, 25 total fat (3 g sat fat), 0 cholesterol, 90 mg sodium, 12g carbohydrate (5 g fiber, 3 g sugar), 14 g protein

Hummus
Phase 1, 2, and Sustainable
Serves 8

15-oz. can chick peas (garbanzo beans), drained
2 Tbsp. olive oil
1 Tbsp. sesame oil
¼ tsp. cracked black pepper
1 tsp. fresh garlic
2 Tbsp. water

Mix all ingredients in a small food processor until smooth. Serve with Belgian endive or brown rice crackers.*

*See our list of recommended resources for purchasing ZOE 8–compliant foods (page 219).

2-oz. serving: 110 calories, 5 g total fat (1 g sat fat), 0 cholesterol, 150 mg sodium, 11 g carbohydrate (2 g fiber, 2 g sugar), 2 g protein.

RECOMMENDED RESOURCES

We have searched and researched ready-made products that are of excellent quality and conform to the guidelines of the ZOE 8 Weight Management Program. Listed below are the products we have used in this appendix. All other ingredients used are whole, natural foods available at most grocery stores.

We have included company information so you may contact the company if you cannot find these items in your area. If you can't find these products, please contact us at www.zoe8.com and we will ship them to you.

Ancient Harvest 310-217-8125	Quinoa
Arrowhead Mills 800-749-0730 www.arrowheadmills.com	Quick brown rice
Avomex 817-431-9308 (fax)	Salsa and guacamole
Bearitos 800-424-4246 www.littlebearfoods.com	Black beans and other products
Bob's Red Mill www.bobsredmill.com	Spelt flour and other grains
Bragg 800-446-1990 www.bragg.com	Liquid aminos and apple cider vinegar
Deland Bakery 386-734-7553 www.delandbakery.com	Yeast-free millet breads
East Wind Nut Butters 417-679-4682	Almond butter
Edward & Sons 805-684-8500 www.edwardandsons.com	Brown rice crackers
Erewhon/US Mills Cereal 800-422-1125 www.usmills.com	Crispy brown rice cereal
Hain Celestial Group www.hain-celestial.com/brands.php	Network of natural food brands

Imagine Foods www.imaginefoods.com	Organic chicken broth, rice milk
KAL Stevia 800-365-5966 www.nutraceutical.com	Pure stevia powder
Lundberg Family Farms 530-882-4551 www.lundberg.com	Brown rice
Madhava Honey 303-444-7999 agave@madhavahoney.com	Agave nectar
Margaritas Tortilla Factory 512-282-5787 www.margaritastortillafactory.com	Spelt tortillas
McCormick Brand 800-632-5847	Cajun seasoning mix
O Bakery 802-985-8771	Sourdough spelt bread
Pure De-Lite 866-410-CARB www.puredeliteproducts.com	Chocolate
Silver Spring Gardens www.silverspringgardens.com	Organic horseradish
Thai Kitchen 800-967-8424 www.thaikitchen.com	Coconut milk
Tinkyada 416-609-0016 www.tinkyada.com	Brown rice pasta
Vegenaise 818-347-9946 www.followyourheart.com	Mayonnaise substitute
Westbrae Natural 631-730-2200 www.westbrae.com	Unsweetened ketchup
West Soy Milk 800-SOY-MILK www.westsoy.biz	Unsweetened soy milk
ZOE 8 888-775-2368 www.zoe8.com	Barbecue sauce and much more

Appendix 4

Dining-out Guide

WHEN it comes to eating out, Elisa and I have a distinct advantage: we have our own restaurant. We travel frequently, however, so we are not strangers to making food choices from unfamiliar menus. Over the last few years we have developed a wealth of helpful hints to share with you, so you can skip right over the frustration we had when first creating our own food plan. On the ZOE 8 Web site (www.zoe8.com) we post actual restaurant reviews for our members, but the following general guidelines will help you adapt ZOE 8 principles to your lifestyle.

Let me assure you that you do not have to throw away your weight-management program just because you are traveling or celebrating a special occasion at a restaurant—or if you just want to get out of the kitchen for an evening. Here are the three most important principles for ZOE 8–friendly dining away from home:

1. Know your food plan.
2. Do some preplanning.
3. Don't be afraid to speak up.

THE BASICS

It's helpful if you can limit dining out until you are familiar with your food plan. The more thoroughly you know your particular dos and don'ts, the easier it will be for you. We offer a brochure-size version of the Body Balance Food Chart that you can take with you as a reference guide when dining out. (See our Web site at www.zoe8.com for ordering information.)

The principle of deconstruction and reconstruction of recipes can be applied to a restaurant menu the same way you use it in your kitchen. This will help you to analyze a restaurant menu and to take authority over what you eat. Most restaurants will work with you—after all, they are in the business of selling food. Be sure to reward the extra attention with an appropriate tip, particularly if it is a restaurant you plan to frequent.

If you have the opportunity, do some research before you dine out. This will help you to determine not only which restaurant to patronize but also which menu items will be the best choices.

There are two basic types of restaurants: chain restaurants and independents. Elisa and I tend to favor independent restaurants because that is the business we are in, and we find them to be a little more flexible than chain restaurants because the food is being cooked on site; there is no central commissary or remote preparation involved. If it is a free-standing restaurant, you know their key ingredients are available in the kitchen. There is nothing wrong with chain restaurants, but we naturally gravitate toward the independents when traveling because they are more open to substitutions.

With national or regional franchises, the recipes are created at the corporate level. While this insures consistency, it does limit flexibility when it comes to making substitutions to meet your particular requirements. I've found that servers and kitchens at the chain restaurants will try to be as helpful as possible, but sometimes they cannot do much because so many dishes are prepared in advance. That does not mean the food is bad; it just means they don't have as many options. You will also find more extensive use of preservatives in the food at a chain because of remote preparation.

One advantage that chain restaurants do have is that they are more likely to have Web sites that allow you to check out the nutritional content of the menu before you arrive.

Whichever type of restaurant you choose, you must learn to speak up for yourself. Ask your server questions, and don't hesitate to make special requests. In an independent restaurant, and to a lesser degree in the chain restaurants, the chef is often very accommodating in leaving off certain ingredients or adapting a recipe. More and more restaurants now have a gluten-free section of the menu, and servers and kitchen staff are becoming more knowledgeable about food issues. So apply the principle of deconstruction and reconstruction to a restaurant menu, and be bold in ordering what is appropriate for your food plan. It is easy to substitute steamed or grilled vegetables for mashed potatoes or french fries, for example.

In most cases the menu is not written on stone tablets—entrées and sides can be rearranged to create a custom dish. The restaurant industry is becoming much more sensitive to food challenges; it is a liability issue for them, and by the time you read this book, legislation will be in place that will require restaurants to disclose common allergens in their foods. (See chapter eight for more information.) As a result, you will find more and more servers becoming educated about the foods they serve and the changes they can make.

In our seminars we teach a restaurant workshop session, and we distribute menus from various restaurants. The participants break into small groups and pick apart the menu to decide what would be best to eat; then they practice ordering and making substitutions and special requests. Since we cannot do a workshop for you, we will do the next best thing—and that is to go through the major cuisine types with specific tips for the healthiest choices.

MENU GUIDELINES BY CUISINE TYPE

Steak houses

Steak houses are generally safe territory when eating out on the ZOE 8 plan because there are plenty of protein choices and some reliable side dishes. The same principles work whether you are dining at a pricey steak house or an economy establishment. In addition to steak, the menu customarily features chicken and seafood, which can usually be broiled or grilled. Vegetables come on the side, which makes them an easy substitution. Skip the baked potato and stick with steamed or grilled veggies. The high-end steak houses will usually have fresh asparagus and broccoli, and those are always good choices. Pass on the Hollandaise or Béarnaise sauces during Phase 1, but you can use them sparingly once you are in Phase 2 and beyond.

A number of the mid-priced steak houses now offer baked sweet potatoes as an alternative to baked potatoes. If served with honey butter or sweetened topping, ask them to leave that off. When slow cooked, the sweet potatoes are naturally moist and sweet, and delicious with no added flavor or topping. If you do want something extra, use a little butter—not margarine, which is an artificial, man-made food. Butter has no additives, and although it is saturated fat, it is much healthier for you than the alternatives.

Steak houses are great places for salads, but you do have to watch the dressings. Ask for a lemon and some olive oil and make your own dressing right at the table. You might also ask the kitchen to chop some fresh basil or other herbs to add to your homemade dressing. Add the herbs with a little salt and pepper, and it will punch up the flavor in your salad. My favorite steak house salad is a sliced tomato and sliced red onion, drizzled with olive oil and seasoned with sea salt, pepper, and chopped basil. Almost any kitchen can put that together for you if it's not on the menu.

Mexican

Some items in typical Mexican food restaurants are problematic—for instance, tortillas, . Even if you do not have a food sensitivity to corn, you have to think about how the tortilla is fried. Some restaurants still use lard, but most have switched to healthier fats. You have to be careful about ingredients. When in doubt, ask your server.

Almost every Mexican restaurant will have homemade charro beans, which are a good choice. Fresh salsas are full of good ingredients, and other whole ingredients on the menu will include guacamole, which is usually just mashed avocado with a bit of lime juice, salt and pepper, and perhaps onions, chopped tomatoes, and cilantro. Fajita meats are grilled and served with peppers and onions; just avoid the cheese and sour cream toppings.

Around Boerne, Texas, Elisa and I have become known for ordering taco salads—hold the taco shell and hold the cheese. That leaves plenty of lettuce, tomato, onions, and all the meat and beans. I use fresh salsa and pico de gallo as a dressing. Even the refried beans are OK if not prepared with lard. Refried beans are simply beans and fat, which are both Phase 1–compliant.

Elisa and I like a new concept in restaurants that we call "Fresh Mex." These are restaurants that use whole ingredients to make dishes to order for each customer. Our favorite is Chipotle Grill (a division of McDonald's, interestingly, so we can expect these to expand rapidly), where you go through a cafeteria-style line and select your ingredients for a "burrito bol." It's very easy to make ZOE-friendly choices at a Chipotle Grill, and chains such as Taco Cabana now offer their Cabana Bowls following the same concept.

Diners and coffee shops

Every city has what I call diners, usually chain restaurants or small independents that offer three meal periods, some of them open twenty-fours hours a day. It is tougher to make ZOE 8–compliant choices here. Breakfast is usually their best meal. Eggs are fine, but you have to watch out for bacon because it is cured in sugar, and both bacon and sausage will be filled with nitrates and other ingredients you want to avoid. Sometimes I will have steak and eggs, because the steak doesn't have additives like other breakfast meats and eggs are a good, whole food. But when breakfasting in a diner I tend to stick with oatmeal. When not in Phase 1, I top the oatmeal with berries.

Lunch and dinner are more difficult. Stick with a grilled pork chop, grilled chicken, or steak. The vegetable choice may be limited to green beans or a steamed vegetable mix like peas, broccoli, cauliflower, and carrots. Often the garnish on the plate is healthier than some of the vegetables they offer. You can always ask for a grilled hamburger patty with lettuce and tomato.

Asian/Chinese

Other than one or two national chains, I haven't eaten Chinese food for three years because almost everything has sugar or cornstarch in it, and the only choice for starch is white rice or rice noodles. However, some of the Chinese restaurants are now offering brown rice because people have started asking for it.

Some of the soups are wonderful, especially in the Thai cuisine. A lot of the Thai and Vietnamese restaurants have great fresh vegetables and a different approach to preparation. Some Vietnamese spring rolls, for example, are wrapped in rice paper rather than wheat. So you can make good choices in these restaurants; it is just a matter of asking the questions and not doing the usual things.

Ask the kitchen to put your vegetables in the wok without any sauce—just oil, or chili oil if you want to spice it up a little. Let the natural flavors of the vegetables create the sauce for you; you're better off that way. One of Elisa's favorites is egg foo yung. It is basically eggs and vegetables, but you can add shrimp or chicken. Just ask them not to put any sauce on it.

Even though most places have stopped using MSG—a big "no-no" as you probably already know—Asian food is customarily prepared with a lot of sodium. Because of this, if you are salt-sensitive you will want to save Asian food for special occasions.

Like "Fresh Mex," there are a growing number of "new concept" Chinese restaurants that feature made-to-order wok cooking. Generally inexpensive, you can request the ingredients you want, and your meal is cooked exactly as you specify. Pei Wei and Fire Wok are two good examples of this new type of restaurant, called QFR (quick-fast restaurant) in the industry. These places are a great alternative to fast food; just be sure you know your particular dos and don'ts before you order.

Barbecue

The year I lost two hundred pounds, I ate a lot of barbecue. In Texas, that is pretty easy to do. The downside of barbecue is the sauce; you have to leave it off because it has sugar and vinegar in it. If the meat is on the dry side, mix it with some pinto beans, or ask them to pour some bean juice over your meat. We recently created our own barbecue sauce that is ZOE 8 compliant, and we will begin selling it in our restaurant and online soon.

The good news about barbecue is that you can get smoked chicken, brisket, ribs—all kinds of meats. They are all basically OK, although you need to watch the rubs. If the rubs have too many ingredients, we recommend avoiding them. But straightforward smoked meat is great. Most barbecue places have either pinto beans or green beans. If they are cooked with bacon, I pick that out and just eat the beans. Balance the protein with some beans, and you will do fine. I lived the better part of a year eating barbecue, barbecue, and more barbecue—and I lost two hundred pounds while doing it.

Traveling through the Southeast is a little more difficult than the Southwest when it comes to barbecue. In this region, sweet and vinegary sauces are the norm, and often the meats are marinated in these sauces before cooking. I don't eat such pre-sauced meats, so I have to be careful when traveling "abroad" (that is, any place outside of Texas). Also, I rarely order barbecue at the big chain restaurants because their entrées are usually focused on sugar-based sauces and rubs. If you keep the deconstruction and reconstruction principles in mind when ordering, you will learn, just as I did, which barbecue restaurants in your neck of the woods are ZOE 8 compliant and which ones aren't.

Fast food

When it comes to the drive-through, Elisa and I always say it is better to drive by—and keep on going! But there are times when fast food may be the only available option. I do have to give them credit for getting better and starting to offer more choices on their menus. Although the choices are still extremely limited, you can find salads and fresh fruit now, or you can order a hamburger patty or grilled chicken. Most of the food has already been prepared elsewhere and the restaurants are merely heating it up and serving it, or cooking pre-seasoned items, so flexibility when ordering is going to be very limited.

If the restaurant has a salad bar, eat your meal inside and choose plenty of fresh greens and veggies. The packaged dressings are a problem, though, because they are loaded with additives and sugar or sugar substitutes. Most of the fast-food places have Web sites, and we encourage you to check out the menu items and nutritional content in advance. Some of them also have nutritional brochures on-site, so you can ask for one when you arrive to help you make the best choice.

Do the best you can, but realize that you will have to limit the times you eat at a fast-food restaurant. The food items are heavily processed, something that is not a part of the ZOE 8 program. If you have been grabbing a quick bite at a fast-food restaurant for lunch, start bringing something from home instead. It is simply a fact of life that your health will improve and your waistline decrease when you stop relying on convenience foods.

Italian

Elisa is Italian, and I love the cuisine as well, so we eat a lot of Italian food. Because of food sensitivities to wheat, discovering brown rice pasta revolutionized our kitchen and brought pasta back into our lives. But outside of our own restaurant I don't know of any that serve it. So although we skip the pasta when dining out, we have found a way to eat at Italian restaurants and do it well. (Our Web site can point you to the manufacturers of brown rice pasta and where to find their products for your home kitchen.)

I am going to break with precedent and recommend a particular restaurant chain here: Carrabba's Italian Grill. They are in several states already and are going national. If you don't have a Carrabba's in your area yet, you can find similar Italian restaurants. These are more in the middle to upper price range because they serve a number of fresh grilled items, including seafood, chicken, and veggies. They are very amenable to making substitutions and adapting recipes for you.

Eating at Carrabba's was a "eureka" experience for me when I was losing weight. That was where I discovered how to make an incomparable salad dressing right at the table. Many of the Italian restaurants serve dipping oil for the bread. They put down a small plate, sprinkle it with herbs and seasonings, then pour extra-virgin olive oil over it. One night I shoved aside the bread, looked at that plate of oil and herbs, and voilà! I knew I had found a salad dressing I could enjoy—it was the principle of deconstruction and reconstruction. Outside of organic apple cider vinegar, these were all of the ingredients I would use to make a dressing at home. So I ordered a salad and dumped the dipping oil over it. It was quite a change of pace from plain old lemon and olive oil; the herbs gave it a lot of flavor. Now when I go to an Italian restaurant, I automatically ask them to double the dipping oil.

At Carrabba's the sautéed spinach with garlic is outstanding. They do grilled salmon and roasted and grilled vegetables. Some of the soups are also ZOE 8-friendly. My favorite is the sausage and lentil soup—it is ZOE 8 compliant because they make their sausage fresh every week. As always, ask your server, and check online to see if your favorite Italian restaurant has ingredients posted.

You will need to have willpower to avoid the pasta and the bread; make a commitment in advance that you are going to stay on your food plan—then go and enjoy a fine, ZOE 8–style Italian meal.

Indian

Indian food is another cuisine you don't have to throw out entirely; you just have to make wise choices. For example, they usually have pappadam, a crispy cracker-type bread made with pure lentil flour—it is wonderful! The tandoori chicken, baked in a traditional clay oven or pot, is another good choice. They will usually have grilled shrimp and some fresh vegetable items. Ask if they have brown rice; like the Chinese restaurants, a few of them are beginning to serve it. As the demand for brown rice increases, more and more places will offer it.

Most Indian restaurants are small independents, and the ingredients and degree of excellence will vary greatly. Get to know the owners of your local Indian restaurant, and let them know what kind of menu choices you are looking for. We have found one such restaurant where the whole buffet is almost all Middle Eastern. It is simply their native cuisine in its whole food form, and they have not adapted it to the Western style. It is delicious, and we have so many healthy choices. Every time we are in that city we go back, and the servers recognize us now.

It may take awhile to discover places like this in your area—whatever the type of cuisine—but don't stop looking. They are out there, and they are worth it!

Pit stops and airports

If you do any amount of traveling, you will wind up stopping at a convenience store or an airport vendor for a snack or meal. These places offer few choices, but here are some tips for that inevitable quick stop.

When traveling by car, or even by plane, Elisa and I try to pack some snacks ahead of time—things like soy nuts and our homemade Cajun nut mix (page 218), which is a travel favorite. If we do have to stop for a snack, we stick with packaged nuts or seeds. Sunflower seeds and pumpkinseeds make a great choice. I love beef jerky, but most of the commercial ones are loaded with nitrates and additives. As always, you have to check the food labels.

Instead of going for that giant 44-ounce soda, grab a bottled water. And that goes for airport vendors as well as pit stops. Choose water, water, and more water!

Some airports will have a breakfast place where you can get a fresh fruit bowl and fresh scrambled eggs. Lunch is tough because there will be a lot of fast food-type choices, and you cannot avoid the smells coming from the grill. Like other venues, some airport restaurants are getting better and starting to provide healthier options. If you can find soup or salad, choose these over a sandwich or fried entrée.

The more you can plan ahead, the better off you will be.

There you go. Keep in mind the three basic rules—knowing your food plan, preplanning, and speaking up—and dining out can be an enjoyable experience that won't derail your weight-management program.

Bon appétit.

Identifying Sugar

MAKE sure you *read all labels carefully*. Four (4) grams equals 1 teaspoon.

OK to use: Fruit/herbal sweeteners

- Agave nectar
- Inulin/Dahlulin
- Stevia (can contain maltodextrin; drops contain alcohol)
- Lo Han
- Ki Sweet

Use with caution: Sugar alcohols

Use the following cautiously, because while they have little or no effect on blood sugar levels, they can cause digestive upset in sensitive people. Consume less than 10 grams daily.

- Erythritol
- HSH
- Lactitol
- Mannitol
- Xylitol
- Hexitol
- Isomalt
- Malitol
- Sorbitol

Avoid: Artificial sweeteners

- Altimae
- Aspartame
  Equal
  NutraSweet
  NatraTaste
  Sweet Thing
- Acesulfame-K (considered dangerous)
  Ace K
  Diabeti Sweet

    Somer Sweet

    Sunnett

    Sweet One

- Cyclamate (banned in 1969)
- Energy Smart
- FruitSource
- Saccharin (has a warning label)

    Sugar Twin

    Sprinkle Twin

    Sweet 'N' Low

- SucraFlore
- Sucralose

    Splenda

Avoid: Natural sweeteners (any word ending in –*ose*)

- Barley malt
- Blackstrap molasses
- Brown rice syrup
- Cane juice
- Cane syrup
- Caramel
- Caramelized sugar
- Confectioner's sugar
- Corn syrup
- Crystalline fructose
- Dextrin
- Disaccharide
- Fig syrup
- Fruit juice concentrate
- Glucose
- Glycerine
- High fructose corn syrup
- Invert sugar
- Levulose
- Liquid cane syrup
- Malted barley
- Beet sugar
- Brown rice sugar
- Brown sugar
- Cane sugar
- Cane syrup solids
- Caramel coloring
- Concentrated fruit juice
- Corn sweeteners
- Corn syrup solids
- Date sugar
- Dextrose
- Evaporated cane sugar
- Fructose
- Galactose
- Glucose polymers
- Granulated sugar
- Honey*
- Lactose
- Liquid cane sugar
- Malt
- Maltodextrin

- Maltose
- Maple syrup*
- Monosaccharides
- Polydextrose
- Rice sugar
- Rice malt
- Sucralose
- Sugar cane syrup
- Turbinado sugar
- White grape juice
- Yinnie syrup

- Maple sugar
- Molasses*
- Muscavado
- Powdered sugar
- Ribose
- Sucanat
- Sucrose
- Table sugar
- Unrefined sugar
- White sugar

* Honey, maple syrup, and molasses are good nutritious products, but they are high on the glycemic index and should be avoided until health conditions have stabilized.

GENERAL NOTE: Some of these ingredients do not have to be calculated as sugar on food labels. Just because a product says "0 grams sugar" does not mean it has no sugar effect. Some of these ingredients may be listed as carbohydrates.

CHAPTER TWO: AMERICA SUPERSIZED: WHY WE ARE GETTING FATTER AND SICKER

1. "Tasty Beverages," Fountain Drinks, 7-Eleven Company Web site, "Tasty Beverages," www.7-eleven.com/products/index.asp (accessed May 26, 2005).

2. "Obesity in the U.S.," American Obesity Association Fact Sheet, www .obesity.org/subs/fastfacts/obesity_US.shtml (accessed May 26, 2005).

3. Greg Critser, *Fat Land: How Americans Became the Fattest People in the World* (New York: Houghton Mifflin Company, 2003), 4.

4. Francine R. Kaufman, MD, *Diabesity: The Obesity-Diabetes Epidemic That Threatens America and What We Must Do to Stop It* (New York: Bantam Dell, 2005), 14.

5. Centers for Disease Control and Prevention, National Center for Health Statistics, "National Health and Nutrition Examination Survey, Health, United States, 2002." Flegal, et al., *Journal of the American Medical Association* 288 (2002): 1723–1727. National Institutes of Health, National Heart, Lung, and Blood Institute, "Clinical Guidelines on the Identification, Evaluation and Treatment of Overweight and Obesity in Adults, 1998." Chart taken from the AOA Fact Sheet "Obesity in the U.S."

6. Critser, *Fat Land*, 10–11.

7. Ibid., 18.

8. Megan A. McCrory, et al., "Dietary Variety Within Food Groups: Association With Energy Intake and Body Fatness in Men and Women," *American Journal of Clinical Nutrition* 69(3) (March 1999): http://www.ajcn.org/cgi/content/full/69/¾40#F4 (accessed June 10, 2005). Data for obesity from K. M. Flegal, et al., "Overweight and Obesity in the United States: Prevalence and Trends, 1960–1994," *Int J Obes* 22 (1998): 39–47. Data for food products from A. E. Gallo, "First Major Drop in Food Product Introductions in Over 20 Years," *Food Rev* 20 (1997): 33–35.

9. Critser, *Fat Land*, 15.

10. Eric Schlosser, *Fast Food Nation: The Dark Side of the All-American Meal* (New York: HarperCollins Publishers, 2002), 3.

11. Ibid., 6.

12. Critser, *Fat Land*, 28.

13. Source: McDonald's USA Nutrition Facts and Wendy's U.S. Nutrition Information.

14. McDonald's USA Ingredients Listing for Popular Menu Items, www .mcdonalds.com/usa/eat/nutrition_info.html (accessed May 26, 2005).

15. Wendy's U.S. Nutrition Information, http://www.wendys.com/food/index (accessed September 22, 2005), current as of April 1, 2005.

16. McDonald's USA Ingredients Listing for Popular Menu Items.

17. Critser, *Fat Land*, 40.

18. Schlosser, *Fast Food Nation*, 122.

19. Ibid.

20. U.S. Food and Drug Administration, Center for Food Safety and Applied Nutrition, "Frequently Asked Questions About GRAS," December 2004, http://www.cfsan.fda.gov/~dms/grasguid.html (accessed May 26, 2005) (emphasis added).

21. Compiled from information in Schlosser, *Fast Food Nation*, 125–126.

22. Russell L. Blaylock, MD, *Excitotoxins: The Taste That Kills* (Santa Fe, NM: Health Press, 1997).

23. Ibid.

24. U.S. Department of Health and Human Services, National Institutes of Health press release: "New NHLBI-Sponsored Study Shows Programs Can Teach Children to Eat Healthier," June 1, 2005, http://www.nhlbi.nih.gov/new/press/05-06-01b.htm (accessed September 22, 2005).

CHAPTER THREE: THE FALLACY OF THE FOOD PYRAMID: WHY THE GOVERNMENT HAS IT WRONG

1. Kaufman, *Diabesity*, 249.

2. Walter C. Willett, MD, *Eat, Drink, and Be Healthy* (New York: Free Press, 2001), 56.

3. Ibid., 57.

4. Ann Louise Gittleman, ND, CNS, *Eat Fat, Lose Weight* (Los Angeles: Keats Publishing, 1999), 11.

5. Ibid., 6.

6. Ibid., 4.

7. Ibid., 5.

8. Willett, *Eat, Drink, and Be Healthy*, 87.

9. Ibid., 71.

10. Kaufman, *Diabesity*, 39.

11. Ibid., 41.

12. Ibid., 37.

13. Ibid., 41–42.

14. Willett, *Eat, Drink, and Be Healthy*, 21.

15. Ibid., 43.

16. Ibid., 18–20.

17. Ibid., 19.

18. Ibid., 20.

19. Ibid., 45.

20. Ibid., 71.

21. Ibid., 17.

CHAPTER FOUR: YOU ARE MORE THAN A NUMBER ON THE SCALE

1. Mary Pipher, PhD, *Hunger Pains: The Modern Woman's Tragic Quest for Thinness* (New York: Ballantine Publishing Group, 1995), 20.

2. Alicia Potter, "Mirror Image," *Boston Phoenix*, Infoplease, http://www.infoplease.com/spot/mbi3.html (accessed June 4, 2005).

3. Erin J. Shea, *Tales from the Scale* (Avon, MA: Polka Dot Press, 2005), 123, 124–125.

4. Bob Greene, *Get With the Program!* (New York: Simon & Schuster, 2002), 55.

5. Ibid., emphasis in original.

6. Shea, *Tales from the Scale*, 96.

7. Pipher, *Hunger Pains*, 25, 90.

8. Ibid., 86.

9. Associated Press, "Athlete Study Exposes Flaw of BMI Obesity Measure," March 8, 2005, http://www.foxnews.com/story/0,2933,149807,00.html (accessed June 7, 2005).

10. Pipher, Hunger Pains, 12.

CHAPTER SIX: "ED, YOU ARE NOT A CANDIDATE FOR CHANGE"

1. Don Colbert, MD, *Deadly Emotions* (Nashville: Thomas Nelson, 2003), 9 (emphasis in original).

2. Don Colbert, MD, *Stress Less* (Siloam, 2005), 4.

3. Colbert, *Deadly Emotions*, 13.

CHAPTER SEVEN: THE "F" WORD: FORGIVENESS

1. John Eldredge, *Wild at Heart: Discovering the Secret of a Man's Soul* (Nashville: Thomas Nelson, 2001), 72–73.

2. "Five for 2005: Five Reasons to Forgive," *Harvard Women's Health Watch*, January 2005. Downloaded from Harvard Health Publications, Harvard Medical School, www.health.harvard.edu (accessed July 11, 2005).

3. Ibid.

4. Jane Lampman, "Forgive and Your Health Won't Forget," *Christian Science Monitor*, December 19, 2002, http://csmonitor.com/2002/1219/p11s01-stgn.htm (accessed January 18, 2005).

5. Jordana Lewis and Jerry Adler, "Forgive and Let Live," Newsweek, Inc. and MSNBC, 2005, http://www.msnbc.msn.com/id/6039585/site/newsweek/ (accessed July 11, 2005).

6. R. T. Kendall, *Total Forgiveness* (Lake Mary, FL: Charisma House, 2002), 12.

7. Ibid., 15.

8. Ibid., 21.

9. Ibid., 141.

10. Colbert, *Deadly Emotions*, 84–85.

11. Kendall, *Total Forgiveness*, 149–150.

CHAPTER EIGHT: HOW TO BREAK THROUGH YOUR WEIGHT-LOSS BARRIERS

1. The National Weight Control Registry is a research study developed by Rena Wing, PhD, at Lifespan, Brown University and the University of Pittsburgh, and James Hill, PhD, at the University of Colorado. For more information visit the National Weight Control Registry Web site, http://www.nwcr.ws.

2. Don Colbert, MD, *The Bible Cure for Candida and Yeast Infections* (Lake Mary, FL: Siloam, 2001), 2.

3. Colbert, *Deadly Emotions*, 8.

4. Ibid., 15.

5. Elizabeth Vliet, MD, *Women, Weight and Hormones* (New York: M. Evans and Company, Inc., 2001).

6. D. Kripke, et al., "Short and Long Sleep and Sleeping Pills. Is Increased Mortality Associated?" *Arch Gen Psychiatry* 36 (1979): 103–116, in Eve Van Cauter, PhD, et al., "The Impact of Sleep Deprivation on Hormones and Metabolism," *Medscape Neurology and Neurosurgery* 7(1) (2005): http://www.medscape.com/viewarticle/502825 (accessed May 5, 2005).

7. National Sleep Foundation, Sleep in America Poll, 2001–2002 (Washington DC: National Sleep Foundation), in Van Cauter, "The Impact of Sleep Deprivation on Hormones and Metabolism."

8. Van Cauter, "The Impact of Sleep Deprivation on Hormones and Metabolism."

9. Ibid.

10. Ibid.

11. Don Colbert, MD, *The Bible Cure for Irritable Bowel Syndrome* (Lake Mary, FL: Siloam, 2002), vii.

12. Rudy Rivera, MD, and Roger David Deutsch, *Your Hidden Food Allergies Are Making You Fat* (Roseville, CA: Prima Publishing, 2002), 7.

CHAPTER NINE: HOW TO CREATE A FOOD PLAN THAT WORKS FOR *YOU*

1. "Health Benefits of Grass-Fed Products," Eat Wild, http://www.eatwild.com/nutrition.html (accessed August 18, 2005).

2. Mary G. Enig, PhD, *Know Your Fats: The Complete Primer for Understanding the Nutrition of Fats, Oils, and Cholesterol* (Silver Spring, MD: Bethesda Press, 2000), 104–105.

CHAPTER TEN: EIGHT WEIGHT-LOSS STRATEGIES THAT SPELL SUCCESS

1. Barbara Rolls, PhD, and Robert A. Barnett, *Volumetrics* (New York: Harper Collins, 2000), 10.

2. Ibid., 14.

3. Ibid., 94.

4. Bob Greene, *Get With the Program*, 68.

5. Ibid., 69.

6. Ibid., 70.

7. Adapted and expanded from Don Colbert, MD, in his book *Stress Less*, 276–278.

8. Dr. Henry Cloud and Dr. John Townsend, *God Will Make a Way* (Nashville: Integrity Publishers, 2002), 271.

CHAPTER ELEVEN: GET UP AND GET MOVING

1. See Bob Greene's book *Get With the Program!* for a good explanation of types of fitness and instructions on specific exercises for flexibility, cardio, and strength training.

2. Paige Waehner, "Perceived Exertion Scale," About.com: Exercise, http://exercise.about.com/cs/fitnesstools/l/blperceivedexer.htm (accessed August 15, 2005).

3. "Exercise in Cold Water May Increase Appetite, UF Study Finds," University of Florida Press Release, http://www.ufl.edu/mobile/news/articles/calorieswim.htm (accessed September 26, 2005).

CHAPTER TWELVE: WHAT TO DO WHEN YOUR ENGINE STALLS

1. Cloud and Townsend, *God Will Make a Way*, 268–269.

Got Zoe? Get It NOW!

The Zoe 8 Support Program

All the Information and personal support to achieve and maintain your health objectives.

24 hours a day / 365 days a year!

Join the Zoe Family NOW

Recipes, Restaurant Reviews, Fitness Acitivities, Motivation & Inspiration, Cooking Video Library, Cookbook, Message Board, Chat Rooms & even Private Chats with Ed, Elisa & Zoe Support Team

CHECK IT OUT!!

www.Zoe8.com

The Zoe 8 Total Health / W8 Loss Program

A **four-hour instructional video** (DVD/VHS format) featuring Zoe 8 founders Ed and Elisa McClure with award-winning actress and health activist Susan Howard; a comprehensive **180-page guidebook**; and the **Body Balance Food Chart**. Everything you need to create your own personalized program to acheive optimal health in every area of your life!

Z.I.P. (Zoe Individual Program)

Be a Zoe Important Person...Z.I.P. is the most flexible, "have it your way" program possible. Create your own health retreat on the dates that fit your calendar with the services and options you desire. With Z.I.P. you can craft a completely individualized program that meets your specific needs for health and weight loss. Includes one-on-one consultation with Ed & Elisa McClure and Zoe's on-site professionals and much more ~ in the beautiful Texas Hill Country at Ye Kendall Inn & Limestone Grille.

CONTACT US TODAY!

1-888-775-2368 ~ www.Zoe8.com

hope@zoe8.com

See YOU Soon!

EST. 1859

TEXAS HILL COUNTRY
HOTEL ~ RESTAURANT ~ TAVERN ~ CONFERENCE CENTER

Home of

z8e

The historical Ye Kendall Inn situated in the famed Texas Hill Country features, 36 beautifully appointed guest rooms, suites & cabins; Aveda Lifestyle Spa: Kendall Halle conference facility; and, of course, Zoe 8. This national historic landmark located in Boerne, Texas on the banks of the Cibolo Creek, is a unique environment for business, pleasure and getting Zoe in your life.

LIMESTONE GRILLE

Home of

z8e

Cuisine

This award-winning restaurant located in Ye Kendall Inn, offers cutting edge "naturally healthy" cuisine; fresh, natural ingredients, modern style, utilizing classic old world techniques. Since 1859, our open-air courtyard, cozy fireplaces and front porches have invited guests to relax and enjoy fine food, service and true Texas hospitality. The Grille is very Zoe.

Let us know when you are coming. We'd love to meet and share our home with you. *Ed Elisa*

Reservations & Information
1-800-364-2138 ~ www.yekendallinn.com

Strang Communications,

publisher of both **Charisma House** and *Charisma* magazine, wants to give you

3 FREE ISSUES

of our **award-winning** magazine.

Since its inception in 1975 *Charisma* magazine has helped thousands of Christians stay connected with what God is doing worldwide.

Within its pages you will discover in-depth reports and the latest news from a Christian perspective, biblical health tips, global events in the body of Christ, personality profiles, and so much more. Join the family of *Charisma* readers who enjoy feeding their spirits each month with miracle-filled testimonies and inspiring articles that bring clarity, provoke prayer, and demand answers.

To claim your **3 free issues** of *Charisma*, send your name and address to: Charisma 3 Free Issues Offer, 600 Rinehart Road, Lake Mary, FL 32746. Or you may call **1-800-829-3346** and ask for Offer # **96FREE**. This offer is only valid in the USA.

WWW.CHARISMAMAG.COM

Charisma
+CHRISTIAN LIFE
www.charismamag.com

5567